WESTERN EUROPEAN ENERGY POLICIES:
A COMPARATIVE STUDY

WESTERN EUROPEAN ENERGY POLICIES:

A Comparative Study of the Influence of Institutional Structure on Technical Change

NIGEL LUCAS
with the assistance of
Dimitri Papaconstantinou

CLARENDON PRESS OXFORD
1985

Oxford University Press, Walton Street, Oxford OX2 6DP

London New York Toronto
Delhi Bombay Calcutta Madras Karachi
Kuala Lumpur Singapore Hong Kong Tokyo
Nairobi Dar es Salaam Cape Town
Melbourne Auckland

and associated companies in
Beirut Berlin Ibadan Mexico City Nicosia

Oxford is a trade mark of Oxford University Press

Published in the United States
by Oxford University Press, New York

British Library Cataloguing in Publication Data

Lucas, Nigel
    Western European energy policies.
    1. Energy policy—Europe
    I. Title   II. Papaconstantinou, Dimitri
    333.79'094   HD9502.E8

ISBN 0-19-828488-8

Library of Congress Cataloging in Publication Data

Lucas, Nigel.
    Western European energy policies.

    Bibliography: p.
    Includes index.
    1. Energy policy—Europe. I. Papaconstantinou,
Dimitri. II. Title.
HD9502.E8L83 1984   333.79'094   84-20540
ISBN 0-19-828488-8

Phototypeset by Taj Services Ltd., India
Printed in Great Britain at the University Press
Oxford by David Stanford, Printer to the University

In memory of my father

PREFACE

The response of Western European countries to the changing structure of energy supplies provides a first-rate opportunity of studying the influence of institutions on technical change. There are three main reasons why this is so. The Western European nations have diverse institutional forms, yet many of them find themselves in similar technical predicaments. The change has been sudden and the rate of reaction therefore relatively fast. Among the alternatives to oil none is outstandingly attractive; all suffer from environmental, political, economic, practical or security disadvantages. Decisions therefore are peculiarly susceptible to peripheral influences, and in particular to the discrimination exercised by the way in which responsibilities are allocated in society, to which I have given the name 'institutional structure'.

This book is based on a series of articles which have appeared in past years in *International Relations*. The factual updating of these articles has been undertaken by Dimitri Papaconstantinou. I am grateful to Miss Mary Sibthorp OBE for her unflagging enthusiasm and to Miss Esmé Allen for her typing of the manuscript.

Any merit which this account may have derives in large part from the assistance which I have enjoyed from many people in the UK and in the countries studied. There are so many people who deserve my thanks that I am unable to list them all, and selection among them would be invidious. I am, however, deeply grateful to them all.

31 August 1982   Nigel Lucas

CONTENTS

ABBREVIATIONS

AEC	Atomic Energy Commission (of Denmark)
AEE	Agence pour les économies d'énergie
AEG	Allgemeine Elektrizitäts Gesellschaft
AFME	Agence française pour la maîtrise de l'énergie
AGIP	Azienda Generale Italiana Petroli
ASEA	Allmänna Svenska Elekriska AB
BNOC	British National Oil Corporation
BP	British Petroleum
BRP	Bureau des recherches de pétrole
BTU	British thermal unit
BWR	Boiling light-water-cooled and moderated reactor
CDF	Charbonnages de France
CDU	Christlich-Demokratische Union
CEA	Commissariat à l'énergie atomique
CEM	Compagnie électro-mécanique
CENTEC	Centrifuge Technology (combined enterprise of the UK, West Germany and the Netherlands for centrifuge technology)
CFDT	Confédération française démocratique du travail
CFP	Compagnie française des pétroles
CHP	Combined heat and power
CIP	Comitato Interministeriale per gli Prezzi
CIPE	Comitato Interministeriale per Planificazione Economica
CNEN	Comitato Nazionale per l'Energia Nucleare
CNRS	Centre national de la recherche scientifique
COGEMA	Compagnie générale des matières nucléaires
COMES	Commissariat à l'énergie solaire
COREDIF	Company formed to build second diffusion enrichment plant to EURODIF (see below)
CRPM	Centre de recherches de pétrole du midi
DEN	Délégation aux énergies nouvelles
DEMINEX	Deutsche Erdölversorgungsgesellschaft
DGB	Deutscher Gewerkschafts-Bund
DICA	Direction des carburants
DKBL	Deutsche Kohlenbergbau-Leitung
DNG	Dansk Naturgas
DONG	Dansk Olieog Naturgas
DUC	Dansk Undergrunds Consortium

DUP	Déclaration d'utilité publique
DWK	Deutsche Gesellschaft für Wiederaufarbeitung von Kernbrennstoffen
ECSC	European Coal and Steel Community
EDF	Électricité de France
EEC	European Economic Community
EGF	Électricité et gaz de France
EI	Elettro-nucleare Italiana
ELSAM	Det Jysk-fynske Elsamarbejde (Jutland and Funen electricity co-operation)
ENI	Ente Nazionale Idrocarburi
ENEL	Ente Nazionale per l'Energia Elettrica
ERAP	Entreprise de recherche et d'activités pétrolières
ESA	(Danish) Electricity Supply Act
EURODIF	European Diffusion Group (combined enterprise of France, Italy, Spain, and Belgium for uranium enrichment)
FBR	Fast breeder reactor
FDES	Fonds de développement économique et social
FDP	Freie Democratische Partei
GBAG	Gelsenkirchener Bergwerks AG
GDF	Gaz de France
GE	General Electric
GEORG	Gemeinschaftsorganisation Ruhrkohle GmbH
GW	Gigawatt
HAO	High activity oxide
HEW	Hamburgische Elektrizitätswerke
HTR	High temperature reactor
IEA	International Energy Agency
IFV	Isefjordvaerket
IRF	Institut de recherche fondamentale
IRI	Istituto per la Recostruzione Industriale
KF	Kooperativa Förbundet
KWU	Kraftwerk Union
LNG	Liquified natural gas
LWR	Light water reactor
Mt	million tonnes
mtoe	million tonnes of oil equivalent
MW	Megawatt
NERSA	Société centrale nucléaire européenne à neutrons
NESA	Nordsjaellands Elektricitet Selskab
NSSS	Nuclear steam supply systems
NVE	Nordvestsjaellands Elektricitets-Vaerk

NWK	Nordwestdeutsche Kraftwerk
OK	Olge-Konsumenterna
OPEC	Organization of Petroleum Exporting Countries
PCI	Partito Communista Italiano
PLI	Partito Liberale Italiano
PS	Parti Socialiste
PSDI	Partito Socialista Democratico Italiano
PUK	Pechinney-Ugine-Kuhlmann
PWR	Pressurized water reactor
RAG	Ruhrkohle AG
RAP	Régie autonome des pétroles
RWE	Rheinisch-Westfälisches Elekrizitätswerk
SEAS	Sydstsjaellands Elektricitets Aktieselskab
SFP	Société française des photopiles
SNEA	Société nationale Elf-Aquitaine
SNG	Substitute natural gas
SNPA	Société nationale des pétroles d'Aquitaine
SOFIDIF	Société France-Iranienne pour l'enrichissement de l'uranium par diffusion gazeuse
SP	Svenska Petroleum
SPD	Sozialdemokratische Partei Deutschlands
SSPB	Statens Vatterfallswerk (Swedish State Power Board)
STEAG	Steinkohlen Elektrizitäts AG
Twh	Terrawatt hour
UGP	Union générale des pétroles
UKAEA	UK Atomic Energy Agency
UNGG	Natural uranium gas graphite reactor
URENCO	Uranium Enrichment Company (combined enterprise of the UK, West Germany, and the Netherlands for uranium enrichment by centrifuge)
VEBA	Vereinigte Elektrizitäts-und-Bergwerks Aktiengesellschaft
VDEW	Vereinigung Deutscher Elektrizitätswerke
VEW	Vereinigte Elektrizitätswerke Westfalen

1
FRENCH ENERGY POLICY

THE INSTITUTIONS

The main actors in French energy policy and the main lines of dependence are given in Figure 1.1 The French Government has exercised close control over the activities of energy supply for 50 years or more. The policy objectives are in part implemented through the large state involvement in the energy industries. Coal, gas and electricity were nationalized in 1946, and there are virtual state monopolies in electricity supply, coal-mining and the sale of gas. The State also exercises a monopoly on imports of crude oil which it delegates to French and foreign companies.

The Evolution of Relationships among Institutions

The relationships among the institutions concerned in energy supply have evolved in a manner conditioned by several factors. Some of these factors are specific to the energy industries, others reflect the wider environment in which the energy industries operate. One can detect four stages of evolution, the boundaries between which are marked by reasonably distinct changes both in energy specific and energy non-specific factors.[1]

These four periods are the inter-war period, the period following the Second World War up until about 1957/58, the period from then until 1970/73, and the period up until the present. During the inter-war period the uses of energy were mostly specific to particular fuels. There was little competition for markets or supplies. Immediately after the War, energy was in short supply, all that could be produced could be sold, foreign exchange was scarce and consequently the production of indigenous energy from high cost coal resources and hydraulic power was encouraged. Competition between fuels for markets was still negligible. At the end of this period, for many reasons, oil began rapidly to displace other fuels, most especially coal; energy prices fell and were generally thought likely to go on falling. In 1970/71, the Teheran–Tripoli agreements and the difficulties of the French oil companies in Algeria, brought home some of the dangers of

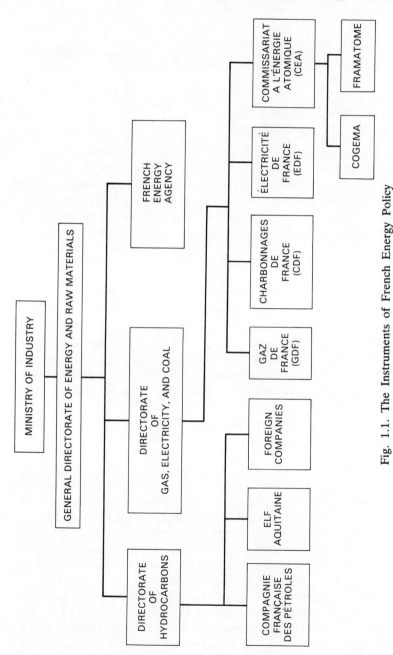

Fig. 1.1. The Instruments of French Energy Policy

relying on petroleum. The events following the Yom Kippur War reinforced this judgement and a new perception of energy supplies became widely accepted. Adaptation to changing circumstances began.

Parallel with this evolution of the energy market, there were changes in the nature of the relationships between and among the various branches of industry and government. The first period was characterized by government control of private industry, mostly proceeding through government departments. After the War the State nationalized large parts of the sector and introduced state agencies into the oil sector. Subsequently the state-owned industries came to resent the irksome and detailed controls of government. New relationships between government and public industry were defined. Private capital began again to be an important part of the energy sector, generally in association with public enterprise.

The final period is characterized by the successful attempts of some of the public firms to control the environment in which they operate. In particular, the companies try to control supplies, markets, future technologies and finance. This behaviour is probably what is meant when one hears certain French public firms described as a state within a state, a description frequently met with in France, especially of Électricité de France (EDF). The boundaries of the four historical stages are not strict, they vary from industry to industry and from function to function; events have not always evolved according to this scheme and there have been other currents. It is nevertheless a possible basis from which to start.

The four stages define a historical dimension in which to situate changes. It is also useful to add a sectoral dimension. The energy industries separate into two groups. There is a group whose activities are largely confined to the nation; coal, gas, electricity, nuclear. There is also a group whose activities cannot and must not be confined to the nation; it comprises the oil companies. In the first group the principal relations are between industry and state. In the second group the dominant relationships are those between firms; the activities of the French oil companies have always been determined in the first instance by the need to operate in an environment controlled by the oil majors. Each subsector has its own internal dynamics, yet interacts with the other.

Between the Wars

The inter-war period was characterized by competition for space; the competition was arbitrated by the State. The end uses for different forms of energy were fairly specific: gas for lighting; electricity for lighting, motive power and electrochemistry; coal for heating, industrial processes and railways; oil for lubrication and road transport. There was little competition for markets. The gas industry countered the potential threat to their lighting market by buying up the nascent electricity companies; gas and electricity in many areas were provided by a joint enterprise. There was little competition for supplies. Electricity came from hydraulic power or was generated by heavy industry and sold as a by-product; gas was manufactured from coal. The use of coal as a feedstock for both gas and electricity did not introduce competition where a joint enterprise operated. The industries were all protected from the competition of imported goods or capital; they did not seek abroad for supplies, technology, capital or markets. In sum, the separate coal, oil and gas/electricity sector existed with little inter-sector competition for markets or supplies.

The principal competition was for terrain. To have permitted competition between similar supply industries within the same area would have sanctioned duplication of expensive supply infrastructures; concessions were therefore allocated by the State both for supply and use. The basic text establishing the regime of concessions for coal mining was the law of 21 April 1810; it conferred on the concessionaire a perpetual right to the mine, subject to certain general rules. A law of 1919 forbade the use of hydraulic energy resources (waterfalls, tides, rivers, lakes) for generating electricity without a concession from the State. Similar concessions regulated the behaviour of the public services of gas and electricity.

Having created local monopolies it evidently required the vigilance of the State to see that the concessions were not abused. This function was the origin of the state directorates, la Direction des mines and la Direction de l'électricité. The well-trained and intelligent engineers of the *grand corps* who staffed these directorates were more competent and acted more coherently than the 'subsistence capitalists' who ran the industries. Responsibility for control of the sector, initiative and what would now be called policy, passed into the hands of the administration.

The best example of the public powers trying to form the industries to their own designs is the perpetual battle during the inter-war period to interconnect electricity and gas supply systems to permit more efficient use of resources. None of the companies had the resources to assure within a single region, and still less throughout the nation, the development and management of an interconnected system of production, transmission and distribution. The syndrome was similar in the United Kingdom. In an attempt to encourage and to constrain the producers to collaborate on the financing of interconnections, the French State introduced a regime of concessions for long-distance transmission of electricity. The attempt was only partially successful. In 1937 the State again took the initiative by establishing a national body within which the producers and distributors of electricity should define a plan of development for the means of production and transport of electricity in a national framework. The State also attempted to harmonize tariffs and restructure the industry. Nevertheless, despite these efforts, by 1946 there were still 54 companies producing electricity from 86 thermal stations and 100 companies exploiting 300 hydraulic stations. Long-distance transmission was practised by 86 companies and there were some 1,150 distribution companies.[2]

Administrative control of the coal-mining industry had a different emphasis. A mine owner cannot be protected from competition by assigning him the sort of local monopoly enjoyed by gas and electricity distributors, but ways do exist and the French State tolerated them. They were not as good; competition broke through. There was, therefore, a natural tendency for coal production to concentrate in a few mines. By 1938 there were 181 pits; eleven companies produced over 64 per cent of the total French production; small companies, although representing two-thirds of the numbers, produced less than 2 per cent of the output.[3] But this degree of concentration was not enough to secure a rational use of resources. In the Nord and Pas-de-Calais regions, especially, the geological circumstances demanded a common use of services; but the concessionaires were reluctant to compromise their individualism. Persuasion was inhibited by the existence of the concession in perpetuity. The State did attempt to force concentration by modifying the regime of concessions and in 1919 it introduced the concept of temporary concession, but it had little effect because most mining rights had been allocated under the old system.

The main thrust of administrative intervention during this period was to concentrate the sectors; this applied in different ways both to the utilities and to coal-mining. In taking responsibility for the strategic adaption of the industry, the State essentially appropriated responsibility for policy.

Circumstances forced the intervention of the French State in the oil industry to take a different turn. France had never managed to secure supplies of oil through the activity of indigenous entrepreneurs. Worse, the known supplies were in the hands of the Dutch and the Anglo-Saxon companies which also controlled the markets and technology. During the First World War the scarcity of fuel supplies to the French troops caused them such distress as to provoke Clemenceau's sad observation, 'a drop of oil is worth a drop of blood'.

To compensate for the deficiencies of its capitalists, the French Government demanded at the end of the War the 25 per cent share of the Deutsche Bank in the Turkish Petroleum Company, which was dominated by the Anglo-Persian Oil Company, itself the result of an initiative of the British Admiralty. It appears that in this affair the French benefited from a variety of rivalries and grudges. It is alleged that Henry Deterding, the President of Royal Dutch-Shell, helped persuade the United Kingdom to agree to the transfer to France of the Deutsche Bank holding. He planned, following an idea of Gulbenkian, to create a joint company with the Banque de l'union parisienne to which the French would be persuaded to attribute their part. In this way Deterding would be on equal terms with the Anglo-Persian Oil Company, then holder of 50 per cent of the capital of the Turkish Petroleum Company, and the ensemble would be dominated by the United Kingdom. But Gulbenkian wanted to frustrate Deterding's ambition and presented to the French Government the idea of a French company to manage the holding.[4]

Be that as it may, the transfer of the Deutsche Bank holding to France was regulated by the San Remo Treaty in 1920. In 1924 France set up the Compagnie française des pétroles (CFP) to manage its interests. The concept of the CFP was an innovation in industry-government relationships. The capital of the company came entirely from private sources, but the Government was the source of initiative and retained some control.

The Government nominated the President of the company before it had been formed —Ernest Mercier. In correspondence dated 20 September 1923, the Foreign Minister, Raymond Poincaré, defined the institutional framework of the company:

As soon as possible the group will take the form of a limited company, whose statutes ... will be approved by the Government.

He went on to specify that the objectives of the Government were:

. . . to create a tool capable of the realisation of a national petroleum policy. The company must be essentially French and remain completely independent. It will do its utmost to develop petroleum production, under French control, in the different producing regions. It may receive from the Government the mission of undertaking such work as the Government thinks necessary. If this should not be profitable the state will accord appropriate remuneration.

Similarly the Minister specified four objectives of the company. They were:

1. To exploit the resources and the advantages which the state would obtain by diplomatic effort or otherwise in matters concerning petroleum.
2. To take whatever holdings were necessary in other petroleum bearing regions, especially Central and Southern America, in order to maintain a balance of supplies.
3. To take up the problem of the Russian concessions.
4. To develop the petroleum resources of France, the Colonies and the Protectorates.

The company was to receive the support of the Government and the co-operation of its administrators. The Minister also insisted on the necessity of ensuring permanent control of the company by French capital. This correspondence is the real genesis of the CFP; the same ideas were later cast into statutes.

Through its part-ownership of the Turkish Petroleum Company, later the Iraq Petroleum Company, the French obtained access to large deposits of oil in Iraq. As this was the result of a diplomatic coup rather than steady industrial and commercial development, it was not easy to dispose of the large quantities potentially available. The CFP had no outlets and was obliged to create them—it could most easily do this in France. Mercier also desired to develop an advanced refining industry in France, counter to the prevailing practice in other European states. For strategic reasons the French Government shared this objective. Government intervention in the market at the time alternated between liberalism and *dirigisme*. After impropriating a monopoly of imports in 1917, the Government returned in 1921 to a free market system which permitted the international societies to strengthen their position and undertake a price war detrimental to the young French company. The majors even imposed a refining quota on the French companies. To help the CFP the French Government drew up some formidable legislation centred on three texts—the law of 10 January 1925 required that petroleum only be imported by companies so authorized by the State; the law of 4 April 1926 attributed to the State a monopoly of crude imports, and the law of 30 March 1928 defined the conditions under which this monopoly would be delegated to the companies accredited by the State. The completion of the legislation was prompted in late 1927 by a discovery at Baba Gurgur which revealed the first and largest Iraqi deposits and made it imperative for the CFP to prepare outlets.

The law of 30 March 1928 required special licences for imports of crude oil, for refining, for imports of petroleum and distribution. The licences for crude oil originally ran for 20 years and were known as A20s. The period was later reduced to 13 years (A13) and now stands at 10 (A10). The licences for refined products ran for 3 years (A3). The idea was to permit the public authorities considerable control over the sector whilst still leaving the companies an adequate guarantee of continuity to permit them confidently to invest in refinery and distribution capacity.

In return, the oil companies operating in France undertook to construct refining capacity in volumes in line with market trends and to build up strategic stockpiles. Later they were also obliged to transport two-thirds of their imports under the French flag.

The first allocation of quotas respected fairly strictly the established market shares of each society, with the exception of the CFP which received, in addition to its own quota, the right to refine the equivalent of one-quarter of French consumption. This gave the company refined products far in excess of its own outlets, but simultaneously ensured that its competitors would buy the surplus. The concept of the French policy is clear; French capital was to operate an oil company in the interest of the nation within limits defined by the State. In turn the State would do its utmost to favour the CFP at home. But among the shareholders of CFP were other distributors of refined products, sometimes working for the foreign oil companies. The insecurity of his control over the company led Ernest Mercier into great difficulties. In December 1928 he offered his resignation to Poincaré. To stabilize the company the State took a 25 per cent holding. There were difficulties with Parliament and it was not until July 1931 that the state holding was agreed; by that time it had been increased to 35 per cent with 40 per cent voting rights.

French oil policy before the Second World War undoubtedly had the effect of increasing national involvement in the industry compared to what would naturally have occured. CFP was responsible for about 50 per cent of crude imports and 50 per cent of all refining done in France, the remainder was controlled by the multinationals.

The issue of licences and the supervision of the petroleum industry was the responsibility of the Office national des combustibles liquides and later of the Direction des carburants (DICA). But the strong international companies, which it would have been undesirable, and indeed impossible, to eliminate from the French market, were a different story from the protected 'subsistence capitalists' operating in the other energy sectors. DICA never achieved a dominance of the energy sector comparable to the analogous Directions for coal, electricity and gas.

The Time of Nationalizations

At the end of the War the conjunction of political and economic circumstances was favourable to a national co-ordination of energy supplies. It was the definite intention of the Conseil national de la résistance to put the commanding heights of the economy into the hands of the State. After six years of armed conflict there was damaged plant in all the industries. A financial and technical reconstruction was imperative. The penury of fuel made rationing inevitable. Heavy investments were necessary to equip new hydraulic stations and to compensate for the neglect of coal-mines.

The dominance of the state directorates within the coal, gas and electricity sectors made it more or less inevitable that the planning and financing of the reconstruction would be led by the State. The combination of technical and political pressures for nationalization was overwhelming.

The coal industry was nationalized by the law of 17 May 1946 creating nine Houillères de bassin and the Charbonnages de France (CDF). The organizations of the first group were regional boards for production, exploitation and sale. The role of CDF was to co-ordinate and direct the ensemble. The group of institutions ' had a monopoly of the production and treatment of coal.

The gas and electricity supply industries were nationalized by the law of 8 April 1946. Electricité de France (EDF) was assigned a monopoly of the transport of electricity, though not of its production; it acquired most of the generating plant and almost all of the distribution facilities. The original intention was that distribution would be entrusted eventually to particular public enterprises with geographically limited competence. This never happened. Organizations such as the coal-mines and the railways, which produced electricity for their own requirements were permitted to sell their surplus to EDF. The Compagnie nationale du Rhône was responsible for the development of hydraulic sites on the Rhône. The national interests in gas production, distribution and supply were assigned to Gaz de France (GDF). Because of the existence of many pre-war joint gas-electricity supply companies and because of the strong interest, within the Ministry of Finance, in restricting expenditure, GDF and EDF were given a common personnel for distribution, known as Electricité et gaz de France (EGF).

The senior management of these public enterprises came, naturally enough, from the great directorates of the State. They could provide men of far greater talent than could the fragmented industries. The policy of the public enterprises was defined by the newly formed Commissariat du plan in its first Plan. The members of this body were also mainly civil servants; they and the civil servants in the technical directorates shared their priorities and ways of thinking with their colleagues among the senior management of the public enterprise who had only recently been civil servants themselves. This common background, together with the general atmosphere of working together for renewal, and the fact that in such times priorities are relatively easy to define, assured a remarkable consensus of opinion. The First Plan designed by these partners was a bureaucratic plan; it was never even formally approved by Parliament.

The natural ease of relationships between the administration and the heads of public enterprise has persisted, although strains have arisen from conflicts of substance. In the post-war years, and really ever since, public enterprise has been more attractive than French capitalism for men of value and ambition.

The generally higher standards of personnel in public enterprise, supported by the enormous real influence that a monopoly buyer could exercise, combined to create a relationship between suppliers of equipment and public enterprise not unlike that which existed between the enterprise and the State.[5] The aim of the First Plan was simultaneously to reconstruct and modernize French industry. Coal, electricity, steel, cement, agricultural machinery and transportation were chosen as priority areas for rapid development. Production objectives were assigned to the various sectors, taking care to ensure consistency. Investment programmes and means of finance were proposed after studies as intensive as the limited time allowed. These served as a management framework for nationalized industries. The First Plan is generally considered to have been a success.[6]

The understanding among the enterprises and between them and the administration was reinforced by the relationship of the industries to one another in the economy of the country. All the energy that could be produced at this time was needed; there was essentially no competition for markets and by now a good deal of interdependence; for example the gas industry and the electricity supply industries relied on coal as feedstock. It follows that the relationship between these industries was characterized by competition for resources, but not markets, and the requirement for congruence in their future plans. The requirement for congruence put limits on the extent to which it would have been healthy for one energy industry to seek resources to the detriment of its supplier or customer.

In broad terms the nature of French public enterprise at this time was therefore akin to that of a branch of the administration. Economic competition was weak, direction was clear, and government control tight.

The oil industry in France was changing rapidly; in responding to events in difficult circumstances a certain lack of logic crept into the institutional structure. Some days before the War began, a fairly large discovery of natural gas was made by the Centre de recherches de pétrole du midi (CRPM). At the outbreak of the War the Régie autonome des pétroles (RAP), a state enterprise, was created to succeed the CRPM. In 1941 the Société nationale des pétroles d'aquitaine (SNPA) was also created, with the mission of prospecting Aquitaine, except for the concessions attributed to the RAP. It was not possible for the CFP to perform this task because the company had been declared an *ennemi technique* by the United Kingdom, on the grounds that its registered office was in occupied Paris; its interests had been sequestered in London.

After the War the political will to attribute the basic industries to the State required that there be some control over a portion of the oil industry. Because of the effective domination of the sector by foreign companies it was not possible to direct the reconstruction through the Plan as for the other energy industries. In October 1945, therefore, the Bureau des recherches de pétrole (BRP) was created, a public enterprise charged with the task of elaborating a programme of exploration and putting it into practice for the exclusive interest of the nation. The BRP was allocated substantial annual subsidies from the specially constituted Fonds de soutien aux hydrocarbures, whose revenues were obtained by a tax on the sales of petrol, gas oil and light fuel oil. There are various explanations why the State chose to overlook the CFP and create a new instrument within an essentially unchanged policy. The CFP had not been a great commercial success before the War; it paid one dividend in 1936. Moreover, it was engaged in difficult negotiations with the United Kingdom and American oil companies over compensation for its revenue lost during the War.[7] It may have been these factors, or the political will for nationalization which prevailed. Later, still more national companies were created, including one named Repal in which the Government of Algeria was represented. Investment companies (REPs) were also instituted with the intention of mobilizing private capital for the purpose of exploration. Their shareholders benefited from tax exemptions.

The licensing system had been suspended at the outbreak of the War; it was re-established in 1950 when the CFP had returned to adequate production levels. In the same year, the State decided to insist that companies possessing the authority both to distribute and refine petroleum should meet at least 90 per cent of their product needs from French refineries. The scope of this ruling was large because the companies falling into this class supplied about 95 per cent of the market. The intention was to oblige oil companies to invest in refining capacity in France if they wished to be part of the French market. To give the international companies an incentive to participate in the French market, prices were permitted to be kept high and competition was restricted by the licensing system. The oil policy after 1939 was administered, and largely devised, by the Direction des carburants (DICA) which had replaced the Office national des combustibles liquides. The DICA was a powerful body at the time.

Another of the post-war state energy institutions (contemporary with the BRP) was the Commissariat à l'énergie atomique (CEA). It was created in October 1945 and given full responsibility for the promotion and co-ordination of every aspect of nuclear energy, both military and commercial. In practice, its priority was to develop the necessary scientific and technical structures, for this reason it had more freedom of action than the commercial institutions.

Competition

The harmonious relationships which existed between the energy industries were disturbed by the events of 1957/58. These years were critical for European energy policies, as it became impossible not to accept that large quantities of petroleum could be produced from the Middle East and carried to Europe at a cost much lower than that of mining indigenous coal.[8] A mild industrial recession coincided with a clement winter; the consumption of energy fell for the first time since the War, but imports of coal and oil continued to increase. The final agony was the wet summer of 1958 which allowed exceptional production of hydraulic electricity. Consequently, the effect of the slight fall in energy consumption was amplified many times on the indigenous coal industry.

It was impossible not to accept that the difficulties of the coal industry were the consequence of structural changes. The operating environments of all the energy industries were modified by the penetration of oil, but none so much as that of the coal industry which was in direct competition with oil for the bulk fuel market.

The important question of the time was: how far to let oil penetrate the market to the cost of social stability and political security?

Restrictive as the oil licensing system may have been, it in no way inferfered with the fundamental determinants of oil policy, the rate of growth of supplies, buying and selling prices, and rates of profit. As a result there was no control over investment because it was almost entirely self-financed. The State in principle could have controlled part of the behaviour of the companies by restricting the allocation of licences. But this would have antagonized the major oil companies on whom the State was relying for a secure and stable supply of oil. This basic weakness in the negotiating position of the State has always prevented it from using the legislation of 1928 to its full effect; it has always been careful to favour French companies whilst still permitting the internationals to grow modestly. This procedure is only possible in a growing market.

The argument that France could not satisfactorily solve the coal problem without exercising a politically undesirable degree of control over the oil companies is part of the story. But it is not enough to explain French policy, because the government never tried—even in an imperfect way. All European coal producing countries offered some degree of protection to their indigenous coal industry; France offered less than any other. She was the only European coal producer not to put an excise tax on heavy fuel oil, and in 1968 she even made the Value Added Tax on heavy fuel oil deductible, so that the ex-refinery price of these fuels became the lowest in the EEC. Relative to French coal, therm for therm, the price of heavy fuel oil fell from a factor of 2.3 higher in 1958, to 1.2 in 1973, a reduction of 50 per cent.

France cheerfully embraced the penetration of oil. She did so because a policy of cheap oil suited three powerful groups for three quite different reasons. It suited the Ministère des finances because it brought low prices and demanded no investment from the State. It suited the Ministère de l'industrie because it engendered an internationally competitive manufacturing industry. It benefited a coalition of Gaullist politicians and oil company executives (not always distinguishable) who perceived an opportunity for creating an extensive and secure structure of oil supplies based on French crude. Let us take these points in turn.

The Ministère des finances, like any organization responsible for preserving financial equilibrium has a near time-horizon. Its priorities are to keep the external accounts in balance, to keep the public accounts in balance and to stabilize, if not to reduce, the price index. To an Inspecteur des finances, a cheap petroleum policy was the answer to his prayer. It provided for low cost sources of energy; it made almost no demands on the public purse for investment capital; it assured that the cost of energy fell in constant francs.

The Ministère de l'industrie was concerned about competitiveness. France had a well-established tradition of non-competitive industries protected by import tariffs, price fixing cartels, tax evasion and like devices. The imminent entry of France into the Common Market and the consequent regime of decreasing barriers to trade was worrying. The Third Plan makes this point in general terms: 'The period covered by the Third Plan is one of fundamental importance in preparing the French economy for European competition.'

French industrialists were conscious of their weakness, especially the men running the traditional and energy-intensive heavy industry. It was precisely in this sector that the links between the politicians and the grand old families of France were strongest. The lobbying for a low price energy policy was persuasive.

The third element of this triangle of forces was the coalition of the leading politicians with the French oil company executives. The compatibility of their expectations requires some explanation.

The enthusiastic encouragement by the State of exploration for petroleum had been fruitful. In France itself, the SNPA had discovered deposits of oil at Lacq in 1949 and then 2 years later the more important deposits of gas which lay underneath. In 1951, Esso had discovered another small oilfield at Parentis. But the greatest success had been in the Sahara where large deposits of oil and gas began to be discovered after 1956. Guidelines for the exploitation of these discoveries were given by the *Code pétrolier saharien*. This edict provided for an equal division of profits between the State (France) and the public and private investors. The code also assigned to the State the priority of supply from the franc zone.

The brilliant success of these explorations in the Sahara posed the problem of how to dispose of the oil. As a result of previous policies, France was endowed with a well-developed refining structure. Technically the obvious solution was to sell the oil on the French market. De Gaulle recognized that international independence in all its forms was an essential requirement of political influence; autonomy in energy supplies was much to his liking. It is also significant that the top men in the state oil industry and administration had been put there by de Gaulle and shared his political perspective. The most influential of these was M. Pierre Guillaumat. M. Guillaumat has undoubtedly been a pervasive and effective influence on all French energy policy. He was a Gaullist from the first; after the Liberation he became Director of the DICA, then Commissaire at the CEA. During the war in Algeria he was Ministre des armées. He was frequently referred to as the *'éminence grise'* of General de Gaulle in the energy sector, and as the 'Minister for Oil'. He appointed men of similar outlook to strategic posts throughout the industry. The alliance of this coalition of politicians and oil companies with the Ministères de l'industrie and des finances was irresistible.

Some of the oil from the Sahara was channelled to France through international companies refining in France, but to supplement that means, a new state organization, l'Union générale des pétroles (UGP) was created, jointly owned by the state producers of crude. In 1960 it organized, with Caltex, a distribution network in France with a market-share of 5 per cent. In 1962, the year in which Algeria achieved independence, the production of crude oil from the franc zone was 23 Mt of which 17 Mt came from the Sahara; it supplied half the needs of the nation.

At that·time, the validity of the concept of *pétrole franc* was not in doubt. The Treaty of Evian was signed in March 1962. Those clauses of the agreement which related to oil proposed that Algeria would give priority to French oil companies in the allocation of permits to prospect and produce, for a period of 10 years. In fact, French diplomacy was later able to exact an agreement for 15 years with the possibility of revision at the end of the first 5 years; this was signed in 1965.

The policy known as *brut franc* or even *brut national* was reinforced in 1963 when the licences for refining were renewed. A decree was issued that permitted the French State to impose an obligation on oil companies to refine crude from French controlled territories in their refineries, with the intention of obliging the majors little by little to eliminate other imports. The objectives of French oil policy were restated by an inter-ministerial Council in November 1964. The producing capacity controlled by French companies had to be permanently equal to French consumption. The origin of the production should be diversified as far as possible. French enterprises should keep more than half the national market in refining and in distribution and should penetrate abroad. These principles were confirmed by the Ministre de l'industrie before the National Assembly in November 1968.

The objectives were largely reached. In 1969, the French companies were producing 80 Mt against a national consumption of 70 Mt; they had slightly more than 50 per cent of the refining and distribution in France and exports of finished products exceeded imports by 14.2 Mt to 5.2 Mt.[9]

The policy of cheap oil naturally had important consequences for the other energy industries. The most important were:

1. The regression of the coal industry.
2. The frustration of natural gas.
3. The conversion to oil of EDF.
4. A slackening of interest in commercial nuclear power.
5. A shift of emphasis to light water designs.

The Third Plan had proposed a target of 65 Mt of coal production by 1965, compared to the actual production of 60 Mt in 1959. The Plan had only been published a few months, when the parlous state of the coal industry and the recognition of the consequences of a low price energy policy made it necessary to prepare a special supplementary plan for the coal industry. This, the Jeanneney Plan, proposed a rapid regression of the industry, and suggested an objective of 53 Mt by 1965. It offered a little protection for coal by requiring oil companies to restrict price reductions from the official price to no more than 5 per cent; this provision was lifted in 1963, thereafter allowing the oil companies full licence. In the same year the miners reacted violently to the regression of the industry. A long strike followed. The Government instituted a 'round table' between themselves, the enterprise and the unions. The State relieved the industry of some of its financial charge but also fixed an enormous programme of regression, known as the *Plan de la table ronde*. The deficit of the industry continued to grow. In 1968 another special plan, the *Plan Bettencourt* confirmed the rhythm of regression.

The penetration of oil gravely frustrated attempts to extend the use of natural gas in France. GDF has never had access to the low cost reserves on the scale enjoyed by the British Gas Corporation, but this material difficulty was reinforced by the policy of cheap oil. The low profit margins and slow rate of growth of sales were inadequate to finance the heavy investments required to expand the industry. By the late 1960s, GDF was heavily in debt. The Ministère des finances imposed a programme of financial recovery which was successful, but at the expense of investment; the consequences are still felt today.

EDF was at first unaffected by the penetration of oil. It did not think in terms of particular markets, but in terms of its growth rate of 7–8 per cent a year which had prevailed since the War and which it had come to regard as a natural law. The penetration of oil into Europe was led by sales of petrol for the automobile industry; in refining crude oil to petrol, large volumes of heavy fuel oil are produced concomitantly. This product had no market at the time other than to large boilers for power generation; it was therefore bound to be sold just below the thermally equivalent price of coal. EDF's first reaction was to launch a programme of fuel oil-fired generating plant; thirty-seven 250 MW (e) generating sets were ordered and put into service in the period 1956–1974. All the sets up to 1963 had been designed to burn coal. Thereafter, all were to burn fuel oil, with the exception of two units on the coalfields. Subsequently CDF negotiated an agreement with EDF to the effect that the annual burn of French coal would reach 15 Mt by 1975, but it was later revised and in the event EDF burnt less than half that figure. EDF began to look at the nuclear programme with an increasingly jaundiced eye. Obsessed now by the criterion of least cost, the enterprise became more and more convinced that the gas graphite line of development being followed by the CEA would have less chance of competing economically with the light water reactors developed in the USA. The CEA had developed their technology with dedication. To understand the extent of their chagrin at EDF's change of heart it is helpful briefly to review the history of the programme.

In 1952, the Chamber of Deputies voted a 5 year programme of research and development of the natural uranium gas graphite reactor (UNGG), and the first elements of a reprocessing factory; this was to be implemented by CEA. In 1956, EDF began its first nuclear programme comprising three reactors of the UNGG type, Chinon 1, 2, 3. In 1958, Framatome, a firm owned by Schneider, took out a licence from Westinghouse to manufacture the pressurized water reactor (PWR). In 1960, EDF undertook an experimental programme of diversification and decided to construct a light water reactor at Chooz; Framatome received the order for the nuclear steam supply system. In 1963, EDF undertook a second UNGG programme, Saint-Laurent 1, 2 and Bugey 1. After this date the UNGG design became the object of steadily increasing attack by EDF not only for the reasons mentioned, but also because the vast bulk of experience of nuclear reactors in the world lay with the light water reactors (LWRs), so that in the event of trouble the costs of retrieving the situation would be shared among many more participants. French heavy industry also favoured the American designs because these offered more scope for export. The apparently better export prospects were the consequence of three factors:

1. The determination of CEA to maintain complete control over the details of design of the UNGG reactors, and the EDF's habit of assuring the architecture of its own stations, impeded the industry from obtaining 'turn key' experience in the UNGG design. With the LWRs for which they had licences, both Schneider (PWR) and La Compagnie generale d'électricité boiling water reactor (BWR) hoped to construct a trading position in France that would facilitate export.
2. The apparent superior economic viability of the LWR designs and particularly the reduced work needed on site.
3. The dominant position in the market already established by American designs.

The CEA took up a position against the EDF and the construction industry and in favour of their own UNGG designs. There had always been tension between EDF and CEA, partly as a result of overlap in their functions and partly due to their attempts to control new areas of responsibility as they arose. The original statutes of the two bodies did not assign responsibility for the construction of nuclear stations. A first CEA–EDF protocol in 1956 gave EDF responsibility for the construction of nuclear stations to CEA's design; this led to interminable disputes over, for example, materials. There were also differences of objective: EDF claimed a duty to cut generating costs even if that meant using American technology. The CEA advocated that energy policy should be guided by wider considerations; in this they received top level political support even from de Gaulle himself who was opposed to the construction of American designs. When the Director General of EDF, M. A. Decelle, resigned in 1967, this was widely attributed to his frequently stated belief in the superior merits of American designs, and to the exhaustion of de Gaulle's patience.

The Government finally sought advice on the choice of reactor from a consultative commission, known as the commission consultative pour la production d'électricité d'origine nucléaire— the PEON Commission. EDF, with a large pool of able engineers and technologists, operated extremely skilfully within the PEON Commission—as it still does within other important committees— to ensure that the decision of the group incorporated the views of the enterprise.

The PEON Commission report[10] was couched ambiguously, but essentially favoured the LWRs. It concluded that after Fessenheim 1 and 2, at that time planned as UNGG stations, there would be no imminent need for further such stations. The LWR design was thought to provide the cheapest electricity and the Commission recommended building a 600 MW(e) prototype. The report is permeated with discussion of the prospects for exporting reactors and fuel reprocessing plant, matters which were then discussed with less caution than now; it is clear these were an important consideration of nuclear policy.

But de Gaulle was not the man to be unduly influenced by the recommendations of technicians if they went against his political aims. The final obstacle to the LWR programme still remained. Senior French administrators laid siege to de Gaulle and, it is believed, were on the point of convincing him when he was defeated in the referendum in 1969. The new President, M. Georges Pompidou, was easier to persuade; by 1970 he was convinced of the need to manufacture American designs. The orders for Fessenheim 1 and 2 were changed to PWRs and given to Framatome.

The disruption of the traditional relationships between French energy industries occurred at the same time as a change in relationships between state enterprises and the State. The apparatus of control of public enterprise by Ministries was extensive. It was employed by the State in the 1960s in a most aggressive fashion. Control was exercised principally by the Ministry of Finance. The power of this department was , and still is, legendary in France. M. Alain Peyrefitte, a minister under de Gaulle, Pompidou, and Giscard, claims:[11]

The administrative omnipotence has two stages. There is that of the administration over all that which is not administration. And then there is that exercised by the [Ministry of] Finance on the rest of the administration. The departments which make others tremble, tremble themselves before the rue de Rivoli—who tremble before no one.

Peyrefitte describes the considerable control exercised by the Ministry officials over the spending Ministries in the budget. Mr. Jacques Chirac (an experienced French politician and ex-Prime Minister) has also claimed that the State no longer dominates its administration, and has drawn attention to the fact as he sees it of the disproportionate power of the Ministry of Finance and its inadequate response to political direction.[12]

Among the nationalized industries , EDF was especially restless under the prevailing regime; its complaints mainly concerned the restrictions placed upon it by the Ministry of Finance. One of the matters which attracted most attention was the control by the Ministry of the salaries of EDF personnel. Discontent led eventually to a strike in which the supply of electricity was cut. Similarly, input prices and tariffs were fixed by Ministries, either exclusively or predominantly by that of Finance; permission to borrow funds from national or international markets was required from the Fonds de développement économique et social (FDES), an institution presided over and controlled by the Ministry of Finance.

These relationships were not untypical of those characterizing public enterprise and government department. There is, however, one aspect, small but significant, which is particular to EDF. EDF regularly showed an annual growth rate of 7 per cent or more in electricity sales; this roughly meant a doubling every 10 years. As a consequence EDF was obliged to finance every 10 years as many new stations as existed at the beginning of those 10 years, and to replace obsolete plant. This programme called for ever increasing injections of capital. The response of the Ministry of Finance was to reduce the requirement by lowering the growth rate. The Ministry was hostile therefore to all advertising and aggressive commercial behaviour on the part of EDF. As a consequence, the allocations for advertising were restricted to 0.5. per cent of the value of total sales.[13] On one occasion a commercial campaign was stopped dead on instructions from the Rue de Rivoli. This was especially irritating for EDF who even at that time perceived their greatest opportunities for expansion as lying with sales of electricity for thermal uses. This large new market could not be penetrated without an extensive and aggressive selling campaign which was denied to them.

The general question of the direction of public enterprise in France was examined by a working party set up in April 1966 by the Prime Minister. The need for this study was attributed to concern for the competitiveness of French industry in the environment of the common market, concern with the finances of public enterprises and the dissatisfaction of the public enterprises with the existing and tiresome system. The study[14] confirmed that effective power to control the affairs of public enterprise was moving consistently towards the Government, partly to the technical *tutelle*, but mainly to the Ministry of Finance. The working party made many recommendations on the whole nature of the relationships involved, but the most essential requirement was seen to be a greater autonomy of public enterprise in pricing policy, salaries and investment. In return the industries would be subjected to more vigorous criteria of management and self-financing.

Specifically, it was proposed to re-establish the industries' finances by setting prices at a level that reflected true costs and eliminating the need for transfer payments from the State, and also to allocate clearly the responsibilities of the technical *tutelle*, the financial *tutelle* and the enterprise. The State could ask the enterprise to undertake certain actions for the sake of wider social and political considerations, but the enterprise was entitled to be reimbursed. Responsibilities were allocated as follows:[15]

1.   The enterprise was responsible for developing markets and making best use of its assets.

2. The technical *tutelle* had the responsibility for elaborating sector policies, particularly in energy and transport.
3. The financial *tutelle* had the responsibility for reconciling sector policies and maintaining the equilibrium of the economy.

EDF, which had participated vociferously in the protests against the existing system, was chosen for an experiment in the new order, both in respect of the new salary policy and the new contractual relationships between the State and public enterprise. In the negotiations leading up to the agreement of the *Contrat de programme*, a principal objective of EDF was to obtain the right and the duty to promote their product and to pursue an effective commercial policy. By this means EDF hoped to increase sales sufficiently to provide more of its own finance and thus assure its own continuing and growing autonomy. This objective was resisted by the Ministry of Finance and according to M. P. Delouvrier, the President of EDF, it took 6 months to agree to this aspect of the contract.[16]

The contract was eventually signed at the end of 1970 and covered the years 1971–75, which were the subject of the Sixth Plan. The results of this new independence of management were expressed in the official vision of EDF as the 'great commercial turning'. The aim of this initiative was to capture new markets, particularly the domestic space heating market, on the basis of the growing price of oil and the qualities of electricity—cleanliness, convenience, absence of pollution, the possibility of heating each room to the required extent—combined with the relative fall of electricity prices. The campaign comprised modifications to tariffs to encourage bulk users, cultivation of relationships with groups acting on the interface between the electricity supplier and user, for example architects, equipment designers and distributors, and town planners, and a vigorous advertising campaign with the slogan '*tout électrique*'.

The severance of the apron strings for which EDF fought so fiercely was forced upon the CEA.[17] After it had been decided to construct American reactor designs, the function of the CEA changed; previously the largest part of its commercial work had been directed to research, development and design associated with the UNGG reactor line. Much of the CEA resented the selection of foreign technology and feared the consequences; the unions were strongly opposed. President Pompidou, making fruitful use of the right to appoint directly the senior positions in French public enterprise, chose as the senior administrator M. André Giraud, a strong and brilliant man, and assigned to him the mission of converting the CEA to an economic institution with commercial objectives and a relatively small spending section. The internal structure of CEA was changed and given the form of a central kernel surrounded by seven units each with a relatively homogenous task and subject to different criteria for good management.

The seven units covered radiological security, scientific research, nuclear materials, industrial co-operation on non-nuclear matters, programmes of national interest, industrial application of nuclear energy and military applications. It was foreseen that certain operational units might take the form of private companies in which CEA would have some participation. The organization was further modified in 1975 by the creation of subsidiaries in which the activities with conflicting management needs could each find the best working environment. The Institut de recherche fondamentale (IRF) was formed to group the units working in basic research; an Institut de sûreté et protection was formed to cover safety matters. The non-commercial activities of the CEA, namely research and development, military applications and safety, were now financed by a direct allocation in the budget of the Ministère de l'industrie or indirectly through a budgetary allocation to defence which was used to purchase services from the CEA. In August 1975 the CEA received authority from the Government to constitute its activities relating to the fuel cycle in a new private subsidiary, wholly owned by CEA, called the Compagnie générale des matières nucléaires (COGEMA). The reasons for creating COGEMA were to facilitate the management of the CEA's industrial activities on a commercial basis, to provide the State with an instrument for ensuring all the stages in the provision of nuclear fuel and to permit France to enter as easily as possible into international markets both for the purchase of raw materials and the sale of products.

A similar trend to independence can be detected in the oil industry. In order to strengthen the instruments available for the execution of the Algerian oil policy, the functions of the existing public groups, BRP, RAP, UGP, were assigned to a new single public organization, l'Entreprise de recherche et d'activités pétrolières (ERAP). ERAP, like its forebears, was created by Ministerial decree, it was never voted for by Parliament. Credit for the conception and construction of ERAP is universally given to the man who filled the posts of President and Director-General for its first eleven years—M. P. Guillaumat.

The analogy between this change in the institutional structure of the oil industry and the later changes in the CEA, is striking. Immediately after the War, new institutions, BRP and CEA, were established to retain the state interest in oil and nuclear energy. In 1966, the BRP was transformed into a state enterprise to operate in a competitive, international sector; 9 years later the commercial interests of CEA were assigned to a new similar institution.

The relations between the State and the major oil companies continued on much the same lines. The licensing system was an irritant to the companies compensated by the high profits on the French market and by the security which the system offered. The issue of licences always anticipated the growth of the oil market. The rapid penetration of oil which was unforeseen by the architects of the Fourth and Fifth Plans was not hindered by any corresponding myopia at the Ministry. Prices were controlled but at levels determined by the world market. Investments were financed without state funds and were not controlled. Again, the Fourth and Fifth Plans grossly underestimated the growth in refinery capacity. The Plans were of no consequence; the oil companies made the running. The pragmatic relationship was lucidly defined by M. A. Giraud, the Director of the DICA. He explained that the law of 1928 'recognized in a realistic fashion the prime importance of the oil companies and delegated to them the exercise of these activities within a flexible framework, reduced to the essential, in which the State and the companies have discovered their interest.'[18]

Adaption

The fourth period of adaption is characterized by an increasingly clear perception of the difficulties and uncertainties of maintaining cheap and secure oil supplies and by the emergence of new ideas about the structures preferred for French industry if it were to flourish in an international environment. Awareness of the dangers of relying excessively on oil began to be seriously entertained at high political and administrative levels in France during the late 1960s. The events in Algeria in 1970 and 1971 gave the French firsthand experience of the weakness of the position of the consuming nations, and caused them to perceive the beginning of the end more clearly than did other European nations; the Algerians had taken over all the foreign companies successively between 1962 and 1970, leaving only the French companies CFP and Elf-ERAP.

Algerian initiatives to control her own petroleum deposits began in 1963 with the formation of a national oil company, Sonatrach. This company amicably acquired the distribution network belonging to BP, and then nationalized Esso and Mobil as, ostensibly, a political reprisal for alleged American collusion with Israel in the Six Days War. The first nibble at France came during the serious disorders in Paris in May 1968; Algeria took the opportunity to nationalize fourteen French oil companies involved in distribution of refined products. In the following ten days, another forty-five French companies, not in the energy sector, were nationalized. *Détente* prevailed and indemnities were agreed for the nationalized companies.

The agreement at Evian in 1965 had put forward to January 1969 a re-examination of the fiscal claims relating to petroleum. The royalties going to Algeria were considerably lower, on average by about half, than those obtained by other oil producers. Negotiations were postponed throughout 1969, because of France's internal changes, but as soon as M. Pompidou became President he sent the Minister of Foreign Affairs, M. M. Schumann, to Algeria to open negotiations. The delegation from the French Government proposed a reduction in royalties of 4 cents a barrel, in reply to the Algerian proposal of an increase of 57 cents.[19] Negotiations made no progress and in July 1970 the Algerian Government fixed the reference price of oil unilaterally. In February 1971, Boumedienne announced the nationalization of 51 per cent of the oil production and 100 per cent of gas production, promising France that her security of supply would not be affected. CFP and ERAP withdrew their personnel from Algeria and tried to organize a boycott of Algerian oil.

The French Government approached the US Government for help in seeing that US companies did not ship oil from the French concessions; it also created problems for Algeria in international bodies such as the Common Market and the World Bank. But Sonatrach proved equal to the task of managing the French companies' production equipment and, although the boycott was largely successful, wider political considerations eventually prevailed and the French Government retreated. It did so by announcing that the position of the Algerian Government made the pursuit of oil negotiations between the Governments purposeless, and that, therefore, it would be up to Algeria to talk to the oil companies directly. This formula permitted the companies to salvage what they could. CFP had a comparatively small interest in Algeria and had plenty of resources elsewhere in the world, which it could develop to replace Algerian oil; it was the first to approach Algeria. ERAP had a much larger interest in Algeria; moreover, it had fewer resources elsewhere, and its President and Director-General, M. Pierre Guillaumat, had a strong personal commitment to the policy of *pétrole franc* and to the whole French petroleum policy of which ERAP's presence in Algeria was the pivot and the proudest symbol. M. Guillaumat's disappointment was evident.[20] Nevertheless, ERAP eventually signed a settlement, in September 1971. As a result the production capacity in French hands fell substantially below the needs of the country.

The events following the Yom Kippur War are well-known and do not require elaboration; they undoubtedly reinforced French fears and stimulated their endeavours to develop new secure sources of energy, particularly nuclear. But it was the events of 1970/71 which marked the change in French attitudes, later events really only reinforced the changes set in motion at that time.

The other determining influence on institutional relationships was the prevailing perception of French industrial policy. French business was seen as being increasingly vulnerable to foreign competition, partly because of material superiority of organization and size of unit, and partly because of the independent, aggressive competitive spirit of foreign firms in contrast to the less self-reliant French firms seeking, and provided with, extensive state direction and protection. It became the aim of French industrial policy to rectify these disadvantageous operating conditions and attitudes.[21] The means employed varied from sector to sector, according to the precise environment of particular industries and the degree of competition and *regroupement* so far attained, but the general principles were to eradicate the paternalistic *tutelle* of the State, to restructure industry into larger units that would be competitive nationally and internationally and then to sell abroad. The final structure would consist of one, or perhaps two, great national firms for each sector, for example Pechiney-Ugine and Penarroya-Mokta in non-ferrous metals, and Rhône-Poulenc and ERAP-CFP in chemistry. In practice, the structure tended more and more to single firms dominating sectors as the principal firms tended to divide tasks between them. It was at the time envisaged that there should be two constructors of reactors, CGE and Framatome, in order to preserve competition, but a monopoly eventually developed in this sector as well. An especially interesting remark by M. Chaban–Delmas was that: 'In any case, the creation of purely national groups can only be a stage, leaving these groups themselves to negotiate balanced international alliances.'[22] Competitiveness was to be preserved by competition amongst international groups.

The heavy electrical manufacturing industry and the turbine manufacturers were a prime target of this policy; three of each shared a French market considerably smaller than that of the UK or Germany which were served by only two firms. The attempt by Westinghouse to dominate the French market through the purchase of Jeumont-Schneider was prevented by a Government decision. The Government preferred to constitute European ensembles around two poles: Compagnie électro-mécanique (CEM) with Brown-Boveri, and Alsthom-CGE, which was also to seek European alliances. Again a monopoly of state contracts eventually developed. Similarly, much of the heavy mechanical engineering industry was grouped into a new ensemble, Creusot-Loire. Part of the rationale for encouraging foreign alliances was to facilitate access to foreign capital. The work on the Sixth Plan had shown a substantial gap between the financial needs of industry to carry out the objectives and the investment funds available in the French economy.

The events following the Yom Kippur War reinforced the existing trend. Although not specifically threatening French industry, they were seen, especially by the small group of people responsible for co-ordinating French industrial policy as a particularly striking example of the gross dislocations of the world industrial and economic system which were likely to become increasingly frequent and which could only be withstood by large firms with international markets and international alliances.

The objectives of public enterprises during this period have been analysed by Professor J. M. Martin.[23] He asserts that the essential principle of their behaviour is to control the environment in which they operate. Specifically they seek to extend their control upstream to secure supplies, and downstream to secure markets, to ensure control of future technologies which they could use or which threaten them, and finally to obtain access to means of finance that would alleviate the control exercised by the Ministry of Finance.

The CEA offers one example of this new behaviour. By means of its participation in joint enterprises with private firms and foreign capital, it now controls the whole nuclear industry, from uranium prospecting, mining, ore processing, enrichment, fuel element fabrication, to reprocessing. It also has considerable influence within the reactor construction industry. Let us examine its activities within the four functions described.

The first function is to secure its supplies. For the CEA this means, in the first place, the access to uranium ore, and through COGEMA, usually in association with foreign partners, it is active all over the world. France's domestic uranium recoverable reserves, estimated at 120,000 tonnes, are significant but not enough to sustain her nuclear programme. They are used sparingly and tend to be regarded as a strategic stock. The chief priority of the CEA is to acquire access to reserves in old French colonies still under the influence of Paris and considered politically secure. The uranium is not actually styled '*uranium national*' or '*uranium franc*', but the motive is identical to the mainspring of French petroleum policy in the 1960s. In April 1974 there was trouble in one of the CEA's most successful prospecting areas—Niger. The President, Diori Hamani, tried to nationalize the uranium deposits and was overthrown by the present incumbent—Lt. Col. Kountche. It is alleged that France had a hand in the *coup d'état*.[24]

COGEMA has production interests in Niger, Gabon, the USA and Canada, mining rights in several Australian provinces, and has shown exploration interest in Mauritania, Indonesia, Senegal, Guyana and Guinea. COGEMA hopes that its initiatives will permit it to market about 10,000 tonnes by 1985, which is considered to be the expected consumption plateau to be reached in 1990.

The next function is the control of the energy market; for CEA its final market is the electricity supply industry at home and abroad. At home, any exercise of control that it can have must take the form of pressure, preferably in conjunction with EDF, on government policy. Since the reorganization of the CEA and the redefinition of its function, the principal sources of discord between CEA and EDF have been removed; these two bodies therefore usually operate together in their attempts to influence government policy.

The control of technology is a particularly important function of the CEA; the company is concerned both to direct the commercialization of existing technology and to direct the development of new technology; in the former group the important elements are ore treatment, enrichment and reprocessing. Conversion operations are carried out by Comurhex, a company owned 39 per cent by COGEMA, 10 per cent by St. Gobain and 51 per cent by Pechiney Ugine Kuhlmann. The production capacity considerably exceeds domestic requirements and it is planned to export these services.

At the beginning of 1972 an enrichment study group with the name EURODIF was constituted by companies from the United Kingdom, West Germany, Belgium, France, the Netherlands, Spain and Sweden. France was not prepared to consider any process for enrichment other than the diffusion process perfected in France by the CEA over the preceding 30 years. The German, British and Dutch partners considered that this technology had been superseded by centrifugation and withdrew from the consortium. In November 1973 the remaining partners agreed to a factory operating on the diffusion principle. The study group was then dissolved and a company of the same name was created with the task of constructing and operating the factory and selling its services. Sweden withdrew in 1974 and the Iranian Atomic Energy Organization took a 10 per cent share by means of a joint subsidiary with the CEA, with the name SOFIDIF. Iran had a blocking minority in SOFIDIF so that, in principle, the CEA did not have complete control in EURODIF. After the revolution in Iran, the Iranian Government wanted to withdraw from the project, but its shares were frozen by a court decision. The dispute is under arbitration by the International Chamber of Commerce in Geneva. Italy also negotiated a reduction in its share in 1981, from 25 per cent to 16.25 per cent, because of a slowdown in its nuclear programme. The present non-French shareholders are shown in Table 1.1.

TABLE 1.1

Foreign shareholdings in EURODIF

	%
Italy (Agip Nucleare, Comitato Nazionale per l'Energia Nucleare)	16.25
Spain (Empresa Nazional del Uranio)	11.1
Belgium (Société Belge pour l'enrichissement de l'uranium)	11.1
Iran	10

The enrichment plant is sited at Tricastin in the Rhône valley. Work on site started in 1974, production began in 1979 at a level of 2.6m SWU/yr and the full capacity of 10.8m SWU/yr was reached in June 1982. The EURODIF company during the course of 1974 successfully negotiated long-term contracts for the period 1979–1990 which covered 95 per cent of the capacity for the period. The shareholders held 89.5 per cent of the contracts and 10.5 per cent were with third parties from Germany, Japan and Switzerland. The project was financed by shareholders' capital, advances from customers, bank loans (mostly French) and a long-term loan from the CEA. France supplied only small subsidies and the overrun on the budgeted cost was small.

Such was the success of EURODIF that a subsidiary company, COREDIF, was formed with the task of launching a second uranium enrichment plant on the same principle. It was planned that the COREDIF plant would reach a production of 5m SWU/yr by 1985 and that this would be increased to 10m SWU/yr as demand justified it. However, because of the world-wide slowdown in the nuclear industry, a surplus of enrichment capacity has developed and the COREDIF plant has been postponed indefinitely. The CEA has also developed a chemical enrichment process and has approached West Germany, Australia and the United States to share the cost of a demonstration plant. The process is claimed to be inherently unsuitable for enrichment to levels of weapon-grade uranium, and thus can be exported without violating nuclear safeguards.

France has two reprocessing plants, at Marcoule and at La Hague. They were built and operated originally by CEA and have now passed to COGEMA. The larger and newer plant is at La Hague; it was originally intended to reprocess irradiated fuel from the gas graphite reactors operating on natural uranium but was later equipped with facilities to handle the irradiated fuel from light water reactors burning enriched uranium. Future developments will be concentrated at La Hague and the reprocessing of spent fuel from the gas graphite reactors has been transferred to Marcoule.

The reprocessing operation is probably the least satisfactory aspect of the French nuclear programme. The factory at La Hague was originally conceived for the purpose of reprocessing natural uranium fuel; in this capacity it was the object of detailed and vigorous criticisms from the socialist union CFDT representing the largest part of the work-force. The plant has now been equipped with a new unit known as the HAO (*haut activité oxyde*—high activity oxide) for the stripping and dissolution of irradiated fuel elements from reactors operating on enriched uranium. This unit, in the view of the union, posed such serious health problems to the work-force that they went on strike in September 1976 a few months after it had come on stream. A major fire in 1980 and other minor accidents in the plant have fuelled the dispute between COGEMA and the CFDT. The union is opposed to fast breeder reactors, believes reprocessing technology has not yet been mastered and would like a ban on the reprocessing of radioactive waste from abroad pending a debate on alternatives, particularly storage. COGEMA claims that the storage alternative would cost almost as much as reprocessing and would close the fast breeder option for France. The Socialist Government set up a twelve-man scientific commission in late 1981 to study reprocessing and alternatives. The report of this commission endorsed reprocessing. Meanwhile, the Government has authorized expansion of La Hague's capacity.

The initial plan was to bring the throughput in HAO from 400 tons/year at present to 800 tons/year and construct a third plant, UP3, with two similar reprocessing lines of 800 tons/year, functioning in parallel. This would give France a capacity of 2,400 tons/year by the end of the 1980s, compared with a national requirement estimated at less then 100 tons/year. Work has begun on an interim expansion to 1,600 tons/year by 1987–1988.

COGEMA has been seeking long-term contracts for reprocessing and storage all over the world to justify this capacity. So far its initiatives have been extremely successful. It has enjoyed a world-wide monopoly of reprocessing services, following President Carter's decision to stop reprocessing in the United States. Plans to build a reprocessing plant at Gorleben in Germany are facing political opposition and the enlargement of the British plant at Windscale is not scheduled to start before 1987. Some of COGEMA's clients were obliged by their governments to find an acceptable means of disposing of irradiated fuel before being authorized to proceed with the construction of nuclear power stations. COGEMA has signed contracts with companies from West Germany, Japan, Sweden, Belgium, Switzerland and the Netherlands for some 6,000 tons of fuel to be reprocessed between the mid-1980s and the mid-1990s, and has used its powerful negotiating position to impose severe conditions on its clients. The client companies will in effect finance the extension of La Hague through a condition in the contracts which obliges them to pay the principal part of the costs before the first deliveries of irradiated fuel. Moreover, the final price for the reprocessing service is not fixed in advance but will be notified to the customer after the operation, thereby removing from COGEMA the financial rises associated with unforeseen operational difficulties.

In 1978 COGEMA started the operation in Marcoule of the first plant for the solidification of liquid nuclear waste; West Germany and the United Kingdom soon showed interest in acquiring the licence. The CEA has a share in Framatome, the French monopoly manufacturer of steam supply systems. In 1980, COGEMA took over responsibility for the fabrication of fuel for fast breeders and graphite-gas reactors, and started, in association with Framatome, construction of a fuel manufacturing plant for a PWR reactor fuel. The CEA in participation with French and foreign capitalism in Framatome and Comurhex does not interfere with the management in any detail, but it does provide political direction.

For the purposes of controlling new technology, the CEA has a wide variety of subsidiaries, the most important of which are shown in Table 1.2.

TABLE 1.2

Subsidiaries of the CEA in fast breeder technology

Company	Shareholdings	Function
Novatome	15% Alsthom-Atlantique 34% CEA 51% Creusot-Loire	To be responsible for the engineering, industrial architecture, and construction of fast breeder reactor plant
Serena	65% joint subsidiary of Novatome and CEA 35% the German society KUG controlled by Siemens, in which Belgo-nucléaire and Neratom (Netherlands) participate.	Exclusive right to commercialize a combined French-West German technique and will have three licences, Novatome and West German and Italian concerns.

CEA has also attempted to acquire the technology of solar energy. It had 20 per cent of a company called Sofretes in which Renault had a large share. The company made solar powered water pumps, technically exciting but commercially disappointing. A large increase of capital was a necessary (but not sufficient) condition to make the company profitable. Renault would not take the risk; the CEA bought their holding and became the majority shareholder. The operation was brought rapidly to fruition in early 1978 a few days before the formation of a Commissariat à l'énergie solaire which might have considered itself a more suitable candidate to hold the state interest.

The final function suggested was the control of finance. Although the capital requirement of the CEA is not high compared to EDF, the rapid rate of growth of its activities, their relatively long lead times and its relative youth as a commerical organization do not permit it to finance much of its own requirements at present. It hopes to do so eventually as a result of its sales of services overseas, especially enrichment and reprocessing; this situation does not pertain at present—the State has to provide much of the capital requirement, while its commercial activities in association with private industry have been financed by loans from consortia of banks.

The CEA has been trying hard to consolidate its position in the nuclear industry, with considerable success. When Novatome was formed, the first intention was to allocate the capital as Alsthom (30 per cent), the CEA (30 per cent) and Creusot-Loire (40 per cent). The CEA wanted a blocking minority but Creusot-Loire objected. The solution finally reached in November 1977 was a compromise; the CEA was given the blocking minority and Creusot-Loire obtained an absolute majority in its own right. The arbitration favoured the CEA. In March 1978, Pechinney-Ugine-Kuhlmann (PUK) was persuaded to concede some of its holdings to COGEMA. PUK, directly or indirectly, was a partner with the CEA in at least twelve companies involved in the mining and treatment of uranium and the manufacture enrichment plant. The agreement covered five of these companies.[25]

The struggle of CEA to acquire a blocking minority in Framatome is most interesting. When Westinghouse was forced to part with some of its original 45 per cent holding in Framatome, the CEA wanted to acquire a blocking minority (34 per cent) and Creusot-Loire objected. The dispute was settled by the Ministre de l'industrie in favour of the private firm and the shareholding structure became: Creusot-Loire (51 per cent), the CEA (30 per cent), Westinghouse (15 per cent), Jeumont-Schneider (4 per cent). In early 1981, Creusot-Loire took up its option and acquired Westinghouse's stake, thus increasing its share to 66 per cent. An attempt later in the year by Creusot-Loire to merge with Framatome was blocked by the Socialist Government and finally the CEA was given 34 per cent of voting rights in Framatome and a veto on all decisions, while its financial stake remained at 30 per cent.

The behaviour of EDF can also be intepreted in terms of control of its environment. In order to attain its objective of a rapidly growing electricity market, EDF has entered into associations with French private industry that all, in their various ways, have the aim of influencing the choice of consumer or of developing new final uses for electricity. These subsidiaries include:[26]

Société française d'etude électrique (SFEE)
Société d'étude de réalisation et d'exploitation du tout
    électrique (SORETEL)
Société électricité isolation (ELISE)

Société maître d'œuvre pour la réalisation d'immeubles tout électrique (SOMORITEL)

Compagnie pour la promotion du transport—véhicule électrique (COTRAVE)

Société auxiliaire de matériaux pour les equipements électriques

Société pour le financement de la protection de la nature et la lutte contre la pollution

By means of these societies EDF is able to influence the choice of those determining the installation of energy using equipment and to create new markets. It has also, as we have observed, launched an aggressive commercial campaign which it had been working on for many years. EDF also publish a splendid magazine, expensively produced in full colour, which is distributed to those whose choice can affect electricity markets and wherein the virtues of electricity are extolled, particularly as a source of heat for homes, commerce, industry, agriculture, swimming pools etc.

The control of its own finances is the other principal aim of EDF's activity. The nuclear programme is, and will be, extremely demanding of capital. For this reason EDF would like to be able to raise electricity prices. Higher prices are not without dangers because they would slow down the rate of penetration into heating markets. On balance the present rate of penetration is regarded as satisfactory and higher prices are seen to be more urgent. However, prices have been deliberately suppressed in recent years for the wider purposes of the economy and the company has been making losses consistently. EDF claims that prices are 20–30 per cent lower than the long-run marginal cost. In 1980 the Government wrote-off a FFr.11.6 billion state-backed loan to EDF and allowed electricity prices to rise by over 20 per cent; EDF reported a small profit of Ffr.272 million. Since then price rises have been made worse by higher interest rates and the devaluation of the franc. EDF's financial position has deteriorated rapidly because of poor sales and the rising dollar.

The requirement for finance could also be reduced by keeping down the cost of stations. EDF has a reputation among suppliers for driving a hard bargain; the prices it claims to be paying for nuclear stations are indeed remarkably low. In 1978–79 it was involved in bitter negotiations with Framatome about a cost overrun of Ffr.1 billion, only a few per cent of the value of the contract but enough to erode profits in both companies. Framatome argued that the cause of the cost overrun was more stringent quality controls than were initially agreed and much stricter safety precautions.

So preoccupied is EDF with keeping costs down that it has refused certain improved safety standards desired by the safety inspectorate on the grounds that this would interfere with economies of scale.[27]

Most of EDF's finance is arranged by consortia of French banks, almost certainly with high level political encouragement, or from the international markets. EDF has put considerable effort into mastering the financial expertise required for these operations.[28] It has made a remarkable entry into the American financial market where it has raised money with an original scheme comprising loans denominated in eurodollars at floating interest rates for a period varying from 5 to 10 years, with the facility for the subscriber to enter the American 'commercial paper' market where periods are short and interest rates lower. As this market is unstable, the borrower (EDF) can reimburse at any moment by drawing on its long-term arrangements. With the help of Crédit Lyonnais, EDF has developed a mastery of the American commercial paper market unparalleled by any other non-American institution. The financial requirements of EDF are nevertheless huge and it is active in seeking new sources. The persistent French pressure for Euratom loans which enable EDF to borrow on the guarantee of the Community is an example of this continual effort.

If the proposed hypothesis of state enterprises working to control all aspects of their environment is correct then it should follow that EDF would attempt to infiltrate the companies constructing reactors. When Westinghouse was obliged to sell the larger part of its holding in Framatome, EDF made representations within the Government that it should be allowed to buy the shares. The dispute with the CEA was arbitrated by M. d'Ornano, the Ministre de l'industrie, against EDF.

The behaviour of the oil companies can be discussed in similar terms. In their case there is little behavioural change because control of their environment has long been a principal guiding the actions of multinationals. The most significant structural change in the French oil industry during the period under discussion was the fusion of Elf-ERAP and SNPA, the purpose of which was to procure funds for ERAP. For a long time the President/Director-General of the two companies was the same man: M. Pierre Guillaumat. Many of their operations were closely linked, but legal barriers prevented transfer of funds between the groups. However Elf-ERAP possessed extensive prospecting rights for oil and gas all over the world and too little money to finance the programme it desired. The State, the only shareholder in ERAP, would not furnish the additional funds. SNPA, on the other hand, had a healthy cash flow from its industrial diversification, undertaken to compensate for the depletion of the Lacq gas field. To direct this flow of funds into prospecting, the two companies were fused to form the Société nationale elf-aquitaine (SNEA). The operation was contested by the French Left because the financial nature of the operation was such as to reduce the participation of the State. From the SNPA (54 per cent state capital) and Elf-ERAP (100 per cent state capital) was created a company owned jointly by private shareholders and the State. At present the state shareholding is 70 per cent.

The CFP has tried to acquire new technology in coal and uranium mining and in solar energy. It is a partner in SOFRETES with the CEA and when Renault withdrew it was a competitor for that holding. It operates with the CEA in uranium prospection. Elf is also active in the solar and other non-energy sectors (cosmetics, pharmaceuticals, paper and packaging). The Ministère des finances, through its representatives on the Conseil d'adminis-tration, tried hard to discourage these new activities and the Government announced major management changes at the board of Elf. The aim was to stop Elf using its big cashflow to bring more private companies under state control, to prevent it from diversifying into non-energy sectors, and to channel its invest-ments into activities which foster the national energy policy.

SECTORIAL POLICY

Oil

France is poorly endowed with hydrocarbons. Natural gas was discovered at Lacq in 1951 and oil at Parentis in 1956. Since then nothing else of significance has been found. Domestic production reached a maximum in 1965, when it was supplying 6 per cent of oil consumed, but the proportion declined to 1 per cent by 1973 and has remained around this level since. Exploration at home was also declining up to 1973, when it started picking up again; an estimated Ffr. 1 billion was spent for exploration onshore and offshore in 1981. The State helps the oil companies in exploration financing by awarding grants from the Fonds de soutien aux hydrocarbures, a special oil-tax fund. The results obtained have not been encouraging.

The French national oil companies have made considerable efforts to secure interests in producing areas outside France. In the North Sea they have interests in the large Ekofisk and Frigg fields, which mainly produce gas, and are about to start development of the North Alwyn field. After the events in Algeria, France became increasingly dependent on oil supplies from the Middle East, which accounted for about 80 per cent of her total oil supplies in 1978. Subsequent events in that area have greatly harmed French interests. Nationalization in Iran after the revolution ended CFP's involvement and, as a result of the protracted Iran–Iraq war, supplies have been almost cut-off from Iraq, where France had worked hard. New stable suppliers have been sought and oil supplies from Mexico, Venezuela and Norway have been increased.

The need for overseas supplies and the expansion of French oil companies' interests abroad were given the full backing of French diplomacy. France has followed a pro-Arab policy since the days of General de Gaulle, after the Six Day Arab-Israeli War in 1967. In 1973 the EC, on France's initiative, adopted a UN resolution directing Israel to end occupation of Arab lands seized in 1967, and France was not subject to the 1973–74 oil embargo. France did not join the International Energy Agency created in 1974, arguing that the industrialized countries should follow a policy of co-operation and not confrontation with OPEC. French initiative was behind the Euro-Arab dialogue between the EC and the Arab League in 1974, and the North–South Conference in 1975–76, although they were not very fruitful. President Giscard supported the right of self-determination of the Palestinian people in his Arab tour in 1980.

On top of the loss of supplies, the French oil companies were hit financially. The result of the huge rise in oil prices in 1973 was to stabilize or reduce the demand for a commodity that had universally been foreseen to grow strongly in future years. New capacity in production, refining, transport and distribution had been planned and commissioned, resulting in a world-wide overcapacity in all branches of the industry. Markets in the United States, Canada, New Zealand, Australia and Japan being either protected or inaccessible to competition, the only region where the consequences of overcapacity can develop fully is Europe. Dumping of oil products in Europe forced prices down to a level below the costs of production of the European companies. Because these companies have relatively few markets outside Europe the total of their operations is a loss. The need to find reserves to replace those lost requires heavy investment in exploration and production, which with a small net income must be financed in large part by borrowing which in itself increases financial problems.

Starting in 1978, a number of measures were taken to liberalize the oil market in France. Prices of several products were freed. Prices of petrol and diesel oil were still controlled, calculated on a formula that took into account the cost of crude and the dollar exchange rate. The mechanisms of 1928 were maintained but their spirit and purpose were abandoned. The system of quotas was suppressed and 3 year import authorizations were distributed more widely. The objective of 50 per cent of the product market for French companies was abandoned. The objective of controlling production equivalent to the national need was also abandoned *de facto*. On the other hand, the State increased royalties on domestic oil and gas production and reduced the depletion allowances. Neither CFP nor Elf was completely happy with the system. Both argued that the choice should be between a fully dirigistic system that would set prices at a level high enough to provide profits for investment, and a completely liberal system; any mixture of the two would not work.

A combination of rising crude prices, government price controls, a weak franc and falling demand has driven the refining and distribution sector in France into a record loss of Ffr. 13 billion in 1981; Elf and CFP accounted for Ffr. 8 billion of it. Losses in 1982 continued at the same rate. The Socialist Government announced its oil policy in April 1982. It is gradually applying a new pricing system; product prices will be allowed to vary within 16 per cent of a cost-based price, with reference to Rotterdam spot prices and average published EC prices, and will be adjusted automatically every month. It also allowed a phased closure of refining capacity, aiming at reducing the huge overcapacity that exists at present; a target of 110 Mt of nominal refining capacity has been set for 1990, compared with 153.5 in July 1982. In return the industry will gradually invest in refinery modernization, with the aims of doubling the existing cracking capacity of 20 Mt.

Gas

Gaz de France appears a relatively timid organization compared to its United Kingdom counterpart. In its relationships with EDF it is usually defensive; this again contrasts with the relationships characterizing the gas and electricity industries in the United Kingdom. The difference is explicable in terms of the profitability of the industries in the two countries and their access to supplies. British Gas had access to low cost supplies in natural gas, which as monopoly buyer it was able to purchase at low price. This fortunate circumstance, allied to the vast volumes of gas available, permitted the industry to penetrate many markets rapidly and easily to finance the necessary infrastructure of supply; moreover the financial freedom which the industry consequently enjoyed permitted it to adopt aggressive and non-commercial marketing policies in other markets to the discomfort of its competitors. In contrast, the resources available to GDF built up more slowly and, with the exception of the deposits in Aquitaine, under less favourable circumstances. GDF has had three main preoccupations; its precarious finances, security of supplies from outside France and adequate markets.

The difficult introduction of natural gas into France was partly a result of material difficulties, but it was reinforced by the policy of low cost oil and price controls as a measure against inflation. The weak cash flow would not finance the heavy investments. As a result, by 1969 GDF was greatly in debt; the total of medium and long-term debt far exceeded its own capital resources. The period from 1969 to 1973 was characterized by a rapid increase in sales (25 per cent per annum on average) and higher prices, particularly after 1970/71 when the price of oil began to rise. But the poor financial state of GDF continued to restrict its growth; in real terms the investments during the period 1969–1973 were no more than in 1963–1968. Emphasis was placed on financial recovery. In this the enterprise was partly successful; by 1976 it was able to self-finance almost all its investment. This result was achieved partly by restricting the volume of investment and partly by increasing the profitability of the organization. After twelve years of losses, GDF made small profits in 1975 and 1976.

The poor financial performance of GDF in the mid-1960s was partly the result of the legacy of debt from the days of coal gasification that plagued all the gas industries of Western Europe and partly the result of the policy of cheap oil. The debts of GDF were not written off by the Government as happened in the United Kingdom; the financial problems were reinforced by the strong competition from heavy fuel oil. The weakness of GDF is undoubtedly one of the deleterious results of the policy of cheap oil.

The original sources of supply for the French natural gas network were Groningen, Algeria and Aquitaine. By 1975 the structure of supplies bought by GDF was: Aquitaine (19 per cent), Netherlands (62 per cent), Algeria (18 per cent). Declining deposits in Aquitaine and prospects of declining production from Groningen meant that the principal areas of future interest for France, and indeed all continental European gas companies, are the northern basins of the North Sea, the USSR, and Algeria. For France, delivery of gas from all these areas is most easily achieved in participation with third countries; most negotiations and contracts therefore involve international consortia. 'Soviet contracted' gas at 2.5 bn m^3/yr started flowing in France in 1976 under an exchange deal that arranged deliveries of Dutch gas, originally intended for Italy, to France, and Soviet gas to Italy. Direct Soviet supplies at a rate of 4 bn m^2/yr started flowing by pipeline via Czechoslovakia, Austria and Germany in 1980. Norwegian gas from Ekofisk entered France in 1977 at a rate of 2 bn m^3/yr, under a contract negotiated by a consortium led by the German company Ruhrgas.

Following the increased importance given to natural gas in the energy plans of both administrations in recent years, GDF started negotiations with many foreign suppliers to contract adequate supplies. Actual gas supplied in 1981 and planned supplies for 1990 are shown in Table 1.3.

TABLE 1.3

French natural gas supply (bn m³)

	1981	1990
Aquitaine (France)	6.5	3.0
Groningen (Netherlands)	8.0	3.0
Algeria	4.0	8.5
USSR	4.0	12.0
North Sea	2.5	5.0
West Germany	1.0	–
Nigeria	–	3.0
Cameroon	–	3.0
Total Firm	26.0	37.5
Possible (Canada, Trinidad, Qatar)		5.0
Total Possible		42.5

Two key contracts were signed at the beginning of 1982. GDF signed for deliveries of 8 bn m³/yr of Soviet gas from the Siberian pipeline for 25 years beginning in 1984, on top of the current 4 bn m³/yr. There was a 40/40/20 gasoil/heavy fuel oil/crude oil price linkage, a minimum price to run for the whole of the contract and the gas was to be paid for in francs. The deal was a good one, since GDF managed to sign on terms similar to the ones achieved by the powerful German utility Ruhrgas a few months earlier and achieved the rejection of the 100 per cent crude linkage, which had been the demand of Sonatrach since the beginning of 1980. In order to press France to accept its demand, Algeria cut her gas supplies to France by about one-third in 1980, but France made up the shortfall with increased supplies from the USSR and Norway and new supplies from West Germany. The dispute was settled a few days after the Soviet contract, in a contract which accepted crude oil parity and payment in dollars, at least in part. The deal was largely negotiated by the French Foreign Office, which incidentally had been opposing the magnitude of the Soviet contract on political grounds. GDF was unhappy with the Algerian terms and the Government undertook to pay for 13.5 per cent of the fob price, partly in acknowledgement that the agreement was intertwined with Ffr. 12.5 billion of contracts to be placed by the Algerians with French firms. Gas from Algeria is now carried by LNG tankers to three large terminals at Fos, La Havre and

Montoir de Bretagne. To safeguard itself against future supply interruptions, GDF aims to more than double storage capacity to 12 bn m^3 by 1990. It will also increase the amount of gas sold under interruptible contracts to 20 per cent of sales, a near doubling over current volumes.

Because of higher contract prices and the delayed introduction of tariff increases, GDF made a record loss in 1981. The effect of the devaluation of the france on dollar-denominated contracts will make things worse, unless price increases are authorized soon. The company has started a vigorous marketing campaign to attract new customers and meet its 1990 consumption goals. It aims to convince industry to adopt dual (oil/gas) burning capability for medium and large boilers, instead of coal conversion, and to equip 35 per cent of new houses with gas appliances.

GDF is hampered in its supply policy by its lack of authority to explore for gas. To the oil companies, gas is less attractive than oil when all else is equal, because the price obtainable for the commodity is lower, the difficulties of exploitation are greater, there is less flexibility for disposal and it is generally a less profitable venture than oil. Oil companies therefore tend to find the marginal gas fields either by accident or in conjunction with oil. GDF has apparently no plans to try to obtain this authority, which would require an alteration in the law of nationalization and would entrain formidable legislatory difficulties.

Electricity

Increasing the part of electricity in the French energy balance requires increasing generating capacity and markets simultaneously. It is not possible to achieve exact coincidence. Generating capacity comes in large units with a long lead time, the capture of markets has a shorter lead time but cannot be made as quickly as the commissioning of new capacity. Consequently the markets must appear before the generating capacity. This has two consequences during the period in which the nuclear stations are under construction; firstly it requires more fossil fuel to be burnt than would otherwise be the case, secondly it makes substantial demands on the existing fossil fuel capacity which, until the nuclear stations come on stream, must meet a higher maximum demand than foreseen.

EDF's fossil fuel burn has continued to increase during the

1970s. After the increase in oil prices, conversion of plant from oil- to coal-burning started. By 1980 EDF had reconverted all oil-fired stations that had once burned coal and it is studying conversion of plant that was designed to burn coal from the outset. Coal burn increased from 5 Mt in 1973 to 18 Mt in 1980, but this is

TABLE 1.4

Nuclear power stations in France

Station	Type	Power output (MW)	Year of commissioning
Marcoule (Gard)	Gas-graphite	40	1960
Phénix (sur site de Marcoule)	Fast reactor	233	1973
Chinon (Indre-et-Loire)	Gas-graphite	180	1965
	Gas-graphite	360	1967
	PWR		1982
	PWR		1982
	PWR	4×870	1986
	PWR		1987
Chooz (Ardennes)	PWR	305	1967
	PWR * *	2×1275	1989
	PWR * *		1989
Monts d'Arrée Brennilis (Finistère)	Heavy water	70	1976
Saint-Laurent des Eaux (Loir-et-Cher)	Gas-graphite	390	1969
	Gas-graphite	450	1971
	PWR	2×880	1982
	PWR		1982
Bugey (Ain)	PWR	920	1979
	PWR	920	1979
	PWR	900	1979
	PWR	900	1980
Fessenheim (Haut-Rhin)	PWR	2×880	1977
	PWR		1978
Dampierre (Loiret)	PWR		1980
	PWR	4×890	1981
	PWR		1981
	PWR		1981
Tricastin (Drôme)	PWR		1980
	PWR		1980
	PWR	4×915	1981
	PWR		1981

TABLE 1.4 (Cont.)

Station	Type	Power output (MW)	Year of commissioning
Creys-Malville (Isère)	Fast reactor	1200	1983
Paluel (Seine-Maritime)	PWR *		1984
	PWR *		1984
	PWR *	4 × 1290	1985
	PWR *		1986
Gravelines (Nord)	PWR		1980
	PWR		1980
	PWR	6 × 910	1981
	PWR		1981
	PWR *		1985
	PWR *		1986
Le Blayais (Gironde)	PWR		1981
	PWR	4 × 910	1982
	PWR		1983
	PWR		1983
Cruas (Ardèche)	PWR *		1984
	PWR *		1984
	PWR *	4 × 880	1984
	PWR *		1985
Flamanville (Manche)	PWR	2 × 1290	1986
	PWR		1986
Cattenom	PWR *		1986
	PWR *		1986
	PWR *	4 × 1270	1988
	PWR * *·		
St. Alban (Isère)	PWR *		1985
	PWR *	2 × 1300	1986
Belleville (Cher)	PWR *		1987
	PWR *	2 × 1275	1987
Nogent (Aube)	PWR *		1987
	PWR *	2 × 1275	1988
Golfech (Tarn-et-Garonne)	PWR * *		1989
	PWR * *	2 × 1275	
Penly (Seine-Maritime)	PWR * *		1989
	PWR * *	2 × 1290	

Note: In the projected figures, power output and the year of commissioning are approximate.
 * In construction.
 * * Approved but construction not begun.

considered to have been its peak. It fell to 15 Mt in 1981 and, despite the fact that four modern 600 MW coal-fired stations are being built, is expected to continue falling as more nuclear power plants come on stream. The present state of the French nuclear programme is summarized in Table 1.4.

Reactor construction

Construction of nuclear steam supply systems (NSSS) in France is a *de facto* monopoly of Framatome. To produce an NSSS requires four factors:

1. A reliable and competitive design.
2. A strong team of engineers.
3. An efficient and advanced electromechanical industry.
4. Certain specific investments for the larger and heavier components.

Framatome was originally owned by Creusot-Loire (38 per cent), Jeumont-Schneider (30 per cent) and by other companies of the group Empain-Schneider (10 per cent). The company acquired the licence for the PWR from Westinghouse in 1958, which met the first four requirements. In 1960 it won, in co-operation with Belgian industry, the order for the NSSS for the light water reactor at Chooz in the Ardennes. Chooz went on stream in 1967. No further order came until 1968 when Framatome was given the task of constructing the first European 900 MW (e) PWR station at Tihange in Belgium; again the work was done in co-operation with Belgian industry. In 1970,France decided to concentrate on the LWR line of development and in September the order for Fessenheim I was given jointly to Creusot-Loire and Framatome. The order was only obtained after severe technical and commercial competition with CGE. Framatome and Creusot-Loire immediately began a rapid expansion of the engineering facilities and personnel associated with reactor construction. By 1971 Creusot-Loire was able to begin an important extension to its heavy mechanical engineering factories at Creusot, to permit the fabrication in series of pressure vessels and steam turbines.

At the same time it prepared, at Chalon-sur-Saône, an investment programme aimed at providing the matching manufacturing capacity for steam generators. Framatome, at that time essentially a design office, increased its staff by 50 per cent. By

1972 the new factories were nearly completed; they had been designed to permit the construction of five to six NSSSs each year. In 1972 the capital of Framatome was augmented from Ffr. 1.5 million to Ffr. 12 million. As part of its increased capital share Creusot-Loire brought to Framatome the two new factories at Creusot and Chalon.

Framatome could now be said to have acquired control of the four factors identified earlier as being essential to the construction of nuclear steam supply systems. The engineering division of Framatome contained at that time about 250 professional scientists and engineers and the number was rapidly increasing. The company had also established an effective working relationship with the manufacturers of the other components, almost exclusively within the Creusot-Loire group; e.g. Creusot-Loire for the reactor internals, which were made in their conventional workshops, Jeumont-Schneider for the coolant pumps. Framatome had risked substantial investments in people and plant, apparently largely on its own initiative. The CGE refused to make similar commitments until after the orders had been passed. Eventually EDF were to choose exclusively PWRs, and Framatome became the monopoly supplier; the principal determinant of that outcome was probably Framatome's initiative between 1970 and 1972. The motivator in the nuclear policy in all other respects seems to have been EDF, but in the choice of reactor manufacturer, Framatome was able to outmanœuvre the favourites.

In a way Framatome was lucky because it was only after the oil crisis that the orders from EDF began to match the manufacturing capacity of their new plant. The company was capable of six units a year; in 1970 it received one order; in 1971 it received three; in 1972 it received none at all; in 1973 it received two orders from EDF and two orders for the pressure vessels alone from Westinghouse. Nevertheless Framatome continued to increase the number of design engineers employed and to make studies of still larger nuclear boilers containing four steam generators instead of the three current at the time. The report of the PEON Commission in April 1973 recommended a programme of between 8,000 MW (e) and 13,000 MW (e) for the period 1973 to 1977, which would have meant an average of two to three orders a year for Framatome. It is unlikely that the revenue from these orders would even have paid the interest on Framatome's debt. The company was relieved by the oil crisis and the programme 'Messmer' for thirteen units in 1974–75.

Framatome's efforts to export were also crowned with success in 1974. Two NSSSs were ordered by Belgium (Doel III and Tihange II) and Framatome received a letter of intent from Iran for two stations. In response to this considerable development Framatome decided that it was necessary to construct a new factory at Chalon and to extend the facilities at Creusot in order to increase the capacity for making pressure vessels to eight units per year and for making steam generators to twenty-four per year. This is the output necessary for eight complete boilers of the three loop system actually on order by EDF. The plant came into service in 1976.

The necessity for Framatome to have some guarantee of future orders is recognized by EDF. That is to say it was conceded by EDF and the Ministère de l'industrie as being a necessary condition for Framatome to undertake the new investments of 1974–76. There are three distinct levels of commitment by the State to buy reactors. These are the general outline of developments provided in the 5 year plan, the multiannual contracts, and specific orders. The first of these is essentially a moral commitment or *obligation ardente*. There is no financial compensation to the suppliers if the obligation is not met.

The multiannual contracts are even more ardent obligations backed by default clauses if EDF should change its mind. The first multiannual contract was signed in April 1974 after the Council of Ministers had authorized EDF to place the order. The contract covered sixteen identical units of which twelve were firm orders and four were options; the startup dates were spread from 1974 to 1976. The second multiannual contract was passed in February 1976 covering ten identical units differing in only a few respects from those in the preceding order. Construction was to begin in early 1977. The third multiannual contract was in fact concluded before the second, in January 1976. It covered eight 1,300 MW units with construction dates beginning from mid 1977; the fourth was announced in November 1979 covering three 900 MW units and seven 1,300 MW units to be ordered in 1980–81, and later a fifth programme covered one 900 MW and eight 1,300 MW units to be ordered in 1982–83.

After, or sometimes within, the multiannual programme come

the firm orders. By this means Framatome has sufficient security to benefit from the economies of series. In a rather more nebulous sense, Creusot-Loire is present in the PEON Commission whose deliberations largely determine the size of the multiannual contracts still to come; the mechanism therefore provides Framatome with some idea of what domestic requirements might be up to 4 or 5 years ahead.

Nuclear siting

Technical factors   The technical factors governing siting can be summed up as follows:

1. France has a favourable geology for siting power stations; there is little seismic activity; she has a long coastline in the North and West with many suitable sources of cooling water; there are several large river basins with favourable hydrology.
2. Planting of stations at the coast is generally more expensive because of high transmission costs; this applies especially to the west coast.
3. The most favourable sites are those near loads on large rivers which will sustain once-through cooling and do not require cooling towers.
4. When the above sites are exhausted the choice must be between coastal sites with high transmission costs and inland sites with cooling towers.
5. As a consequence the development of nuclear power will be concentrated in the existing industrial areas of France especially along the Rhône. There will be severe limitations on the amount of power available in the present less developed regions. This will reinforce the already severe regional imbalance in France, broadly between the West and the East.

Local opposition   A variety of interests may be threatened by the planting of a nuclear station; the principal sources of genuinely local opposition have been the owners of second homes, people engaged in the tourist industry and agriculturalists, especially peasant farmers. The owners of second homes are rumoured to exert a strong influence on siting decisions and there are stories of sites being abandoned by EDF as the consequence of well-directed letters from senior *Polytechniciens* with property nearby. It is difficult to prove or disprove allegations of this nature. Certainly EDF recognizes that the influential owners of second homes do contribute significantly to the forces forming their decisions; the owners of second homes, however, are not to be seen in the demonstrations on the streets and it is difficult to gauge the consequences of their clandestine operations.

Farmers and people making their living from tourism are closely related groups in rural France. Their opposition is founded partly on fears that the installation of a nuclear station will disturb the practice of agriculture and prevent people coming to the region, but more strongly on the fact that the plant will disturb their traditional communities and lives without bringing them any commensurate benefit. Typical of this attitude is a peasant farmer at Malville who complained that as a result of the fast reactor he would no longer be able to drink at the well where his father and grandfather had drunk before him.

Local councils in these areas frequently oppose the siting of nuclear plant in their communes. This is particularly true of the stubborn, proud, contrary councils of places like Languedoc and Brittany. Privately, officials of EDF maintain that these councils are in practice easily 'bought' by the material attractions of the *patente*. The *patente* is an annual tax to which anybody exercising a profession in France is subjected and which is paid by EDF to the commune where an installation is sited. But this claim is probably a way of casting doubt on the integrity of the opposition; the practical evidence points to strong and sincere opposition at those sites. There is a tendency for these difficult councils to be in the declining agricultural regions where the other socio-political and technical determinants combine together to inhibit nuclear developments. Again the effect is to aggravate the regional imbalance in France.

Universal opposition   This is a title which one might give to that part of the opposition which broadly objects to the development of nuclear power at any place and at any time in the foreseeable future. The complexity of this movement as expressed in the often conflicting expectations and objectives of different components, the grave dissensions about the means to be employed, the differing relationships perceived between the anti-nuclear movement and other contemporary topics of political significance, the association with a search for new forms of organization and lifestyle, the wide range of social backgrounds from which the members are drawn, and the sheer number of groups comprising the movement—this complexity almost defies taxonomy. But one can distinguish elements of the conventional left, the radical *gauchiste* wing, an ecologist movement and an anarchic *autonome* fragment.

Of the conventional left the PSU is the only political party of national significance to have taken up a robustly anti-nuclear attitude. This attitude is faithfully reflected in *Le Nouvel Observateur*, a journal that was formally linked to the forerunners of the PSU and which is still closely associated with the party. The arguments of the PSU are essentially that the nuclear programme is unacceptable because of the deleterious environmental effects, because of its risks for the work-force and the population, because of its irreversibility, and because of the type of society which underlies it, ever more centralized, more secret, more repressive, more heavily political, more militarized.

The general attitude of the PSU and the broad basis of its arguments are similar to those of the CFDT, the Socialist trade union. Officially, the CFDT seeks to avoid violent confrontation with the public authorities; the majority of its elected representatives respect and repeat that line, but a minority of militants from regions where nuclear plant is planned or under construction are probably to be found at meetings and demonstrations not sanctioned by the union.

Although the militant anti-nuclear members of the CFDT have been crucial in the anti-nuclear movement through their role of informing opposition they are very much a minority within the union. The persistent opposition of the CFDT is animated by a relatively few extremely sincere, well-informed and active members, some from the CEA and other nuclear companies.

Gauchistes comprise the revolutionary parties of the French left. On the whole, but by no means exclusively, these organizations favour violent (revolutionary) action not only against the nuclear programme, but also to achieve their other objectives. These groups are not opposed to nuclear energy *per se*, as much as to its quality as the most perfect expression of the sacrifice of the people to capital. To stop the nuclear programme for these groups is a secondary objective to destroying capitalism; in some cases their anti-nuclear attitude is a straightforward cynical and opportunist attempt to exploit a topic of insignificant direct interest but which they perceive as rousing hostility in the populace. In other cases the anti-nuclear attitude is an integral part of a Marxist analysis which has identified a broad range of ecological abuses as a principal contribution to the oppression of the people.

In the rapidly changing, undocumented and often ill-expressed life on the margins of the extreme left it is not easy to make an historical analysis. It is plausible to say that the historical origins of the *autonome* movement can be traced back to the events of May 1968 even though few of the *autonomes* of today would have been more than fifteen at the time and took no active part. But if the movement is seen as part of the anarchist tradition its development can be taken much further back.

It is to this layer of the anti-nuclear movement that the gross acts of violence are mostly to be attributed. Among such incidents are the bomb attack on the home of M. Boiteux, arson practised against offices of EDF and the sabotage of machinery having some relation, however remote, with the nuclear programme. A typical *autonome* is rather badly informed about almost all aspects of nuclear power, but does not find this a hardship. His opposition is sufficiently grounded in the idea of nuclear power as a perfect incarnation of the violence of the State, imposed without consultation, propelled by lies and force.

The discontent bred in the left and extreme left after the events of May 1968 was not confined to those who abandoned the extreme left to sow the seeds of the *autonome* movement. Others on the left withdrew from traditional political formations and began to develop a new apolitical movement, without real coherence or formal structure but held together in practice by three themes: feminism, anti-military sentiments and opposition to nuclear power. Up to the end of 1973, the anti-nuclear movement was a marginal movement in French society. The second stage of development began with the dramatic acceleration of the French nuclear programme.

The ecologists have animated the latent opposition of many parties and there have been demonstrations all over France. In many respects the opposition has shown a rich cultural quality; each regional committee has its own magazine often in an attractive, typically French style—witty and elegant. A variety of ingenious and gentle ways have been found to raise money, the sale of balloons at free fêtes, the sale of anti-nuclear stickers and posters. The humorous surface to the ecological movement should not be permitted, however, to obscure the deep conflicts between State and individual which lie beneath—that is why it is a radical movement.

Authorized procedures

The technical factors determining the siting of nuclear power stations and the socio-political origins of the opposition have been sketched. The outcome of these conflicting interests will be influenced not only by the nature and strength of the forces at work, but also by the administrative framework in which they interact. An account of the procedures for obtaining authorization is therefore necessary.

Nuclear installations in France can only be begun after authorization has been obtained in the form of a decree based on a report by the Ministre de l'industrie with the consent of the Ministre de la santé publique (public health). The application for authorization is first directed by EDF to the Minister responsible for atomic energy who then informs those of his government colleagues who may be concerned. The application is then sent to the prefect of the department where it is planned to site the installation. The prefect organizes a form of public inquiry, *Déclaration d'utilité publique* (DUP). A representative of the prefect informs the public and consults the local authorities, in particular the mayor of the commune directly concerned. The procedure of the DUP is far more one-sided than that obtaining in a public inquiry in the United Kingdom which has, despite original intentions, an adversarial quality; both sides put a case before an arbitrator. In the French scheme the State, through the prefect, *informs*. The municipal council must give its opinion within one month. The conclusions of the inquiry and the views of the local representatives of the competent government departments are sent to the prefect, who passes them on with his own opinion to the Minister.

During the course of the DUP a preliminary safety report on the application is made, in principle, by a committee of experts, in practice by EDF. This report is appraised by the safety department of the CEA and passed on to a Nuclear Safety Inspectorate which prepares the authorization decree.

Up to 1973 the procedure operated fairly slowly but without hindering the relatively small French programme. Successive accelerations of the programme subsequently made it necessary to find many sites rapidly and put sufficient strain on the procedure to contribute to delays. In some cases these delays caused EDF to begin work on a site without the DUP; whether this was legal is a controversial point, but it shows considerable confidence in a successful conclusion to the inquiry.

Forceful implementation of the authorization by the police and the almost complete lack of opportunity to challenge a decision through the courts means that opposition to nuclear sites has had no perceptible influence on the progress of nuclear policy. Violent demonstrations have led to many colourful and some tragic confrontations but no delays.

It is interesting to examine the changing nuclear attitude of the Socialist Party before and after it came to power. In January 1981 it unveiled its energy plan, *Energie: l'autre politique.* It proposed freezing the country's nuclear programme, only completing those plants under construction. As a result, there would be only 39 GW of nuclear plant in 1990, providing 48 mtoe of energy. It also proposed to put the whole nuclear issue to a national referendum, reiterated the Party's opposition to fast breeders and accused the Government of imposing its massive nuclear programme without democratic debate. The Socialist trade union, CFDT, called for more cuts in nuclear plant construction and only 23 GW to be installed. This compared with a government target of 65 GW and 73 mtoe for the year 1990. The Socialists' plan certainly helped to win the ecologists' vote, a small but crucial part in the voting coalition which brought them to power in June 1981.

The new Government's first step was to announce the cancellation of the controversial power station at Plogoff in Brittany, involving four 1,300 MW units. In July it announced suspension of work on five sites, involving eighteen 1,300 units, and an energy debate was scheduled for October. By then the Socialists had changed their minds considerably. It was decided not to put the nuclear issue to a referendum, not to rule out eventual industrial use of fast breeders, to press ahead with expansion of the La Hague reprocessing facility and only to trim the former Government's 1982–83 ordering programme by three 1,300 MW units. By declaring that the vote on its proposals would be a vote of confidence, the Government assured the approval of the Assembly. The Government left the decision to resume work at the five suspended sites to the local and regional councils and they all decided favourably by the end of the year. Initial opposition at Golfech and Le Pellerin was won over after a promise that local contractors and work-force would be favoured during the construction and operation of the stations. The targets under the approved programme are 56 GW and 60–66 mtoe by the year 1990. It was also decided not to abolish the preferential tariffs accorded by the previous Government to industrial and domestic consumers of electricity near nuclear power plants, although the Socialists had criticized the measure when they were in opposition.

The Government's energy programme assumes an improved role for coal, conservation and renewables in the energy system. Developments and programmes in the three sectors will be described in the following sections.

Coal

Domestic coal production had been decreasing steadily during the period before the Socialists came to power and reached about 20 Mt in 1980, while coal imports had been increasing and reached about 32 Mt in 1980, making France the second largest coal importer in the world, after Japan. The previous Government saw coal's role in energy supply as a static one, with domestic production continuing to decline to 10–12 Mt by 1990, and imports increasing. Several French ports invested heavily in new coal terminals to cater for the expected surge in imports. Dunkerque and Le Havre aim for about 12 Mt by 1990, hoping also to act as a major transhipment port for Mediterranean coal imports.

The Socialist Government has promised to reverse the decline in domestic production. Its current programme foresees domestic coal supplying up to half of a consumption target of 53–60 Mt for 1990. If the domestic production target is achieved, some of the coal port expansion might have to be trimmed. But increasing coal production above 20 Mt, possibly up to 30 Mt, will be a formidable task. French coal is uneconomic and attracted Ffr. 5.2 billion in government subsidies in 1981. Despite a small increase in production in 1981 (the first since 1964), the downward trend resumed in 1982. Stocks are high and higher subsidies are requested by CDF.

Imports are also falling and were expected to be about 25 Mt/yr in 1982–3, mainly because of lower imports by EDF. The Government is counting mostly on industry and district heating for the projected increase in coal use. Loans have been made available to finance central heating projects based on coal or other non-oil sources and grants for coal-related research have been increased. Nevertheless, the targets for 1990 look optimistic.

French companies tried from the start to gain a foothold in the growing world coal market. In 1981 CFP bought a US coal mine with 600 Mt of reserves. CFP, CDF and COGEMA have interests in mines in the US, Canada and Australia. CDF controls 165 Mt of reserves and hopes to increase them to 400 Mt by 1990. France is also involved, with other European countries, in the development of the huge coal resources of China.

CONSERVATION

The Agence pour les économies d'énergie (AEE) was created in 1974, after the first oil crisis, to pursue France's vigorous energy conservation programme. The Seventh Plan set a target of 45 mtoe savings a year by 1985 and forecast annual investment in energy conservation running at Ffr. 5 billion a year, half of which would need to go into industry. Savings were large in the first couple of years, estimated at 12 mtoe in 1975, but they began to tail off and reached only 16 mtoe in 1978. Investments in conservation were less than half the levels forecast in the Plan. This is partly due to the trouble that the AEE had in getting its legislation accepted. In February 1977 the Council of Ministers unexpectedly rejected a package of measures, including the establishment of an institution for the finance of heat recovery from power stations, contracts with automobile manufacturers binding them to produce vehicles with better performance and a financial penalty to be paid by electricity and gas consumers that consume more than a specific amount related to past consumption. A proposal to impose a tax of 2 per cent of their expenditure on energy on the country's 5,000 largest consumers, unless they invest more than a related amount in energy conservation, was rejected in December 1977, after hard lobbying by the Confédération nationale du patronat Français who opposed it. Another proposal for waste heat recovery was rejected in June 1978, after several thousands of EDF's employees demonstrated against it. The divergence between the objectives of the Plan and progress in energy conservation was worrying.

The second oil crisis renewed the effort for energy conservation; related investment was increased and new measures were taken. Investment grants of Ffr. 400/toe saved were made available to industry and stricter rules for insulation in buildings were approved. A commission was established to draw up a national heat plan, including waste heat recovery, and heat production or recovery projects would qualify for the Ffr. 400/toe saved grant. People installing heat pumps receive a Ffr. 3,000 grant from EDF and tax relief of Ffr. 7,000 and EDF and AEE started a campaign to have 800,000 heat pumps installed by 1990. A Ffr. 1 billion programme was approved to develop, by 1990, a car capable of travelling 100 km on 3 litres of petrol. Legislation was passed to enable Sofergies to be set up, financing companies exempt from tax aiming exclusively at energy-related investments. The measures, helped by higher energy prices, contributed to an acceleration in savings and 27.5 mtoe were saved in 1981.

The Socialist Government puts more emphasis on conservation and set a national target of a further saving of 30–40 mtoe a year by 1990. Its most important move was to create a new agency in April 1982, the Agence française pour la maîtrise de l'énergie (AFME), which is now responsible for renewables and conservation. The intention was to create a body strong enough to compete with the four established state energy concerns, namely CDF, EDF, GDF and CEA. The new agency will be partly financed by a Ffr. 0.01/lt petrol tax rise planned to apply from November 1982. AFME has been very active since its creation. It is asking the Government to put a special tax of Ffr. 0.04/kwh on gas and electricity use to provide funds for its needs, estimated at Ffr. 5 bn/yr. AFME launched a campaign in June to publicize its new measures. The Ffr. 400/toe saved is being phased out in favour of a Ffr. 8,000 tax credit for energy saving or oil-substitution investments. Other measures include subsidies of up to 70 per cent on energy audits, discounted loans for installation of energy efficient equipment and special loans to install high efficiency insulation.

RENEWABLES

Serious interest in renewable energy sources in France has mostly developed since the Yom Kippur War. The initiative has come both from the State and private capital; in both cases the potential for exports of hardware and services has been a significant incentive.

The earliest leader in solar energy research was the Centre national de la recherche scientifique (CNRS), mainly because of the dedicated work of Professor Felix Trombe, who started working there at a time when the subject was not encouraged and resources were few. The main work was on solar ovens, the best known of which, at Odeillo, was begun in 1968; work was also done on the technology of heating buildings. After the first energy crisis the CNRS designed a programme for solar energy research using the facilities of its existing laboratories. The State established the Délégation aux énergies nouvelles (DEN) in April 1975 whose function was not to research but to promote the idea of renewables and to help in the definition of objectives for industrialists.

The initiative for the establishment of a more powerful state organization came from President Giscard, who reasoned in an interview with *Le Monde*:

In this domain [renewables] France is among the world leaders. In particular solar energy is going to become a very important business. That is why I consider a Commissariat à l' énergie solaire (COMES) to be necessary, to co-ordinate efforts, as was done in 1945 with the CEA.

It is probable that the decision was advanced, and possibly even determined, by the Presidential desire to recuperate the ecological vote at the legislative elections, only 2 per cent but important in the context. The functions of COMES were to promote research and development, to develop new markets abroad by monitoring energy needs of foreign countries, to conclude collaboration agreements, to increase the energy component of French aid to developing countries and to create a market in France for French solar products.

Intentions were not fulfilled. As in the conservation sector, spending on renewables was less than half the level forecast in the Seventh Plan, although France was the second largest spender, per capita, in the world after the United States. A small and uncertain domestic market did not encourage industry expansion. Most manufacturers were small firms with financial problems, there was a shortage of experienced personnel to install and maintain solar equipment, and the cost of the equipment was still high.

After the second oil crisis, spending was increased and many new measures were taken to speed up developments. Property developers installing solar units were able to avoid payment of a Ffr. 3,000 non-refundable advance payable on all-electric homes. Private home owners were entitled to low interest 25 year loans, up to Ffr. 41,000 for heaters installed in single homes and up to Ffr. 3,000 for multiple dwellings. Subsidized loans became available from most major banks, covering 80 per cent of installation costs and repayable over 5 years. Up to Ffr. 7,000 tax relief was allowed on solar installation expenses. 'Growth contracts' were concluded by state bodies with companies producing solar collectors, thus guaranteeing a market. A study was conducted to identify the solar potential of all buildings owned by the Ministry of Defence. A number of public pools were to be equipped with solar heating systems. COMES began running training courses for solar installers.

The Socialist Government campaigned on a platform promising an even greater support for renewables, and has kept its promise. The targets for 1990 were increased slightly to 10–14 mtoe of renewable energy contribution, most of it coming from biomass. Spending on renewables was further increased, making France the world's top spender per capita. The new agency AFME, which absorbed COMES, is to have a special regional structure, in view of the Government's desire to decentralize energy decisions. AFME signed the first regional solar plan with Provence-Alpes Côte d'Azur which involved the installation each year of solar water heaters in 5,000 houses and 30 swimming pools and the incorporation of passive solar architecture into 2,500 newly built low cost homes, as well as into all new local government buildings. Tax credits were also increased to Ffr. 8,000.

There are many companies involved in solar energy. The CEA has also shown a marked interest in mastering the technology which at some distant date might threaten it and which in the meantime permits it to employ the numerous scientists and engineers released by reallocation of, and changes in, the responsibility for nuclear research. It is engaged mainly in fundamental research on the properties of materials for use in photovoltaic devices and flatplate collectors, and is the principal shareholder in Sofretes, a private company making solar powered pumps for use in developing countries. CFP is the principal shareholder in Giordano, France's leading manufacturer of solar collectors, and in Photon Power, which is building a pilot plant in Texas for the manufacture of cadmium sulphide photovoltaic cells. Following a nationalization move initiated by COMES, a new holding company, Société française des photopiles (SFP), was formed to sell photovoltaic solar cells, owned by CGE (51 per cent), Elf (35 per cent) and Radio technique compelée (14 per cent), which is a subsidiary of Philips and provided the technology. EDF also spent more than Ffr. 100 million in 1981 on renewables.

REFERENCES

1. This chapter has been influenced by the work of Professor J.M. Martin. See J.M. Martin, 'Les Industries de l'énergie en France', *Chronique sociale de France*, April-May 1975; J.M. Martin. *L'évolution des relations état-entreprise dans le domaine des activités énergetiques en France*, Université des Science Sociales de Grenoble, October 1973. See also N.J.D. Lucas, *Energy in France, Planning, Politics and Policy*, Europa Publications, London, 1979.
2. Electricité de France, 'Entreprise nationale, industrielle et commerciale', *La Documentation française*, Paris, April 1976.
3. J. Lepidi, Ingénieur en chef aux charbonnages de France, 'Le Charbon en France', *La documentation française*, Paris, April 1976.
4. 'La CFP à cinquante ans', *Pétrole Informations*, 29 March 1974.
5. J. Bour, 'La Passation des commandes et des marches de l'électricité de France', *Revue française de l'énergie*, 1959.
6. J.H. McArthur and B.R. Scott, *Industrial Planning in France*, Harvard University Press, 1969.
7. '1939–1945: le Purgatoire', *Pétrole Informations*, 29 March 1974.
8. N.J.D. Lucas, *Energy and the European Communities*, Europa Publications, London, 1977.
9. Jean Choffel, 'Le Problème pétrolier français, *La Documentation Française*, Paris, April 1976.
10. *Les Perspectives de développement des centrales nucléaires en France*, Rapport de la commission consultative pour la production d'électricité d'origine nucléaire, December 1968.
11. A. Peyrefitte, *Le Mal Français*, Plon, 1977.
12. J.Chirac, 'La Réforme du Ministère des Finances', *Le Monde*, 12 May 1977.
13. 'Face à face avec Paul Delouvrier', *L'Expansion*, October 1977.
14. *Rapport du Groupe de Travail sur les Entreprises Publiques*, April 1968.
15. M.R. Garner, *Relationships of government and public enterprise in France, West Germany and Sweden*, National Economic Development Office, London, 1976.

16. 'Face à face avec Paul Delouvrier', op. cit.
17. 'Reorganisation du commissariat à l'énergie atomique', *Energie Nucléaire*, December 1970.
18. A. Giraud, *Revue française de l'énergie*, Paris January 1966.
19. A. Francos and J.-P. Sorein, *Un algérien nommé Boumedienne*, Stock, Paris 1976.
20. Interview with Pierre Guillaumat, *Nouvel Observateur*, 12 February 1973.
21. Face à face avec Paul Delouvrier, op. cit.
22. 'La France, a-t-elle une politique industrielle?', *L'Expansion*, December 1970.
23. J.M. Martin, 'Les Industries de l'énergie en France', op. cit.
24. 'Une victime de l'uranium', *Le Nouvel Observateur*, 22 April 1974.
25. 'PUK céde à la Cogema plusieurs de ses participants', *Le Monde*, 31 March 1978.
26. J.M. Martin, 'Les Industries de l'énergie en France', op. cit.
27. *Le Monde*, 16 February 1977.
28. *Le Monde*, 28 June 1977.

2
DANISH ENERGY POLICY

INTRODUCTION

What, one might ask, is of interest in Danish energy policy? What consequence for the world at large is there in the choice made by a country of five million people? It may well be that the decisions made in Denmark do not have an appreciable effect on the markets for energy throughout the world, but the subject of this book is the relation of the form and content of energy policy to the institutional structure of the country. The importance of a particular example is independent of size; the institutional structure of Denmark exhibits attractive and special features whose influence on energy policy it is instructive to trace.

Preliminaries

During the nineteenth century Denmark was passing from the practice of subsistence farming to a still largely agricultural, market economy. The farmer was obliged to transact business with suppliers and buyers and to keep records; the need for literacy was recognized and rural education largely inspired by an outstanding Christian philanthropist—Grundtvig.

Not only the economic environment, but the structure of Danish agriculture was changing; livestock farming encroached on arable farming; specialization in butter, bacon and eggs developed, often for export. The new markets required standardization and quality control. The needs were met by a network of retail co-operatives, originally initiated by philanthropists but soon taken over by the farmers. Subsequently, co-operatives were created to purchase the equipment for large units of production or for mechanization. The ability of farmers to organize and manage these co-operatives was in large measure a result of the high standards of literacy and education consequent on Grundtvig's activity.

But what has this to do with energy policy? The consequences are indeed considerable. To exaggerate frivolously, if Napoleon is the single biggest influence on French energy policy, then Grundtvig occupies the same position in Danish energy policy.

The model of the agricultural co-operatives for production, processing and marketing of goods was soon adopted by urban trades, although urban co-operatives have never had the same social and economic importance as agricultural co-operatives. More importantly for the immediate purpose the model was adopted for much of the service industries, water, electricity and district heating.

The principal instigators and agents of electrification in Denmark were the farmers and the municipalities. The farmers were more influential in rural areas and naturally adopted the co-operative model for the new enterprises. The utilities which developed from an urban stimulus were generally owned by the municipal authorities; the most important was the municipal utility in Copenhagen. The principal exception to this municipal or co-operative ownership was the company, Nordsjaellands Elektricitet Selskab (NESA), in Northern Zealand; it started in 1902 as a tramway company which bought electricity to power its trams; subsequently it began to supply electricity from its overhead lines, found this to be better business and moved into electricity distribution. The principal shareholders in NESA are now the municipality of Gentofte and the County of Copenhagen. The substantial differences in origin of the various companies still exercise an influence as we shall see later.

These small utilities were on the whole successful in making the alliances necessary to benefit from integration of the means of production. The events in Zealand are illustrative. Three large rural distribution companies emerged out of a competitive market process by gaining the territories of their competitors, NESA in the North, the Nordvestsjaellands Elektricitets-Vaerk (NVE) in the North East and the Sydøstsjaellands Elektricitets Aktieselskab (SEAS) in the South. Within the territories of these companies there persisted various islands wherein the municipalities preferred to go it alone. Before the war, NESA had a power station north of Copenhagen; at the same time it bought supplies from Copenhagen and mainly from Sweden where there was an industrial or hydro based excess (the first link to Sweden was in 1915). At the end of the 1930s new power stations were necessary to meet expected increases in demand. A station of 2 x 30 MW (e) sets was proposed. To share the cost and ensure maximum utilization NESA proposed to construct it in association with other utilities including SEAS. Eventually only NESA, NVE and the municipality of Frederiksberg participated. The co-operation developed into a joint company Isefjordvaerket (IFV), founded in 1937. Other municipalities came in later; the company now owns all power stations in Northern Zealand and sells electricity to its constituent distribution companies. The IFV, SEAS and the municipality of Copenhagen subsequently began to co-operate on the planning of future generating units and the operation of the existing power station pool; co-operation took place within an organization, Kraftimport, finally converted in 1978 into a new company (Elkraft) in charge of planning, construction, operation and financing of conventional power stations as well as the primary high voltage system.

A similar pattern of events occurred on Jutland and Funen out of which evolved a partnership, Elsam, with the responsibility to co-ordinate system planning and operation, to purchase fuel, to construct power stations and main transmission lines. Elsam is the Electricity Co-operation of Jutland and Funen (Det Jysk-fynske elsamarbejde); it has seven partners, each of whom owns one or two power stations and each of which is owned by its particular group of between three and fifteen municipal or co-operative distribution companies.

In short, integration of the means of production took place naturally from the bottom up. Whether the next level of co-operation, between Elsam and Elkraft would have been achieved naturally will now never be known. It has been precipitated by government action, which will be discussed later. A new joint company will be formed for nuclear construction and possibly additional joint companies for the purchase of fuel. A natural rivalry and the wish to preserve a means of competition will prevent the companies from merging, unless the political grouping in favour of nationalization should get its way.

The new technology of electricity was absorbed more smoothly in Denmark than in most other countries. It is interesting to compare the reception in Sweden, France and the United Kingdom. Sweden has extensive resources of hydropower which became feasible to develop towards the end of the nineteenth century, when long distance transmission by means of alternating current became economic. Development of these resources required new legislation on rights of way for transmission lines and rights of expropriation of the land required for hydroelectric development. The cheap hydroelectricity was a great advantage and a powerful stimulus to industry. The necessary Acts were backed by powerful industrial interests, but opposed by rural communities for whom the costs of the transition outweighed the benefits. The question of electrification was thereby caught up in the dominant political conflict of the time, between the rights and needs of rural and industrial life. The political implications prompted the state to take an active part in the development of hydropower through the Swedish State Power Board, which institution has subsequently come to dominate the production of electricity. The advent of electricity in Sweden was in short highly political and controversial and led to institutional innovation.

In France and the United Kingdom, production and distribution was initiated by private industry and controlled by Government. A system of concessions for distribution, long-lived in France, short-lived but disastrous in the United Kingdom, impeded the agglomeration of utilities and the proper utilization of resources. In both countries series of legislation were passed to encourage co-operation, with little success. To manage the schemes of regulation and supervision, large and technically skilled government departments were created which led, naturally enough, after the Second World War, to the assumption of rigorous control by nationalization.

In Denmark, by contrast, the initiative for electrification came in large part from the municipalities and from relatively small farming co-operatives. The technology did not become identified with the conflict, also strong in Denmark, between countryside and city, although that conflict did leave some marks, mentioned later. Co-operation between utilities was not impeded by Government; there was a minimum of regulation and no concessions, other than for minute hydro resources and the first undersea lines to Sweden.

Expropriation laws were introduced to permit the utilities to obtain way leaves for transmission and distribution lines, but they were rarely used; the normal procedure was for the companies to agree compensation with the landowner in private negotiation.

The dual origins of the Danish utilities in the towns and countryside is still detectable in the different personalities of the two institutions. Elsam is the more technocratic; it has been the more vocal and active proponent of nuclear power and it was the first of the two companies to improve coal handling facilities after the oil crisis. Kraftimport is the more mercantile and more sensitive to the political environment. The farmers, being by far the most influential group within the utilities on Jutland, have always controlled Elsam; there has been little internal or external resistance to the spirit of the technostructure which accordingly prevails. Kraftimport is a more heterogeneous assembly of companies; the farmers' co-operatives are outvoted by the utilities; the necessity to satisfy two sets of owners with different motives and priorities has posed the management of Kraftimport political problems of a kind not found at Elsam and reminiscent of the conflicts of interest between countryside and city which were a principal influence on the development of electricity supply in other countries. The outcome has been to make Kraftimport technically more cautious than Elsam and more sensitive to the views and reactions of the consumer.

The co-operative institution has also been of great importance for the development of district heating in Denmark. Of all countries, Denmark has the greatest amount of district heating in proportion to the population. This is frequently explained by allegations that Denmark is colder than the United Kingdom or that energy there has always been high in cost. But the first argument is false and the second is an unsatisfactory explanation, because in the 1960s district heating flourished in Denmark even though oil was cheaper than in the United Kingdom. The different institutional tradition and simple matters such as the trust individuals have in co-operatives (very low in the United Kingdom) are more plausible explanations.

Analogous to the development of electricity supply there have been two distinct lines of development of district heating, municipal and co-operative. The practice of district heating began in the 1920s in some larger towns, generally on the initiative of a municipally owned electricity utility which saw a way of profiting from the heat in the cooling water of its diesel generators. This was a strictly municipal initiative. District heating through co-operatives is not associated with electricity production.

Development of district heating has accelerated rapidly since the early 1960s. About 15 per cent of housing was connected in 1963, 30 per cent in 1977 and 40 per cent in 1981. In the early 1960s about half of these supplies were provided by power stations. Because of the large expansion of co-operative district heating in the 1960s, the proportion supplied by power stations declined temporarily to about a quarter by the mid 1970s. It rose again to 40 per cent in 1981.

The relation between the electricity supply and district heating is one of conflict and co-operation. Broadly, the municipalities favour district heating and combined heat and power because they fit well into the areas of responsibility attributed to city authorities in Denmark. The attitude of the utilities varies. The power station owners are often in favour of combined heat and power, but the planning institutions which co-ordinate activity are generally less well disposed. The basic conflict between the municipalities and the utilities is over the control of the means of production; the conflict in markets for space heating is not acute. By and large, the municipalities have been able to force combined heat and power schemes on the utilities, through the implied threat that they would go ahead anyway and prevent the electricity utilities having access to the prime markets for electricity within the city bounds. This is true, for example, of Odense Municipal District Heating System, one of the largest in the world. Negotiations in 1945/46 between the several electricity supply utilities and the dominant single city of Funen proceeded much along the lines sketched. The technological debate was settled by power politics. It is fascinating to compare the history of combined heat and power in Sweden, where a finer balance between the powers of the municipalities and the utilities has led to a more obscure outcome.

Post-War

The dominant feature of post-war energy supplies throughout Europe was severe scarcity. Denmark, being dependent largely on imports of coal, was especially badly affected because the War shattered established trading patterns. The Danes reverted to the exploitation of peat and wood; everyone suffered from the shortages, but consumers attached to district heating suffered less than others. Consequently, at the end of the War, district heating enjoyed great marketing appeal; it was also seen as an efficient way of using scarce resources of fuel. The combination of consumer demand and political support encouraged a rapid growth in district heating. Most of the large municipal combined heat and power (CHP) schemes originate from this period. As already mentioned, CHP was not the first choice of the utilities as a means of production of electricity; it was imposed by the municipalities, but the shortage of fuel tended to take the edge off this conflict. The priority of the utilities was to obtain supplies of electricity, free choice of techniques was, at that time, a luxury. The difficulties of meeting demand also helped disguise the potential conflict between district heat and electricity for markets. Everything that could be made could be sold; competition for sales was not a determining feature.

The War made no fundamental change to the structure of the institutions involved in energy supply, in contrast to the changes experienced in France and the United Kingdom. The means of energy production lay mainly outside the shores of Denmark and therefore beyond the reach of Danish institutional change. The utilities were the only institutions of significance within the influence of the Danish State. For the reasons discussed in the previous section, there was no compelling logical support for state control. An additional point is that the ownership by co-operatives and municipalities was already, in a sense, public ownership. The crucial difference between this kind of public ownership and nationalization was that the utilities could not, in the former case, be effective instruments of state policy as was intended in France and the United Kingdom.

The period following the War can be summarized as confirming the relatively decentralized structure of the energy industries. The poor availability of energy was almost certainly an important influence on the character of Danish industrialization. In 1957 the average cost of power to the consumer in Denmark was six times as great as in Norway. The fact that today, the majority of Danish industry is of a type which uses little energy is almost certainly a reflection of the poor availability of energy in the past.

THE PENETRATION OF OIL

Unlike the effects in France and the United Kingdom, the penetration of cheap oil into Denmark did not destabilize relations among energy industries. Previously, energy supply had been based on imported coal and the products of coal conversion (electricity, gas, hot water); afterwards it was based on imported oil and the same products of oil conversion. Oil simply replaced coal as a fuel, with less trouble than when coal displaced peat and wood; the transition caused almost no political reaction. The restructuring of alliances, the reorganization of markets that was experienced in France and the United Kingdom had no parallel in Denmark. There were no indigenous mines to worry about, no violence or discontent in mining regions, no nascent nuclear or natural gas industries to protect.

The only potential source of friction was the possible conflict of interest between the coal distributors and the oil companies, but here again the existing structures were adapted to the new use. The first oil companies to start large scale operations in Denmark (Texaco, Chevron) came in without existing markets; they therefore bought up the existing coal distributors and began dual distribution. Progressively, as the distribution infrastructure for oil was established so the oil companies priced their own coal interests out of the market. The oil companies' sole objective in taking over the coal distribution was to transfer the markets to oil, but the result was that there were never any bad relations between the coal and oil suppliers. By the early 1960s almost all facilities for the distribution of coal had been closed down leaving the electricity utilities as the only free agents in the coal sector.

One consequence of this enthusiastic embrace of oil was that the price of energy in Denmark fell rapidly; the utilities, exhibiting the commercial shrewdness for which the Danes are famous throughout Scandinavia, bought fuel oil cheaply on the spot market; electricity prices in Denmark became the lowest in the world.

The consequence of all this was that, by 1972, 94 per cent of energy supplies to Denmark were imports of oil. This, it is important to note, was in no sense a national political decision; it was the result of cumulative decisions by industry and individuals.

There were two events during this period which later were seen to be significant and where abandonment to the joys of cheap oil may have impaired the judgement of the State. These were the allocation of petroleum concessions and the establishment of a nuclear research station at Risφ.

The first prospection for oil in the Danish subsoil was in 1935. An American, F. Ravlin, had been granted the concession for the whole Danish subsoil. Later the concession was transferred to Gulf, who drilled eighteen wells between 1947 and 1957. In 1957

Esso took over the concession and drilled eleven wells in 2 years; then they also gave up. A German company wanted to take over the concession in South Jutland because oil had been found at Schleswig-Holstein. In 1960 Mr A. P. Møller, a nationalistic Danish ship owner, approached the Government with the argument that if a Danish company would take it on, then the application should be considered.

He proposed that the concession should be allocated to him and his companies, but that to provide money as well as expertise the oil companies should be brought in as partners in the exploration. He got the concession in 1962 on essentially the same terms as Gulf and Esso. The Dansk Undergrounds Consortium (DUC) was formed in 1962 between the concessionaires, Gulf and Shell. In 1963 Denmark extended its sovereignty over the Danish continental shelf *inter alia* in the North Sea, and at the same time ratified the Geneva Convention. The A. P. Møller concession was extended accordingly. Chevron and Texaco joined DUC in 1965, but only with regard to the Danish North Sea continental shelf area. The new companies were brought in because the extended concession was riskier and needed more capital. The DUC comprised three joint ventures, one each in the south-western and the north-eastern parts of the Danish North Sea, and the third comprising the land and remaining off-shore areas. The interests of the individual members varied slightly in each venture. Gulf left DUC in 1974. So far oil has only been found and produced in the south-western part of the Danish North Sea.

The concession entitled the holders to explore for 10 years. If, during that period, discoveries were made which could be exploited economically, then the holders were obliged to start production to secure the concession. The concession also stipulated that if production began, the concession should remain in force as long as production continued, but should expire at the latest in 2012. A royalty of 5 per cent for the first 5 years and 8½ per cent thereafter was payable. A 50 year concession to a single operator over all Danish territory, with an 8½ per cent royalty, seemed generous a few years later. The terms attracted much criticism within Denmark, leading finally to renegotiations and substantial changes in the terms in 1976 and in 1981, as will be described later. Little thought was apparently given to them at the time; the exploration history had been poor, cheap oil was pouring in from the Middle East. But nevertheless it is an area where, with hindsight, one can trace a connection between the policy vacuum engendered by cheap oil in the early 1960s and some of the problems facing the makers of Danish energy policy today.

The Danish nuclear effort was similarly a victim of an absence of policy. The Atomic Energy Commission (AEC) was created in 1955 at the instigation of Danish industrialists and politicians, particularly the then Prime Minister, Viggo Kampmann, a Social Democrat. A research centre was established at Risø. Niels Bohr was asked to head the effort. The principal incentive was the enormous enthusiasm, world-wide, about the prospects for nuclear power. The reputation of Niels Bohr and his collaborators could attract key physicists; whether the Danes could have managed the engineering (which was the principal stumbling block in France) one will never know. Occasional attempts were made to examine the possibility of joint manufacture with Sweden, but it was all academic because the utilities showed no interest. As elsewhere in Europe the utilities were more influenced by the immediate low cost of heavy fuel oil than by prospects for nuclear power. The lack of interest of the utilities was well emulated by the Folketing. When the AEC was formed, a parliamentary committee had been established to receive its report, but it aroused no political interest. Indeed, as time went on, Risø became the object of attack by the right-wing parliamentary parties representing small farmers and businessmen who claimed it to be a luxury the State could not afford and did not need. Without interested utilities and without political support, Risø was ineffective. There is no evidence of a trace of political will even to explore the possibility of encouraging the commercial birth of nuclear power in Denmark; in the absence of this political will, the establishment of Risø seems more a whim of fashion than a part of policy.

The State Stirs

From the late 1960s and early 1970s there is evidence of a growing belief in the administration, and some political circles, that all was not well in the State of Denmark. The events which stimulated this reassessment occurred in the North Sea. Unfulfilled Danish expectations from the North Sea have been a principal motor of institutional change in the energy sector, more so than the oil crisis in 1973/74.

The offshore concession had scarcely been granted to A.P. Møller when Britain and Norway issued licences in 1964/65 and almost immediately gas was found in the southern basins of the North Sea. Expectations about the potential of Danish waters were high and for the first time the terms of the concession looked generous; the State began to take an interest in the activities of DUC. The first well drilled off the Danish shore found oil, the first oil in the North Sea. Gas was found in 1968. But exploration was interrupted by a boundary dispute. In 1964 Germany proclaimed that she did not accept Denmark's claim to rights over part of the continental shelf; Germany argued that equidistant lines were not appropriate because of the shape of the German coastline forming a bay, which in the German view resulted in a disproportionately small German shelf area compared to those of her neighbours. In February 1967 the two countries took the dispute to the Hague; in 1969 the court judged in favour of Germany and asked the two countries to agree a settlement. In 1970 agreement was reached; the boundary lines now have an odd shape because Denmark succeeded in keeping the area where she had spent money and made finds. Exploration drilling in the area had stopped in the Spring of 1969 after the court decision, activity eventually resumed in 1971 and almost immediately the Dan and Gorm fields were discovered. Dan was viable under the prevailing economic conditions; the exploration period expired in July 1972, consequently the DUC had to be producing by that date in order to keep the concession. The companies felt badly treated because of the delays; they asked for an extension of the exploration permit which was granted for two years. In the event Dan was producing oil in time.

The results of exploration made elsewhere in Danish waters during the period of the boundary dispute were disappointing. The DUC drilled three holes in the north-eastern part of the Danish sector, but all were dry. There is a view within the Ministry of Commerce that DUC could reasonably have made a more sustained exploration effort away from the disputed area, but the oil companies had better prospects elsewhere, so that national and company interests diverged. At the same time it is apparent that the possible influence of the State was inhibited by an inappropriate division of Ministerial competence. Up to 1974 all resource matters were within the competence of the Ministry of Public

Works, whose personnel apparently regarded the North Sea exploration as peripheral to their main responsibilities. The importance of energy supplies was more clearly perceived in the Ministry of Commerce and it was perhaps this Ministry which first began to appreciate how the terms of the 1962 concession, which did not permit the State to explore on its own behalf nor to force DUC to explore, restricted the achievement of national objectives.

In 1968 the Ministry of Commerce investigated the prospects for a natural gas supply to Denmark; it concluded that natural gas was of increasing importance in many industrial countries and that the Dutch and British discoveries encouraged hopes that there would be finds in the Danish sector.[1] The lacuna in indigenous exploration success meant that the first opportunity came in 1970 when the Phillips group was arranging the sale of the gas from Norway. Denmark was unprepared for the proposal. It negotiated as part of a consortium with Ruhrgas and Swedegas AB, Ruhrgas being the main prospective buyer, but there were no prospective consumers within Denmark willing to meet the price Phillips could get elsewhere, moreover there was no infrastructure for distribution. The only possibility of absorbing gas was if the utilities could be persuaded to burn the largest part, but they believed oil prices would remain low and they refused. Eventually the gas was sold to another consortium, headed by Gas-Unie and Ruhrgas and landed at Emden. It is still arguable that, even if no gas were sold in Denmark, it would have been more sensible to land the gas in Denmark and take it through Jutland to Germany. This route would have required a shorter sea line and avoided some difficult seafloor structures with which Phillips did in the event have problems. The Danish price for way leave was an option to take up to 15 per cent of the gas. This would have been the ideal solution for Denmark, permitting a slow build up of distribution. But Phillips declined. It could well be that not enough effort went into pushing that option. Certainly in any similar future circumstance the administration appears resolved to try to force a land line through Jutland by putting onerous environmental and safety conditions on any proposed sea line.

But the Norwegian Ekofisk negotiations had important consequences. First, Dansk Naturgas (DNG) was created as a legal entity to participate as a buyer in negotiations; second, legislation on natural gas was passed. DNG was formed in February 1972. The Minister and a civil servant went to the State Attorney on a Sunday and drew up the statutes; an application to the Finance Committee of the Folketing for funds of DK 5 million was granted during the following week. This significant extension of state intervention in the energy sector, and indeed in Danish industry, was made overnight without the proposal ever being debated by the Folketing. Moreover the Minister was a Conservative Minister in a non-Socialist coalition Government. An important part of the motive for attributing the responsibility to a state company seems to have been a deep seated resolve in the officers of the Ministry that never again would they cede control on this vital sector as they had done with the DUC.

Similarly, the legislation in the Natural Gas Act was prepared by a Conservative Minister who lost office before putting the legislation to the Folketing. The Minister who carried it through was a Social Democrat, who apparently took the papers as prepared without changing a word. The Act was passed in June 1972 without opposition; not only the Ministry, but a consensus of political parties supported this important precedent of state intervention. The Act requires a concession from the competent Ministry for the transport, storage, import or sale of natural gas. It was made clear when the Bill was presented that DNG would have the sole right of transmission and that the distribution would be given either to municipal or private companies, probably the existing electric and gas utilities. The political issue was that distribution should remain under local control, consistent with Danish practice in electrical distribution and in harmony with Danish political tradition. The important role of central government was at once consolidated and limited.

Subsequently the Ministry of Commerce was approached by Petronord to discover what would be the conditions for transmission of Frigg gas through Denmark. But at that time the principal continental buyers could not absorb the extra supplies and the gas was sold to the British Gas Council.

The difficulties with the DUC, and the history of the unsuccessful negotiations for gas, persuaded the administration, (the civil service is especially influential in political systems where Ministers change frequently), of the necessity for an informed and able state involvement in energy planning. Not only was it necessary to exert influence directly on the petroleum sector, but it was necessary to influence the whole energy market into which new sources were to be introduced.

Post Oil-Crisis

The oil crisis was a great shock to Denmark; it caused some fairly obvious changes in behaviour conditioned by the new economic circumstances, but the most important effect was to reinforce the dawning belief that government should exercise more influence throughout the energy sector and maybe remove it a little from the discipline of market economics. There were several immediate political responses of no great import; DNG was charged with the authority to purchase oil abroad and the name was changed to Dansk Olieog Naturgas (DONG); it did in fact buy a few cargoes and made a loss on them; a parliamentary committee for energy was established with powers relating to the import and export of oil; there were debates in the Folketing and a preliminary report on energy policy options.[2] But the sustained action flowed from three initiatives, one from the utilities proposing a large nuclear programme and two from the Ministry of Commerce to introduce natural gas and to implement a heat supply plan.

In 1974 the utilities proposed a programme of roughly one nuclear station every 2 years, comparable in proportion to the size of the population with the large programmes in France, Sweden and Germany. The existing legislation on nuclear power dated back to 1962; it provided for all relevant matters to be settled by administrative decision—the route to a nuclear power station only requiring one signature, that of the Minister of Education. The decision-making system was a closed circle of politicians, civil servants and technicians; the AEC was both the design and licensing agency. Rumours spread in 1974 that the Government proposed to operate this mechanism; an agitated public debate blew up. Opposition was revealed inside and outside the political parties; many members of the Folketing who supported nuclear power still insisted that the decision should be seen to be taken by that institution.

The defined administrative path no longer being politically acceptable, new legislation was necessary. A revised version of the 1962 Nuclear Power Act was presented to the Folketing by the Social Democratic Minister for Education in October 1975; it became law in May 1976 with the title, Act on Safety and Environmental Matters in Connection with Nuclear Installations. This legislation contains a clause to the effect that the entry into force of the Act has to be decided by a separate Act, the only exception being certain paragraphs giving the Environmental Agency powers of investigation over existing nuclear installations, which came into force upon the publication of the Act in the official journal. The intention of the decision Act is to permit the technical and administrative aspects to be agreed by the Folketing in anticipation of a nuclear programme, whilst still permitting the political question of the acceptability of nuclear power to be put to a referendum, should the need arise, as a simple question of whether or not to authorize the decision Act. The decision Act was scheduled for debate in August 1976, but was withdrawn, ostensibly because of reservations about the disposal of radio-active waste and the availability of investment funds. Other, possibly more plausible, reasons we shall come to later.

The Nuclear Power Act is essentially an environmental Act; the institutional framework within which nuclear power was to be developed was defined in a separate piece of legislation—the Electricity Supply Act. The first version of this Act was tabled in November 1974 by the minority Liberal Government (Venstre). Early in 1975 the Folketing was dissolved and after the elections a Social Democratic Government took over. The second version of the Electricity Supply Act was then tabled by the Social Democratic Minister for Commerce in March 1975. The Folketing did not finish with the legislation before the summer recess and in accordance with Danish rules of procedure it had to be tabled again. The third and final version was presented to the Folketing by the same minister in October 1975. It became law in February 1976 and came into force on 1 January 1977.[3]

The ESA is an interesting piece of legislation which essentially attributes to the State very considerable influence on the physical structure of electricity supply in return for generous commercial concessions to the utilities. Extensive negotiations between the utilities and the Ministry preceded the drafting of the Act; during the course of negotiations the proposals of the Ministry for control were, apparently, weakened and larger concessions made. The ESA only permits there to be one concessionaire for the construction of nuclear plant; this provision will oblige Elsam and

Elkraft to co-operate in the construction of nuclear plant. It will probably also oblige them to install a link between their systems across the Great Belt. (The absence of such a link is controversial; the utilities claim that there is no technical or economic justification; quasi-popular opinion attributes it in part to a certain desire for independence on the part of the companies.) The Minister of Commerce may also order the utilities to build their plant to burn prescribed fuels, to use particular fuels to a prescribed extent on the existing system, to construct plant in such a way that it permits heat recovery for district heating and to maintain stocks of fuel to a stipulated extent. The Minister has also to approve major alterations in existing plant and the establishment of new installations for production, transmission or distribution. These are extensive powers. In return the utilities are put outside the usual mechanisms of price control; their prices are to be negotiated with a special committee, but it is established that they must cover their costs including depreciation as stipulated by the Ministry of Commerce. At present, terms for depreciation are generous and the utilities, are able to self-finance all their investments.

The final form of the Act strongly suggests that state influence has been 'bought' by commercial concessions, a procedure which reflects the outcome of rather equally balanced forces in favour of, and in opposition to, increased state control. A large part of the Ministry of Commerce considers state influence as an essential part of the apparatus necessary to operate any energy policy which it may construct; these ideas arise naturally from the early experiences already described which showed clearly the lack of means of influence of the State on energy policy. Political support for state control comes from the left-wing parties and factions of the Social Democrats, which is not thought of as a left-wing party; on the right wing of the party there are people sitting on the boards of the utilities who are opposed to state control. The Electricity Supply Act was supported by the Liberals who are basically opposed to state control; their support was apparently part of a bargain with the Social Democrats whereby state control of the utilities was conceded for the development of nuclear power. Later events suggest that the Liberals outmanœuvred. The utilities are in principle opposed to any extension of state control, but apparently they considered that further resistance would engender political opposition to them and they were reasonably content with the commercial concessions.

In addition to these two important pieces of legislation there occurred a reallocation of administrative responsibilities from which the Ministry of Commerce benefited. A section of the Folketing wanted to convert the AEC into an Energy Commission with a broader brief. The Government was opposed to the idea of a powerful Energy Commission and the Ministry of Commerce was equally reluctant to share responsibility for energy. In April 1976 the AEC was disbanded; the research establishment at Risφ became an independent entity with a new mandate that extended to all energy matters. The Secretariat of the AEC formed the basis for a new Energy Agency (Energistyrelsen), and to neutralize the idea of the Energy Commission, an Energy Council was created to give independent advice. The terms of reference of the Energy Council are restrictive and it is not a principal influence. The Energy Agency was established as a directorate under the Ministry of Commerce, thereby greatly extending the personnel available to handle energy matters and providing the administration with the means to operate the interventionist policy which it was constructing.[4] The principal beneficiary of the rearrangement was the Ministry, from where the initiative most likely came.

In order to avoid a situation in which the same Minister would be responsible both for promoting and supervizing nuclear power, the powers of the AEC which related to safety were transferred to the Ministry for the Environment along with the Nuclear Inspectorate that had previously been established as a separate body under the AEC; the Ministry of Environment also took over the task of revising the 1962 Nuclear Power Act.

The growing importance of the energy problem for Denmark led to the establishment of a separate Ministry of Energy at the end of 1979. It is headed by a Cabinet Minister and a Permanent Under-Secretary and has a staff of about fifty. The Energy Agency was transferred to the new Ministry and today has a staff of about 150.

The assumption of these new powers by Government has so far had little obvious effect on the behaviour of the utilities. The principal change in the industry has been the conversion of plant to dual firing (coal and oil). This change is favoured by the Ministry, but so large is the commercial incentive that the utilities have performed the transition at a rapid rate on their own initiative. In 1973, 80 per cent of electricity delivered was produced from oil and 20 per cent from coal. In 1980 the ratio was reversed, achieving a change that was not expected until 1985. The utilities are pursuing plans to improve coal importing facilities. Elsam is the majority partner in a consortium that plans to build a port at Aarhus able to unload ships of up to 150,000 dwt. The other partners are BP, Shell and Portland Cement. Dredging will enable Elkraft's port at Stigsnaes to take ships of up to 170,000 dwt. The Government is also participating in discussions with the other Nordic countries about a joint central coal importing port.

The utilities have followed a policy of diversification of coal supply sources for several years. This enabled them to adjust without many problems to Poland's production cutbacks in 1981, mainly by switching to imports from the USA, which is now the country's largest supplier. South Africa remains the second largest supplier and a continuing source of embarrassment for the Government, which has appealed to the utilities to reduce South African coal imports on political grounds. Elsam has signed a 15 year contract with Exxon to take 2 Mt a year of Colombian coal, starting from 1986, and Elkraft is negotiating with Exxon for supplies of 300,000–500,000 tonnes a year. Elsam has also ordered two 132,000 dwt coal carriers for delivery in late 1982 and mid-1983.

The only detectable effect of the new powers of Government has been to influence the siting of plant to facilitate combined heat and power, for example IFV has sited a new plant near Copenhagen rather than on North West Zealand near the new coal port; this was not in response to a direct instruction from the Energy Agency, but in anticipation of intervention.

One result of the transition from oil to coal in power station fuelling is that nuclear power, if and when it arrives, will displace mostly coal and little oil. A decision on nuclear power, however, is not expected before the mid-1980s. Two major studies were initiated in 1976 on radioactive waste disposal and reactor safety. The Social Democrat-Liberal coalition Government announced in August 1979 that the studies were expected to be concluded in Spring 1980, the Folketing would then vote on the nuclear question and the outcome would be put to a referendum in 1981. But in January 1980 the successor Social Democrat minority

Government called off the referendum. The reason given officially was that the studies had not satisfactorily answered doubts on these problems. The studies were therefore extended and have not yet been completed. Meanwhile, because electricity consumption has not risen as quickly as expected, there is no need to have any decision on nuclear power for a few years yet. Unofficially, the reason for the postponement of the referendum is that although there was a majority in the Folketing for nuclear power, the government party, the Social Democrats, were divided. There was a large enough minority in the Folketing to force a referendum and the Social Democrats were terrified by the prospect of a repeat of the performance that took place over the Common Market, which caused a public and acrimonious split in the party.

The second principal stream of events has flowed from the attempt to introduce natural gas. The Ministry of Commerce had first investigated the prospects for a natural gas supply to Denmark in 1968; its disappointment and mounting discontent with DUC has been sketched. At this point we again take up the story of the offshore concession, which we left as Dan came on stream. The concession distinguished between oil and gas: the concessionaire could have either oil or gas rights separately. The Ministry, backed by the Minister, argued that the DUC had made gas finds in 1968 which could have been put into economic production: therefore the DUC had not fulfilled the conditions of the concession and had lost the gas rights. This point of view was sustained by the consultants appointed by the Government to monitor the activity of DUC. Political support for the proposition came from the Social Democrats and some parties of the left. The DUC disagree. It argued that economic conditions had been different in 1968: experience at the time was limited; the finds were small and far from land and Denmark had no gas market, further discouraging profitable exploitation. Moreover, the DUC argued that legally it was up to them to decide whether a discovery was economic. The concession provided that if one of the hydrocarbons was found, then a 5 year extension would be given for the other; DUC claimed that it had fulfilled the terms and should be given the extension.

The case never went to court and it is likely that the Ministry was not entirely convinced that they had the better of the legal arguments. It appears that a majority of the Folketing at that time also sympathized with DUC. As a compromise the terms of the concession were renegotiated.

The objectives of the Ministry are not entirely clear. There is a view that the Ministry thought that it could get the gas cheaply if it could force A. P. Møller to relinquish the concession. A more plausible motive was to force participation or, failing that, to get an increased effort in exploration and production; this explanation is consistent with the realization by the Ministry that the fundamental weakness of the 1962 concession was the absence of any work commitment.

Logically enough, given the fundamental basis of its concern, the Ministry tried during the renegotiation to introduce incentives to explore, rather than higher royalties or in any sense a larger government take; it asked for provisions to relinquish parts of the concession and amendments to the internal workings of the consortiums, so that unanimity was no longer required. The attitudes of the partners were not identical; A. P. Møller would probably have liked more exploration, but the oil companies had better prospects elsewhere.

Part of the 1976 agreement was that the concession should be divided into blocks and these blocks should be relinquished progressively, the first ten being due back in 1981.[5] Most importantly, DUC should present, by May 1978, a final report on the possibilities of starting natural gas production from the Cora, Brent, Dan and Gorm fields, together with a production and development plan and an estimate of investment and operating expenditure. DONG was granted first right of negotiation for the purchase of gas finds in these or other structures in the concession area. Negotiations should follow the industry's standard provisions with regard to floor price, escalation, minimum quantities, and compensation for unpurchased quantities. The exploration rights for gas were also extended to 1984.

DUC submitted its report in March 1978, which confirmed that there was an economically viable basis for initiating natural gas production. The recoverable reserves of gas from the four fields were estimated to be 53–75 bn m^3. Consultants deGolyer and MacNaughton carried out an assessment of the DUC report for the Government and presented their report in May 1978. They concluded that the size of the reserves had been underestimated and the likely amount of recoverable reserves from the four fields could be in excess of 100 bn m³. This is adequate to cover Danish natural gas requirements for a 25 year period, starting in 1984, achieving a plateau rate of 4 bn m³/yr in 1995 and sustaining it until the year 2009. The consultants in a later report in 1979 concluded that a further 60 bn m³ of natural gas could be recovered from other structures.

After lengthy negotiations DONG and DUC concluded a contract for the supply of 55 bn m³ natural gas between October 1984 and October 2009 from the four fields. An annual volume of 2.5 bn m³ has been agreed between 1986 and 2001. The volume contracted constitutes about half the estimated recoverable reserves in the four fields and only about one-third of the potential reserves indicated in the consultants' 1979 report. The indications are that DONG will receive another offer for about 1–2 bn m³/yr of gas from the late 1980s. The basic price is regulated according to changes in fuel oil and gas oil prices in West Germany, Denmark and Rotterdam. The agreement provided also for a minimum price, which has now been rendered irrelevant following energy price escalations since 1979.

DONG will buy the natural gas on the DUC platform at the Cora (now renamed Tyra) field. DONG will construct, own and operate a 200 km 30-inch subsea pipeline that will transport the gas to the Nybro processing plant on shore. From there a 320 km west-east pipeline will transport the gas to Copenhagen and it will be crossed at Egtved with a north-south pipeline that will interconnect the Danish and the West German system and run north up to the salt dome storage facilities in Lille Torup.

The project was approved by the Folketing in May 1979 and is divided in two phases. In Phase I, sales start in October 1984 and build up to 2.5 bn m³/yr within a year. In Phase II, consumers in mid and north Jutland are connected to the system in 1988, increasing sales by an estimated 1 bn m³/yr. Recently the Folketing voted to speed up development of Phase II of the project. All other aspects of the project are currently on schedule.

The project is one of the biggest investments ever undertaken in Denmark. The main difficulty was how to absorb the new fuel rapidly in the large quantities necessary to give good use of the expensive infrastructure, especially in a country like Denmark where there is little large energy intensive industry. This problem was recognized by the Government and formed part of the

perspective for the Committee on Heating Methods set up by the
Danish Ministry of Housing, a Committee whose work was later
continued by the Ministry of Commerce and of which we shall
have more to say later. The Committee recommended zoning of
areas for specific forms of heat supply to prevent wasteful
competition between natural gas and district heating.[6] The
Ministry of Commerce, with assistance from the banking firm
Kuhn Loeb Lehman Brothers International (KLLB), carried out a
national economic evaluation of the project. The capital return is
estimated to be only 6 per cent calculated in fixed prices, but rises
to 11 per cent if real increases in the price of oil and the possibility
of transporting more than the contracted 55 bn m^3 of gas are taken
into account. In a later report in December 1980 by DONG and
KLLB, following the increases in oil prices, the return on the
investment was calculated as 15–16 per cent.

KLLB advised that the project could be carried out on a
commercial basis with a net capital of approximately 20 per cent
and the equity capital in DONG was increased accordingly by the
Folketing. The attractiveness of natural gas is enhanced further by
its environmental advantages and its contribution to diversity of
supply. It therefore has strong political backing especially from
groups opposed to nuclear power.

One of the obstacles to the introduction of natural gas detected
by the Ministry of Commerce in its preliminary studies, was the
complete unawareness and disinterest of the municipalities. The
Ministry had concluded at an early stage that the gas industry
should not be vertically integrated as in France or the United
Kingdom, but that distribution should be made by local companies. This notion is evident in the Natural Gas Supply Act of
1972; its logical support is that local companies fit better into the
planning mechanism.

By 1977 little had been done to organize the downstream end of
the industry; the contenders for management of the new distribution companies were the local electricity distributors, either
co-operative or municipal, the few existing gas distributors, the
municipalities and district heating co-operatives. None was really
interested. The electricity distributors had relevant expertise, but
were unwilling to devote much effort to preliminary paperwork.
The Government finally bribed the municipalities by granting
them DK 20 million for heat planning activities. The Ministry

mentioned that it was unnecessary to give a grant to the utilities because they had the resources, but there is little doubt that the Ministry favoured the municipalities because it was reluctant to see a further extension of the power of the utilities. In the perennial struggle between the utilities and the municipalities the Ministry plays a game of divide and rule. The money was allocated by the Folketing on the initiative of the Ministry. Again, the crucial act in determining control of a sector came from the administration, not the Folketing. Since then the municipalities have dominated preparations and walked away with the negotiations.

In Spring 1978 five regional planning companies for natural gas were established by the municipalities. In 1979 four of them were replaced by regional distribution companies for natural gas; the fifth one will be replaced before Phase II of the project. Their principal functions are the distribution of natural gas to consumers within their regions, the direction of construction and the operation of facilities required to distribute gas from the transmission lines to the ultimate consumer and the establishment, in concert with DONG, of reasonable load factors. The regional companies may deliver gas either to local municipalities or directly to the consumer. They should generate funds from their operations to meet corporate obligations but they are not permitted to accumulate profits on a long-term basis. In July 1980 the KOMGAS, a common body representing the five regional companies, was established in order to co-ordinate planning, marketing, standardization, international borrowing and negotiations with other authorities.

In February 1979 DONG signed a contract with the West German utility Ruhrgas to purchase 750 m^3 of gas during a 2 year period starting in October 1982, at a price of about 25 per cent above the DUC price. This will ensure a smoother start for the project before Danish gas flows into the system from the North Sea. DONG has the option to return the gas to Ruhrgas at a later date. The parties also agreed to provide each other with emergency volumes of gas in the event of interruption of supply.

In March 1980 DONG and Swedegas exchanged contracts covering sales and transportation of natural gas, according to an agreement reached by the Danish and Swedish Governments. DONG will deliver to Swedegas a total of 3.1 bn m^3 of Danish gas in the period 1985 to 2002. After an initial 5 year period, the quantity will steady at 200 m^3/yr and could rise to a maximum of 440 m^3/yr, if there is excess gas to sell. Swedegas has a prenegotiation right to purchase at the prevailing international market price any gas in excess of Danish consumption produced in the Danish North Sea. Swedegas also has the right to transport up to 2 bn m^3/yr of gas from other sources, mainly Ruhrgas, through the Danish system, in return for contributing DK 220 million towards the construction cost.

In parallel developments to the natural gas sector, the Government intensified efforts to develop the oil resources in the Danish North Sea. In October 1977 the Ministry of Commerce requested consultants DeGolyer and MacNaughton to appraise the Danish potential for hydrocarbons in the North Sea and evaluate the feasibility of establishing an oil pipeline to the west coast of Jutland. The consultants submitted their report in 1979. Reserves of almost 50 Mt of oil in the Dan, Gorm and Skjold fields alone proved the pipeline feasible. Another 40 Mt of oil may be discovered in the same area. The pipeline improves security of supply in Denmark, allows recovery of condensates from gas fields and permits exploitation of marginal oil fields which might be uneconomical otherwise. With an appropriate pipeline tariff, the pipeline would be mutually advantageous to the Government and the DUC. The state will construct, own and operate the pipeline. The construction contracts were awarded in 1981; the work should be completed by 1984. The pipeline will run from the Gorm 'A' platform to the west coast of Jutland and then to Shell's Fredericia refinery. Production from the Gorm field started in early 1981 and the Skjold field is expected to come on stream in 1982. Oil is now transported to shore by tankers. Oil production from the Danish North Sea could reach a figure of 3.5–4.0 Mt/yr at its peak.

Because the Government was still dissatisfied with the rate of exploration by DUC, it started new negotiations and finally concluded an agreement with DUC in March 1981. According to this, DUC would relinquish 50 per cent of the concession area in January 1982, 25 per cent in January 1984 and the rest in January 1986, except for a small compact area in the south-western part of the North Sea amounting to about 1 per cent of the original concession where there are favourable indications. This part will also be relinquished progressively between 2000 and 2012, the date when the original concession expires. The state gained the right to buy 40 per cent of all oil produced by DUC, and DUC agreed to submit an exploration programme every 3 years.

The first 50 per cent of the concession area has been relinquished and the Government plans to offer the next concessions in the North Sea in 1983. A new Oil Tax Bill was passed in 1982, which borrows ideas from the legislation in force in the United Kingdom and Norway, but imposes a lower overall tax rate in order to attract oil companies into the sector. A new oil tax will be introduced, incorporating unchanged royalty at 8.5 per cent and corporation tax at 40 per cent, which will be allowable against the oil tax. The theoretical maximum tax rate is 83.5 per cent, but the rate applicable to 'marginal fields' is only 41.7 per cent. Oil tax and corporation tax will be assessed on a 'norm price' decided by an independent tribunal. An allowance of 25 per cent for 10 years is also made, to guarantee a minimum return on investment. The Bill tries to balance reasonable state incomes from hydrocarbon activities with higher exploitation of Danish resources. DONG is expected to participate in exploration activities, probably in partnership with other companies. In September 1981 DONG signed an agreement with the British National Oil Corporation (BNOC) involving joint licensing applications, exchange of information and provision of technical advice by the BNOC to DONG. Norway's state owned oil company, Statoil, also has an agreement with DONG, providing for technical advice on the exploration of the Danish shelf.

The third of the major initiatives identified earlier in the chapter was that of the Ministry of Commerce to formulate and implement a national heat supply plan. A Heat Plan Committee was appointed in April 1977 with the task of carrying out the investigations. One of the main conclusions reached by the Committee is that there is room in the Danish energy supply system for both the introduction of natural gas and a considerable increase in supplies of power heat. About 60 per cent of the country's total heating requirements in 1995 can be covered by natural gas or power heat, 35–40 per cent by power heat and 20–25 per cent by natural gas. The remaining 40 per cent will be covered by oil, electricity and renewables; these sources are appropriate to sparsely populated areas where it is uneconomic to distribute piped energy. The densely populated part of the country has been divided into three areas suitable for power heat, natural gas and free competition respectively. The central piece of legislation is the Heat Supply Act 1979[7], which places the main responsibility for the implementation of the heat supply planning with the local councils, county councils and the Minister of Energy. The Minister of Energy is responsible for the 'national heat supply planning' and can issue 'heat plan directives indicating whether the heat supply in an area is primarily to be based on natural gas or on power plant heat'. The local councils, in consultation with energy supply companies, provide 'local heat supply plans' for the municipality and suggest proposals for their implementation. The county council then proposes a 'regional heat supply plan' together with guidelines for the areas in which specific heat supply methods shall be given priority and for siting large-scale plants and transmission lines. The Minister approves the regional plans and the local councils prepare an actual heat supply plan for the municipality with time schedules for the establishment of new, and extension of existing, collective heat supply plants. The regional council ensures that the local plan is in accordance with the regional plan. Heat supply planning should be co-ordinated with the other planning of the local authority.

The local councils were given significant powers by the Act, which will ensure that they are able to implement their heat supply plans. The local council must approve all new collective heat supply plants or extensions and modifications to existing ones and can order a supply undertaking to structure its production plant to enable the use of specific forms of energy and to use specified forms of energy in defined quantities. However, if a plant owner thinks he will not be able to comply with the order, he can request that the municipality take over the plant. The local council can request new and existing buildings to be connected to a heat supply plant and can demand contributions towards the cost of the plant. It can also prohibit certain forms of heating in new buildings, if the heat plan assumes other forms of heating. These powers may be softened by certain temporary exemptions for newly installed plant and by subsidies for replacement.

It is remarkable in a country which places considerable value on individual freedom that this intrusive legislation is tolerated. No other democratic country has been able to generate adequate political support for such measures. The Energy Report from the

Ministry of Commerce in 1979 described the Bill as 'epoch making'.[8]

An account of Danish energy policy should include the measures taken to conserve energy and to promote the use of renewable energy. Many measures have been predicated on the grounds of conservation, but there have been other motives behind them as well. Speed limits imposed during the crisis were kept to improve road safety. Subsidies to insulation and district heating were introduced to boost employment, since unemployment is an important topic in the Folketing.

A variety of subsidy schemes have been in force for energy conservation measures in existing buildings since 1975. During the period 1975–77 a total of DK 810 million was given in government grants, causing investments totalling DK 2,700 million. These grants were popular but, on account of a lack of effective control of how investments were spent, it has been estimated that economies were in fact rather modest. New subsidies were introduced for 1978–80 and DK 1,500 million was set aside, with the expectation that it will produce total investment of DK 5,500 million. Owner-occupiers were entitled under the scheme to deduct 50 per cent of the cost of the energy-saving measure from their taxable income, and a grant equal to 30 per cent of the cost of the measure was given for rented dwellings. In all cases the measure should be included on a government approved list of economically worthwhile measures and in some cases one of approximately 700 authorized energy consultants should be called to provide expert guidance. Progress with the scheme was disappointing in the first half of the period. Less than 50 per cent of the grants were taken up. The scheme has also been criticized for its relatively strict control procedures. It became clear that the energy conservation objectives for 1985 of the Energy Plan 1976 could not be realized.

Interest in the scheme increased in the second half of the period, mainly because of heavy increases in energy prices and the imposition of taxes on oil and electricity. The higher prices also had a direct effect on consumption. Consumption of gasoil decreased by almost 30 per cent and consumption of petrol decreased by 15 per cent in 2 years. Since 1981 a new scheme of direct subsidies has been introduced, designed to induce rapid action on the part of the house owner. From a rate of 20 per cent (maximum DK 7,000 for each house) in 1981 and 1982, the grant will go down to 15 per cent in 1983, 7.5 per cent in 1984 and it will be withdrawn in 1985. The Ministry of Housing is also proposing legislation that will make the achievement of minimum standards of insulation compulsory upon practically all house owners. It is believed that the renewed effort will make it possible to achieve the objectives for energy consumption for space heating in 1995.

The Ministry of Energy is supporting a research and development programme in renewable energy and is promoting the use of various forms of renewable energy through direct subsidies, amounting to DK 100 million a year, towards the necessary investments. A grant of 20 per cent of the total cost of the investment is given and the approved systems include solar panels, windmills, heat pumps and biogas systems. By 1981 some 15,000 heat pumps had been installed, and about 1,000 solar panels and 1,000 windmills. Installations for burning straw, wood chips etc. were included in the first subsidy programme of 1978 but they became so economical that subsidies have been withdrawn. The Government's objective in the Energy Plan 1981 is to ensure that 6 per cent of primary energy consumption is covered by renewable energy, including 1.5 per cent from the burning of refuse. A possible breakdown would be 60,000 solar energy units, 150,000 heat pumps, 120,000 straw and wood-burning units, 5,000 biogas units and 60,000 small windmills. The last two would contribute some 10 per cent of annual electricity consumption.

We turn now to energy planning. The history and structure of institutional relations have determined the type of planning to evolve. There exists as yet in Denmark no general planning mechanism, though the Ministry of Finance does try to collate and supervise the planning of other Ministries. Central government planning started in the 1960s with a Perspective Plan which was finished in 1972; it defined the possibilities in the state sector for the next 15 years. The plan was enlarged in 1974 to take in private industry. There exists almost no mechanism by which the State can influence events to conform with its plans. The Perspective Plan never appears to have been used and seems to have left the Ministries wondering why they have made it. One effect was to persuade Danish planners of the prior necessity of systematic planning for sectors. The Ministries of Education and the Environment were pioneers of sector planning.

The first long-term plan to appear was for energy. In April 1976 the Folketing approved a law which requested the Minister to present a report on energy each year. The Minister whose initiative this law was had anticipated the requirements of his own legislation in the document known as 'Danish Energy Policy, 1976'.[9] The principal purpose of the plan appears to have been the need to make clear the necessity for nuclear power within the framework of a comprehensive energy policy.

The Energy Plan was created in a few months by a small number of people and drew heavily on work that was fortuitously in progress at the Niels Bohr Institute; it never seems to have been taken seriously, although obviously, because it exists it is quoted, cited and used in political negotiations. The progress with the Plan was reviewed in Energy Report ER 79 by the Ministry of Commerce in March 1979.[10] The Report acknowledged that the objectives for nuclear energy in 1985 were no longer possible and that there was a delay in the national gas project, which was still awaiting the Folketing's approval. Furthermore, conservation of energy had fallen so far behind that consumption in 1978 had exceeded the level foreseen for 1985 (19.1 mtoe).

The reasons why the Plan did not become a mechanism for the State are twofold. Firstly, the State simply did not have at the time the means to operate the Plan, although it was acquiring them. Secondly, there was no political consensus on nuclear power, nor, to a lesser extent, on natural gas. This second problem illustrates the limits of the stabilizing influence of the civil service in political systems where power genuinely rests with a house of elected representatives whose composition and outlook reflects the mobility of popular opinion.

In 1976 part of the justification for postponing the parliamentary decision on nuclear power had been doubts about available investment. To provide a basis for decision, the Ministry of Finance made a report on available finance and competing investment requirements. In fact it said little about nuclear energy, except that there was room for it. This conclusion arose mainly because the investments for nuclear energy lay beyond the horizon of the investment report. The report did detect a conflict between the natural gas programme and the proposal to construct a bridge across the Great Belt. The Ministry of Finance was broadly favourable to the bridge and unenthusiastic about natural gas, which it wanted to postpone for at least 2 to 3 years. But the Government's investment programme,[11] prepared on the basis of the Ministry's report and presented to the Folketing on 16 May 1978, assumed that the project would go ahead in two phases, which in the event happened. Debate of the programme in the Folketing revealed a considerable majority in favour of natural gas and a distinct preference for gas rather than the bridge.

The second oil crisis of 1979 strengthened the State's determination to implement its Energy Plan. Important pieces of legislation have been approved since and the Government reiterated its objectives in Energy Plan 1981.[12] This Plan conceded that there was a need for much greater investment, co-ordination and direction.

These attempts at indicative planning are a wholly new departure for the Danish State: they are directly motivated by the oil crises and as such they are important to the present examination of the relation between energy and institutional change. They are not, however, markedly original, except that they exhibit, to an unusual extent, the ambiguity always attaching to plans detached from any means of operation. But not only does the necessity to deal with energy problems induce institutional change, the form of institutions determines the perception and treatment of energy problems. For outside observers, the truly original aspect of Danish energy policy is the incorporation of energy into physical planning, which is so natural a result of the division of responsibilities in Denmark.

The reaction of Denmark to the energy crisis exhibits exactly the same fundamental shift in the balance of power between the State and the individual that has occurred almost everywhere throughout the non-communist world. This has happened despite the long-established tradition of free markets and decentralized decision-making. In some ways the change is even more distinct in Denmark than elsewhere, precisely because of the contrast with the past. Many interventionist measures have flown straight from the oil crisis; the control of the utilities, the reorganization of the AEC and the strengthening of the Ministry, the renegotiation of the offshore concession, the Oil Tax Bill, the Energy Policy 76, the Energy Bill 1981, the investment report, the heat plan, the subsidy of district heating and insulation. But the oil crises only reinforced a process that was perceptible in earlier years with the participation of the State in negotiations for gas supplies, the formation of

DONG and the Natural Gas Supply Act. These observations are a record, they are not meant to imply that state intervention is unnecessary; it may well be that state intervention is essential to secure national interests; indeed, it is arguable that the earlier lack of state concern with the Danish offshore activity has seriously restricted subsequent choices.

It can also be seen that the reverse influence of institutions on the perception of energy problems has led to the proposals for the incorporation of heat supply into physical planning which are unique in the non-communist world. They are in fascinating contrast to the United Kingdom, where the local authorities again have extensive powers, but historically have relinquished interest in energy supply. It is the character of Danish institutions which permits them to elaborate a plan for energy use, whereas other countries can only make plans for energy supply.

Finally, one can ask whether the ostentatiously democratic process in Denmark has restricted the options. It is obvious that the retraction from the purely administrative decision-making cycle which did actually exist in Denmark, and which was similar in many ways to the system operated in France, was in anticipation of an effective political protest: it has certainly postponed the introduction of nuclear power.

REFERENCES

1. Danish Natural Gas, reply to a question in the Folketing, 9 February 1968.
2. *Denmark's Energy Supply-Energy Policy Objectives and Measures*, Ministry of Commerce, April 1974.
3. *Electricity Supply Act, 1976*. Monopoltilsynets Meddelelser, 1978 (i), pp. 37–42.
4. *Notice No 236*, 10 May 1976, Ministry for Trade and Industry. English translation and summary, 5 May 1977.
5. Agreement of July 15 1976 between Concessionaires according to sole concession of July 8 1962 and the Ministry of Commerce.
6. *Introduction to a Heating Plan for Denmark*, Ministry of Housing, December 1975.
7. *Act on Heat Supply*, Act No. 258 of 8 June 1978.
8. Energy Report from the Ministry of Commerce—*ER 79*, Copenhagen, March 1979.
9. *Danish Energy Policy, 1976*, Ministry of Commerce, May 1976.
10. *Danish Energy Policy, 1976*, op. cit.
11. *Redegorelse fil Folketinget em de offentlige investeringer*, Ministry of Finance, 16 May 1978.
12. *Energy Plan 1981*, Ministry of Energy, November 1981.

3
SWEDISH ENERGY POLICY

The per capita consumption of energy in Sweden is one of the highest in the world. There are four main reasons for this—the large Gross Domestic Product; the bias within that output towards energy intensive industries, especially steel and paper; the economic geography, which requires extensive transport services; and the climate. There is no indigenous production of oil or gas; coal reserves are small and of low quality; a few thousand tonnes are mined annually as a by-product of the ceramics industry. The only indigenous resource of any consequence is hydro, which accounts for 13.5 per cent of energy consumption. Oil is imported to meet 70 per cent of demand.

The change in the terms of trade of oil has, for Sweden, coincided with the appearance of stresses within the social system which has been the basis of Swedish prosperity. A remarkable coexistence of a capitalist wealth-generating sector and a comprehensive welfare state has contributed to the ability of the economy to adjust to changing circumstances. The increase in the cost of imported oil is a direct tax on the wealth of the country, the profitability of the private sector and the real value of state revenues. The costs accruing to the State, as demands for welfare and support for industry, have increased as revenues dropped.

A second principal characteristic of the Swedish case is the variety of alternatives to oil among which Sweden may choose; she has a strong nuclear industry, huge uranium reserves, a large potential for generation of electricity from hydropower, extensive deposits of peat, vast forests, and a favourable solar regime in that clear winter skies make solar heat available at times when it can be used. In addition to all these options she has a choice among conventional alternatives—imported coal, natural gas and conservation.

The third characteristic of the Swedish case, and perhaps the one which makes it especially fascinating, is the institutional structure. The main elements of this structure are a nicely balanced central and local competence and a political system, in the broadest sense, which effectively represents popular currents of opinion.

It is the interaction between these factors—the need for change, the variety of choice and the particular structure of decision-making—which this chapter seeks to explore. The account begins with an explanation of the institutional structure; it then describes some crucial historical developments in energy supply and goes on to discuss the content of present policy and to emphasize some especially interesting aspects.

THE INSTITUTIONAL STRUCTURE

Municipalities Keynes is supposed to have claimed that all practical men are slaves of some defunct economist; that is no doubt the case, but they are slaves of much else. To understand Swedish energy policy it is necessary to know something of the nature of the relationship between central and local government. The present structure of local government is little more than a century old, but there is a continuous tradition back to pagan times when the owners of farms would meet in the village to decide on matters of common interest. At an early stage definite responsibilities were attributed to local administrative units; to the *härad* for the military and the highways and to the *skeppslag* for the navy. With Christianity, the basis of the local religious community became the parish, the religious administrative structure was fully developed by the twelfth century and has hardly changed geographically since. Medieval Sweden preserved a decentralized structure; the provinces·tendered·allegiance to a single king who provided cohesion for the nation, but they enjoyed considerable autonomy. The population at large made their views known through local meetings.

In the seventeenth century the positions, privileges and duties of this array of units of local government were defined by King Gustav Adolf and his brilliant Chancellor, Axel Oxenstierna. The *härads* survived for overseeing purely local matters, each with its own jury or committee; the parish and parish meeting were made responsible for religious matters and care of the poor. A hierarchical structure at regional level provided the administrative mechanism for taxation and accountancy. In this reform can be seen the definition of relations between local and central government, the delegation of decisions locally and the use of local administrative units as a means of implementing central government policies—important features which persist to this day.

As the cities grew they developed an internally regulated society over which the burghers quickly took control, exercising judicial and administrative functions. The leading official, the burgomaster, was elected or nominated locally.

The novel administrative demands generated by social changes in the nineteenth century were met by an extension of local powers and responsibilities. Elementary education was the most important. As in Denmark, the initiatives were closely associated with agriculture and the Church; Karl Ifvarsson, a farmer from Scåne and a member of the farmers' Estate in the Riksdag, the Swedish Parliament, was a persistent advocate of mandatory primary education run by the parish under state supervision (his ideas were partially absorbed by Grundtvig in Denmark). His activities brought about the passage of a law in 1842 whereby the parish was explicitly permitted to raise money not only for its church but for the school, poor relief and public health.

The present structure of local government was defined in the reforms of another able Minister, Louis de Geer, in 1862 which established new geographical boundaries and empowered local authorities to raise taxes to finance undertakings of common interest—a unique Swedish phenomenon. The legislation permitted representative bodies to be substituted for general meetings, but interestingly it took some 50 years for representative government to be widely adopted. In cities the reforms replaced rule by the burghers and guilds with a general city meeting or representative body which took decisions.

Interesting though the structure is in the way in which it balances local and central functions, it should not be thought that it was in any way democratic. The franchise depended on the volume of taxes paid, consequently *de facto* the burghers and landowners continued in virtual control until well into the twentieth century. What is important is the legitimacy and authority of the local organizations *vis-à-vis* central government.

The local communities were further strengthened by the reforms of the parliamentary structure—again by Louis de Geer—in 1866. He replaced the four estates by a two-chamber house, with the intention that the first chamber should represent 'propertied conservation' and the second chamber should represent reform and serve the common people and farmers.

It was necessary to find an electoral basis for the first chamber and, because the franchise in the local communities ensured strong conservative tendencies, Louis de Geer chose them to elect indirectly the first chamber. Once established in the Constitution as electoral bodies, the local authorities were able to exercise increasing influence on the decisions of central government and to consolidate their role in the implementation of policies.

During the Second World War the local authorities became accustomed to implementing the rationing of resources and their administrative scope increased accordingly. After the War, new reforms reduced the number of local authorities from some 3,000 in 1950 to less than 300. The number of local politicians declined proportionally, which was a trauma for all political parties other than the Social Democrats who initiated the reforms. The Social Democrats had their particular local organizations, the unions and co-operatives, and were less dependent than other parties on the municipalities as a focus for their local political structure.

As a compromise the Social Democrats delegated and decentralized many functions. In the 1970s an enormous effort was made to decentralize and much legislation of that period has a form which specifically prevents central government intervention. It is now almost impossible for government to implement policies.

This lengthy preamble is necessary for an appreciation of the influence exercised by local authorities on the formulation and implementation of policies. The Riksdag is unlikely to pass a law against the interests of the municipalities because it would not be implemented if it did. The sentiment is constantly reiterated: 'it is difficult to exaggerate the strength of the communes'; 'the Organization of Swedish Municipalities is stronger than Government itself'; 'it would be absolutely impossible for the Government to push legislation that did not have the support of the municipalities'. These are all quotations from those experienced in the formulation of Swedish policies.

A few figures will indicate the extent of the resources controlled by local government. Today there are 23 country councils and 277 municipalities; they account for roughly two-thirds of the total consumption and investment within the Swedish public sector; in 1975 the central government contributed 12 per cent of GNP and local government about 20 per cent. The municipalities have three streams of finance: they have the right to tax the incomes of residents within their boundaries (an average of 29 per cent in 1979); they receive government grants for both discretionary and obligatory functions delegated by the State, e.g. education, energy conservation; and they have a right to charge users for services, e.g. in energy supply, waste disposal etc. The municipalities exercise an influence on the implementation of energy policy through their interests in energy supply, their local monopoly of physical planning and their opportunity to take initiatives in energy conservation. Some functions of municipalities are mandatory, others are optional; energy supply and conservation are optional, some responsibilities in energy planning are mandatory.

The municipalities supply all district heating in Sweden, amounting to about 25 Twh of energy. District heating schemes exist in about 25 per cent of municipalities; there are many plans to expand old systems and begin new ones. The municipalities distribute about 40 per cent of electricity—about 35 Twh—and produce about 15 per cent themselves, mostly in cogeneration plants; they serve about 70 per cent of electricity consumers. These operations are carried out by organizations of various legal forms; they are directed by a board comprising local politicians and the chief technical executive. Formally they are subject to much the same financial disciplines as private companies, but in practice there appears to be an opportunity to borrow relatively freely, and consequently a wide range of financial structures has developed. Some energy companies finance their expansion 100 per cent by loans, others by retained earnings of up to 80 or 100 per cent. Tariffs for the sale of heat and power are set by the companies; consumers can register complaints with a state arbiter, but he judges whether tariffs are reasonable given the immediate economic situation of the company, not whether the company is tolerably efficient and providing a satisfactory service. The upshot of all this is that there is a wide range of performance with the best companies exhibiting considerable entrepreneurial initiative and management efficiency.

The State has no power to force a municipal energy company to undertake any particular investment, except where safety is concerned. The municipalities hold fast to their independence. In practice, however, the State acts in a quite different fashion.

Construction of plant above a certain size requires various licences from the State which can be withheld; it has happened that the State has rejected applications to build oil-fired cogeneration plant. A second string to the bow of the State is the dispensation of grants. Different authorities give a variety of grants to all types of oil-substituting installations and while these persist they can influence investment. For example some municipalities are investing in novel wood or peat-fired cogeneration plant because of extensive subsidies; others are installing equipment to clean and burn coal for the same reasons. Finally, the Government generally controls or influences the means of finance one way or another and this is especially persuasive when municipalities are highly indebted. The capital requirements for district heating and solid fuel boilers are so great that few companies can afford to neglect the specialized government funds and avoid the strings attached.

The incorporation of energy as a factor in physical planning is one of the most instructive peculiarities of Sweden. The municipalities' responsibilities here have been formalized by recent legislation, but they are really only a logical consequence of their monopoly of physical planning and their intimate association with the supply of energy. All construction must be approved by the competent local councils; this monopoly is exercised within certain negative constraints applied by central government, but the municipalities can veto all development except that proposed by the Ministry of Defence. The consequences of the municipalities' power could be great; almost any policy could be implemented by refusing to allow developments which went against it. Central government has occasionally been embarrassed by difficulties in siting obnoxious projects. Linkage of issues, whereby municipalities would be compensated for disagreeable projects by pleasanter developments offends the Swedish sense of integrity in government; it does not, and probably could not, exist. A proposal is in the offing to introduce an overriding central government power to impose projects of national interest, the need for such a power is widely accepted in principle. Implementation in practice in specific cases would be quite another matter. Although the logic of local energy planning has been implicit for a long time, it was not until the early 1970s that the appropriate government agency (the National Board of Swedish Industries) recognized the necessity for municipalities to associate the planning of the built environment with the planning of their district heating companies. The idea owed nothing to the energy crisis; it sprang from a conviction that more efficient centralized heat supply systems could be designed through this process. In 1974 the agency decided it would be wise to extend the notion to energy planning in general; it created a committee to study the question, which after due consultation with interested parties, proposed a law on energy planning which would oblige municipalities to promote energy conservation and take measures to ensure a safe and sufficient supply of energy. The Bill was agreed by the Riksdag in 1976. The administrative circum-stances of most countries would make this a startling charge to lay upon a local authority, and there is a long way to go before this general instruction brings about a substantial change in behaviour. It is relatively easy for municipalities to satisfy the letter and neglect the spirit of the law, and informed opinion in Sweden differs in its assessment of the consequences of the Act. On one view the practical consequence has been nil; the National Board of Swedish Industries has not been given sufficient staff to penetrate and monitor the planning of the municipalities, and the latter have shown little spontaneous response. The most reasonable positive statement is that the law lends authority to the relatively few entrepreneurial and enthusiastic officers and politicians in local administrations who are eager to achieve something; it makes it more difficult for others to oppose them. In many authorities there will be no immediate change, but the front runners show what can be done and others will learn from their example.

Energy conservation policy is implemented through municipal-ities and co-ordinated through a central government agency. A law in 1978 made SK 40 million available to finance specialists in energy conservation in local authorities. (The budget was later increased; SK 130 million are now available for 5 years.) About 70 per cent of the municipalities have advisers, one has fifteen people. The money was aimed not at the energy supply com-panies, but at the building committees; in some cases the supply companies have managed to absorb the functions and the finance. These resources could also be used for energy planning; their availability has apparently had a substantial effect on the volume of activity.

The law on energy planning was extended in 1981 by a new paragraph which increased the responsibilities of the communities and obliged them to present, by July 1982, a detailed plan for the reduction of oil use. It obliged the municipalities to take a more active role in questions of transport and industrial development from an energy perspective.

As matters stand, a local energy plan might comprise guidelines for the expansion of district heating; observations on the energy consequences of industrial and residential development; and plans for saving energy in existing buildings, drawing on some analysis of the nature and performance of the existing stock and its means of heating. There is scope for different approaches; Malmö has produced a plan for conservation based on a physical analysis of the building stock; Göteborg has broken down the housing stock by types of ownership and assessed the possibilities for action on that basis.

The powers of local authorities to enforce plans are limited. Although municipalities have powers to impose the choice of district heating, the law has never been applied. They can withhold the sale of electricity for space heating in areas where they want to promote district heating and there are fairly small subsidies towards the costs of joining a heating network; more positive powers of heat planning are likely. The thermal performance of existing buildings is strictly regulated; there is no power to improve the performance of existing building mandatorily and none is contemplated. It is compulsory for oil companies to divulge deliveries of fuel to large consumers and for firms to divulge consumption; this information in principle could allow local authorities to detect uses well above the norm for particular tasks, to detect opportunities for the substitution of oil by solid fuels and the incorporation of industrial processes into heat supply networks as sources or links. It could also be of assistance in locating new residential and tertiary developments near sources of industrial waste heat. In general it provides the essential information by which a local authority can scrutinize energy use in its area. Little use seems to have been made of this possibility so far, but it is too early to judge whether or not it will prove a valuable and effective form of control.

There is, however, evidence of how municipalities can play an active and entrepreneurial role in energy conservation. In Uppsala the energy supply company was vested by the municipality with the conservation function and set up a group to seek out opportunities for conservation and to arrange quotations from suppliers for 'wholesale' improvements. The company approaches the owner or developer telling him what can be done, what the result will be, and how to arrange finance from the State.

It is reasonable to ask whether there is not a conflict of interest between supply and conservation and whether the prosecution of one or other function will not suffer if they are controlled by one agency. This is an intriguing question. If there is an economic rent from energy conservation then it should be possible to arrange to share that rent between the consumer and any entrepreneur who puts the deal together, even if it is an energy supplier. In the USA some utilities finance energy conservation measures and lease the facilities back to the consumer. No such arrangement has been made in Sweden, but some companies appreciate that the cost of expanding services greatly exceeds the average cost of existing services to which prices tend to be related. Whether the supply company benefits from a consumer saving energy depends on whether the tariff properly distinguishes between fixed and variable costs; if the latter are too high then the company will lose revenues in excess of the cost savings. A tariff which accurately reflects fuel costs is therefore an indispensable requirement for removing the conflict of interest within the supply company. Tariffs which load the recovery of revenue excessively on to the unit costs eventually cheat the public as well because the fall in demand brought about by the price signals causes financial disaster for the utility which is then forced to increase prices to the not unnatural displeasure of the consumer.

An institutional system which forces its local politicians to penetrate the cost structure of electricity supply and use to this extent cannot be entirely without merit.

State Agencies

In the nineteenth century the doctrine of Montesquieu on the separation of powers contributed to the design of the Swedish constitution and institutional reform. With time the separation of powers was transformed into a separation of functions. This characteristic is especially evident in another peculiarity of Swedish government structure: the policy-making function is vested in the Ministers and separated from the execution of policy, which is assigned to specific boards and agencies (often in turn working through municipalities). These agencies are not formally responsible to a Minister. This arrangement is intended to avoid patronage; it leads to a sparse government administration.

Among government bodies responsible for various aspects of energy policy there were the Energy Research and Development Commission, the National Swedish Industrial Board (responsible *inter alia* for energy forecasts and advice on conservation and oil substitution in industry), the Oil Substitution Fund (responsible for grants and loan schemes to promote oil substitution and energy conservation), the National Swedish Board for Energy Source Development (responsible for research and development relating to indigenous and renewable energy sources), the National Swedish Board for Technical Development (responsible for that part of the energy research programme dealing with energy use in industrial processes), the Committee on Energy Conservation (responsible for information activities aimed at promoting energy conservation) and some others. Many of these functions were absorbed as from July 1982, into a new governmental agency—the National Swedish Energy Board.

There is a curious continuum between these administrative agencies and commercial state enterprises having an agency form (such as the Swedish State Power Board, SSPB—or Statens Vatterfallswerk), and the state enterprises having the legal form of a private company. The main group of public enterprises in the form of a company are subsidiaries of a holding company (Statsforetag AB) whose shares are held by the Ministry of Industry, but the public enterprise in the form of a company with most significance in energy policy is the Swedish State Oil Company (Svenska Petroleum), owned 50 per cent each by Statsforetag and the Swedish State Power Board.

The thrust of government control appears to be directed exclusively at ensuring the efficient use of resources. Swedish Petroleum operates in principle in a competitive market and the State Power Board coexists with private and municipal power producers. The competitive environment (which in both cases may be more apparent than real) is presumed to impose a certain level of efficiency. The National Audit Bureau (itself an agency of the Ministry of Finance) exercises *a posteriori* controls over commercial and administrative agencies but is designed only to audit efficiency and not adherence to national policy.

As with the agencies, the Ministry has little direct control over the activity of public companies other than to prescribe broad objectives and financial performance over a rather long period. For commercial agencies such as the SSPB, the Riksdag must approve the annual revenue budget, the annual investment programme and acquisition of shares in other undertakings; changes in electricity tariffs have only to be reported to the Ministry. Even these relatively limited powers are of restricted significance in that neither the Riksdag nor the Ministry seems ever to have defined the political objectives of the State Power Board and therefore has no set criteria, other than profitability, by which to judge performance.

Superimposed on this formal mechanism of control is an informal procedure which is said to be significant: Sweden is a small country and most of the people concerned know each other well; for 40 years government remained in the hands of the Social Democrats which helped to stabilize the composition of the top decision makers. But even this familiarity appears to have served more as a means of determining whether or not institutions were tolerably well run rather than as a surrogate for formal political control. Broadly, public enterprise appears to have been required to be reasonably efficient and has then been allowed the resources and the freedom to provide an adequate standard of service, whilst surviving in an environment with some element of competition. In several respects this relationship has been stressed by the energy crisis; the Government has attempted to use state agencies as instruments of policy without (it is argued later) having the means of analysis and control that then become necessary.

Central Government

The central government consists of a loose federation of departments, with fairly small staffs. It is difficult to detect a formidable arbiter like Les Finances in France or the Treasury in the UK. No department appears to be able to summarize the costs of an energy policy and even less to subject policy to budgetary constraints in an organized fashion. The task is made more difficult because of the administrative and commercial agencies not formally controlled by the Ministers. The Ministry of Finance appears to see itself as responsible for the broad fiscal, monetary and economic policies and not as the perpetuator and ubiquitous moderator of the policies of other departments. In recent years this arrangement has worked satisfactorily, aided by an expanding economy and 40 years of government by one party.

With such stable government both the ability of, and the need for, the central administration to impose policies on their Ministers discreetly is attenuated. Genuine political control can be exercised. To allocate a steadily growing amount of resources by political judgement within a stable political environment was a relatively easy task. The recession caused new stresses on public finance—novel in their political character and magnitude. The coalition Government in 1976 reinforced the disintegrative tendencies within the administration; the Prime Minister's office was governed by one party, the Ministry of Finance by another. The net result was to weaken the coercive forces of government with regard to the municipalities and agencies, not least in their capacity to monitor and control the financial consequences of this policy.

In short there does not appear to exist in Sweden, at least in any comprehensive manner, the policy of the Ministry in contrast to the policy of the Minister. Still less is there a powerful department of state, before which the others tremble, arbitrating the conflicts of lesser Ministries.

Industry

The underlying theme of Swedish industrial policy has been that the State creates the environment conducive to change and pays some of the costs but leaves it to others to take specific decisions; this has been in many respects a great success and it is my view that this model has had a considerable influence on energy policy. Because of this and because the strains of industrialization still exercise an influence on modern events it is useful to review the main features of industrial development.

Industrialization has occurred recently and rapidly. Over the last 100 years Sweden's industrial production has increased one hundred times. An analysis by the Royal Swedish Academy of Engineering Sciences attributes the success and rapidity of the process to four main factors: an ample supply of raw materials and hydroelectric power, the high technological level of Swedish industry, participation in international specialization of activity, and a pronounced ability to adjust to change.

The principal episodes of change separate approximately into five periods:

1. Up to 1890, the industrial economy comprised basic processes; saw milling, smelting and simple metal working; mainly in the North.
2. 1890–1913, period characterized by increasing product refinement and specialization, e.g. in ball bearings and telephone equipment; shift of emphasis to South.
3. Inter-war, Sweden became a net exporter of capital; structural change towards chemicals and engineering and away from textiles and timber.
4. 1946–1965, productivity increased rapidly, but profitability and extent of self-financing fell.
5. 1965–, deteriorating growth, further drop in self-financing, social resistance to change.

Since 1965 growth rates have fallen from 5 per cent to 2 per cent, the self-financing ratio has dropped to 20 per cent because of low profitability and the capacity of industry to adjust has fallen away, in part because of government intervention to support ailing concerns and in part because the investments in social infrastructure surrounding work places have come far to exceed the capital committed to the productive process itself; these two reasons evidently interact and reinforce each other.

From a different perspective we see again that the need to cope with energy changes has occurred at the same time as the Swedish industrial structure has been losing its capacity to adjust, both economically because ·of declining profitability, and socially.

The recommendations of the Royal Academy in its study of Technical Capacity and Industrial Competition are most illuminating of the attitudes of at least some of industry. The Academy concludes from its study that adaptive mechanisms have become much less effective since 1965; it argues for new forms of co-operation between Swedish Government and industry; it asserts that Government should develop an industrial strategy and policy, to include support for innovation and research and development, and should provide an overall assessment of the long-term development of Swedish industry modelled after the French Plan.

No doubt it would be wrong to associate the whole of Swedish industry with these ideas, but they do demonstrate what has developed through tolerance and even an expectation of the Government's initiatives. An industrial class that resisted intervention now turns to the Government to solve its problems. This mood extends, I think, into energy policy, where similar expectations of Government are now widespread.

CRUCIAL HISTORICAL DEVELOPMENTS

Electrification

The history of electrification in Sweden illustrates most effectively the balance between central and local competences which is so much a feature of the institutional structure. The early nodes of growth of electrification were the heavy industries in the North and Centre and the municipalities of the South. The sawmills and iron and steel works of North and Central Sweden grew up from the availability of forest products, charcoal and low cost hydropower; much of the forest and river banks were purchased by these industries at an early stage. They quickly developed surplus power production which they wanted to sell. The big municipalities entered energy supply through the manufacture of town gas from imported coal and when it became possible to produce electricity from the same feedstock they took over that activity. In the smaller towns and countryside the municipalities did not initiate electrification, and electricity in these districts was marketed by the industry-based production companies with varying success.

The exploitation of hydro resources rapidly introduced a novel dimension of conflict. The mode of industrialization of Sweden through forest products promoted an especially clear struggle in the late nineteenth and early twentieth centuries between the interests of industry and the countryside. Access to forest, river banks and water for agriculture and fishing was prevented or reduced by the use of rivers for transporting wood and *a fortiori* by the construction of dams which destroyed the fishing as salmon could no longer move upstream. Superstitious beliefs about the effect of electricity on cattle played a not insignificant part. The conflict of town and countryside promoted a curious coalition of political interests between Conservatives and Social Democrats, in favour of industrialization and against farmers and liberals who wanted to preserve rural interests. This type of *ad hoc* alliance between Social Democrats and the right, excluding middle interests, is still detectable today, not least in nuclear policy.

The town–country conflicts became especially strong when industrial entrepreneurs attempted to develop remote hydro resources for the service of towns. The first test case came over a hydropower development east of Göteborg. The Conservative Government was of the view that a reasonably fair development of hydro resources which respected all interests required a socialization of the function. It managed to impose this with admirable legal subtlety. The political basis was the concept of the king's stream; this attributed rights over a fixed width of the middle of any waterway to the king; this right the State took to entitle it to dispute the rights of the owners of the river bank and to make the king part of any development of the stream. The Swedish State Power Board was created in 1907 as the agent of the State in this respect; it began its first large power plant in 1910.

Socialization of the function did not of itself guarantee a rational development of resources. To mediate conflicting interests an early form of welfare cost–benefit analysis was applied to appraise each scheme. Exploitation of hydro resources was allowed if the benefit was three times greater than the damage to cultivated land and twice the damage to other property.

The centrepiece of the physical structure was the Swedish National Grid designed to link regions of cheap production, especially in the North, with regions of high demand, mainly in the South. In 1936 the tasks of deciding what to do with the existing transmission lines, what future needs would be and how to provide for them, were entrusted to Axel Granholm, at the time Director of the Swedish Railway System and a man much employed by the State as a member of investigating committees. He had created the idea of a railway system made up of local systems initiated by municipalities and linked by a state-owned system of long range lines; this organizational concept he transferred to electricity. The Social Democrats and Conservatives agreed on the necessity and desirability of this but differed on ownership; the former wanted public ownership and the latter wanted private. The initial compromise was a separate entity jointly owned by private interests and the Swedish State Power Board. After the Social Democrat consolidation in 1945 it became ideologically difficult for them to accept this scheme and they tried to transfer ownership to the SSPB. The SSPB was unwilling to accept the responsibility because it preferred to keep marginal private interests in being to avoid charges of monopoly. In the event the ownership of the grid was turned over to the unwilling hands of the SSPB, but its operation was entrusted to a Central Dispatching Board owned by a co-operative body of producers in which the SSPB predominated. Ownership of lines above a certain voltage was vested in the SSPB and they were made responsible for maintenance and decisions on pricing. The running of the system was decided jointly.

The basic structure of the electricity supply industry to which this process of compromise gave rise persists to this day; private municipal and state-owned producers coexist; the transmission grid is state-owned and jointly operated, distribution is through municipalities or the producers. In this respect the SSPB has a social function, distributing in sparsely populated areas with the help of subsidies from its more profitable activities.

Chief among the producers after the SSPB is Sydkraft, a private company created by the municipalities of Skåne in southern Sweden to develop hydro resources for the towns. There is no formal authority with the responsibility to co-ordinate the investment plans of the producers but the twelve largest producers collaborate within a central planning group and exchange plans voluntarily. In recent times the SSPB has tended to own about 50 per cent of new capacity.

In principle the producers compete to sell to distributors but in practice they act as a cartel, following the SSPB's price setting. Such competition as does exist is rarely exercised through prices; occasionally a private industrial producer may make the location of a new factory conditional on the town switching to it as a supplier of electricity. Even with the present overcapacity (demand is 95 Twh and stationary, potential supply is 107 Twh and growing) the cartel functions well. In return for this discipline the SSPB protects other producers; it is unknown for a producer to go bankrupt. The SSPB enjoys a large economic rent from its old hydro schemes and is the most profitable part of the electricity supply industry.

Relations between the cartel and distributors vary. Smaller distributors tend to bow to the inevitable; relations with larger municipalities, with more resources, can be abrasive. By its control of trunk lines and the terms on which the municipalities can enter the system the SSPB exercises a crucial strategic influence. Six larger municipalities in the middle of Sweden have formed their own power procuring company to get better terms from the cartel. The same group went to the market with a bid for an existing private producer. The bid failed but as a consequence the shareholding was restructured so that the municipalities in the area now have a majority of votes in the company. There has been a lengthy conflict of interest over cogeneration which is described in detail later.

It is interesting to digress and compare the structure and origins of this system with those of other countries. As described earlier, Denmark enjoys an electricity supply system which is vertically integrated but in which the sense of ownership flows from the bottom up. The density of population favoured widespread rural electrification; local interests, often expressed through co-operatives, initiated electrification. There was never any conflict between surplus and deficit regions or country and town for the State to arbitrate. As a result utilities created their own alliances and hierarchic structure. In France the concept of a centrally organized nation state leads naturally to a centrally regulated system and eventually to a state owned utility. The influence which local and central interests can exercise on the formulation and implementation of policy is crucially affected by the nature of the structure and is a principal determinant of technical choice.

Nuclear Power and Cogeneration

Sweden's nuclear energy programme dates back to the mid-1940s; it was the first direct large scale intervention by Government in the economy, outside the military sector. Government exercised an influence in three ways: it contributed heavily to the R & D programme through Atomenergi, a research organization created in 1947 owned four-sevenths by Government and three-sevenths by industry; it established a nuclear construction company ASEA-ATOM in a 50/50 partnership with ASEA the principal Swedish heavy electrical engineering company; it attempted to influence SSPB's procurement policy. Government participation in all three phases of the research, manufacture, and use did not smooth the path. There were the usual demarcation disputes over responsibilities and choice of reactor. The Government was unsuccessful in its attempts to influence the SSPB which could and did claim that it operated in a competitive sector and could not afford to make judgements other than on a commercial basis. Here as at other times the private rump of generators was convenient to the SSPB.

In 1954 the first Swedish research reactor was commissioned and in the late 1950s plans for a national energy policy were drawn up with nuclear power as an important element. International optimism about the future of nuclear energy was shared by Swedish scientists and the few politicians with detailed interest. The Swedish development programme was based on a heavy water design using natural uranium and avoiding the need for enrichment. Sweden has the largest known reserves of uranium in Europe and this design of reactor would have made her independent of outside supplies. The programme was a terrible flop; and although in the initial stages the SSPB was obliged to participate in pilot projects, when it came to ordering, the Board refused to accept the design. The SSPB and other producers concluded jointly that the whole concept was commercially unacceptable and they forced the Government to accept a switch to US technology marketed by ASEA. The ASEA design of BWR was broadly a General Electric (GE) design, but developed independently by ASEA, not licensed from GE. The state development programme provided 80–90 per cent of the technical knowledge and therefore was in the end a significant and perhaps determining influence on the capacity to develop nuclear plant if not on the choice of technology. There are two anecdotes from this period which give some insight. One of those who began to criticise the programme during the 1960s was the Nobel physicist Hannes Alfven; he has since revealed that a principal factor stimulating his dissent was the determination with which the protagonists of the Swedish line pushed its development, long after it was clear that the concept was neither technicially nor economically sound. He was apparently deeply impressed by the extent to which occult coalitions could operate so successfully against public interest. He later played an important part in the politicization of the topic and the origin of his motivation is not without interest. The heavy water project was eventually abandoned in 1970.

The second incident illustrates the effect which private industry could exert on policy at that time. The chairman of ASEA-

ATOM, the powerful industrialist Marcus Valenburg, was also influential within a private consortium of power producers and his efforts were apparently significant in persuading the consortium to place the order for the first nuclear reactor on their site at Oskarshamn, choosing foreign inspired light water technology. No doubt this coup was mainly of dramatic interest—once ASEA and the power industry had made up its mind there was little the Government could do, but it does remind one that not so long ago private industry interests could still initiate policy in this area.

For some years afterwards the power producers took the decisions. Sydkraft were next to order a reactor, the SSPB trailing behind disconsolately. The Government has tried to persuade the SSPB to place orders with ASEA, but the Board has preferred to buy the Westinghouse design PWRs. The private producers have shown themselves more willing to take into account the interests of Swedish industry and have bought from ASEA—blood in this case being thicker than water. It has been suggested that the SSPB would have preferred not to have had a Swedish supplier at all, but to have had freedom to purchase where they thought best. The status of the Swedish nuclear programme is summarized in Table 3.1.

TABLE 3.1

Status of nuclear power plant

Station		Capacity MW(e)	Operating Date	Owner	Manufacturer
Oskarshamn	1	440	1972	OKG	ASEA-ATOM
	2	580	1974	OKG	”
	3	1060	1985	OKG	”
Barseback	1	580	1975	Sydkraft	ASEA-ATOM
	2	580	1977	”	”
Ringhals	1	760	1975	SSPB	ASEA-ATOM
	2	820	1975	”	Westinghouse
	3	900	1981	”	”
	4	900	1982	”	”
Forsmark	1	900	1980	FKA	ASEA-ATOM
	2	900	1981	”	”
	3	1060	1985	”	”

Notes: The Oskarshamn consortium comprises nine partners including Sydkraft to 33 per cent.
The Forsmark consortium is largely owned by the SSPB with a minority interest held by some of the partners in OKG.

The Government's objective behind the nuclear programme was to reduce oil consumption; the producers' objective was commercial. It is interesting to speculate why Sweden decided on nuclear generation when Danish utilities, after an equally enthusiastic preliminary dalliance, chose oil-based generation. ASEA of course had more realistic expectations of exporting systems and components than could any Danish constructor, but the Swedish producers had cheaper sources of electricity through hydro than did the Danes. Without ever being able to prove conclusively the validity of the explanation, one is struck by the fact that the Swedes—a practical, highly organized, industrial society—chose to develop nuclear power and the Danes—a shrewd, trading society—chose oil.

In the 1960s the long-term planning of the SSPB came up against the ambitions of the municipalities. The plans of the producers for nuclear expansion depended on an assured market for electricity in the cities where the growth was, but where distribution was controlled by strong municipalities. The municipalities in contrast to the producers planned to supply much of the increase from their own cogeneration plant; in Denmark, where a similar conflict had arisen much earlier the municipalities had, by and large, won; in Sweden the result was much closer.

The plans of the municipalities sprung from two quite different considerations: firstly from a fairly short tradition of district heating and cogeneration; secondly from a desire to build up their negotiating strength relative to the producer cartel.

The history of district heating is shorter in Sweden than in Denmark because of the hydropower available from Swedish rivers. The first arrangements to transport heat and sell to third parties were for industrial process heat. In 1939 the electricity utility in Norrköping began to supply heat to a textile firm and in 1948 the local utility at Karlstad began to supply hot water to a nearby factory. After the War, interest in cogeneration from district heating began to develop rapidly, motivated by experience of fuel shortage during the War and a belief that the capital requirements of developing new hydro resources would limit exploitation. In 1951 Malmö started to supply district heating and commissioned its first cogeneration plant in 1953. Developments in many places in Sweden began to advance rapidly and the latent conflict with the plans of the utilities emerged. The decisive

incident was the decision by the municipality at Västerås to go
ahead with a large cogeneration scheme in the early 1960s. At that
time the SSPB underestimated the municipality, which called the
Board's bluff and went ahead and built and managed well. Several
other towns had similar intentions and were watching closely. The
success of the venture at Västerås caused the SSPB to offer
electricity under long-term contracts to other municipalities at a
price which discouraged cogeneration (these contracts are now
beginning to expire). This behaviour is that of a discriminating
monopolist; it is apparently well identified in Sweden and
tolerated. The result is that there are four groups of *de facto* tariffs
in Sweden:

1. Northern Swedish cities with access to low cost hydro to
   which the SSPB relates its price.
2. Larger cities in Middle Sweden with cogeneration.
3. Municipalities around Stockholm with contracts pitched at
   a level to discourage cogeneration.
4. Other regions with no negotiating powers.

This situation soon became apparent and the appraisal by
municipalities of cogeneration as an investment began to be
determined by whether or not the economic expression of the
improved negotiating position justified the outlay. It has even
been said that the most cost-effective cogeneration scheme is the
one which is not run.

Apart from the first large CHP plant at Västerås, the operation
of which is determined exclusively by the municipality, the
compromises struck between the cities and the SSPB included an
agreement that the SSPB would decide the operation of the
cogeneration plant. Details of operations differ from city to city.
The principle of operation is to dispatch plant to minimize system
costs and on this there can be no dispute. It is the distribution of
the rent from cogeneration which is contentious. When a
cogeneration system exports, it is credited with a value for
electricity intermediate between its own marginal cost and that of
the central system; when it imports then it again pays a price
between the marginal cost on the system and its own marginal
cost. The argument is not about the efficiency of dispatching the
existing system; it is about how to determine the intermediate
prices and consequently how to distribute the economic rent.

There is no criterion of economic efficiency or justice for determining this split and it is a matter of negotiating power. It begins to matter if it is planned to increase cogeneration; if the cogenerator does not receive the full economic rent he will be dissuaded from expanding his system. These arguments are, in a way, the most eloquent expression of the delicate balance of central and local power; cogeneration is established but its scale and operation restricted.

Later, during the 1970s, this *modus vivendi* was reinforced. The capacity of many municipalities to finance cogeneration plant was limited and for this and other reasons they sought to collaborate with the power companies in the construction of plant. The result was not so much to remove the creative tension as to shift its emphasis. An example of current controversy illustrates this. Several projects exist for heating Malmö. At one time it was intended to tap heat from the nuclear reactor at Barseback and this idea was close to realization when the referendum intervened. Now that Barseback is commissioned, Sydkraft have lost interest, they propose instead to extend the cogeneration plant they own jointly with the municipality and to supply heat to Malmö and Lund. Malmö opposes this and prefers to build its own heat-only boiler. Their arguments are nominally technical, but in reality they are worried about ceding too much control to Sydkraft (a company in which they have the largest holding). In this case the boundary of conflict has shifted; the municipality has a limited aim of ensuring complete control over the heat producing side; the initiative for cogeneration is coming from the power producer. It does seem that there is increasing diffidence in municipalities about collaborating with the strong, determined and resourceful power companies and an increasing perception of the conflict between requirements of controlling the local physical planning of heat supply and development and the requirements of centrally controlled utilities. If there has indeed been such a shift in boundaries it would signal a retreat by the municipalities and a territorial gain to the producers.

The Penetration of Oil

The penetration of oil into the Swedish economy can be described in two phases—three, if we include the present phase of transition from oil. During the first phase, in the period between the Wars, oil products were used at high prices for specialized functions, mostly for transport fuels and lubricants; the volume of use was negligible, but important parts of the institutional structure were put in place. In the second phase, from the end of the Second World War to the early 1970s, oil met all the increase in demand for energy and eroded the markets for fossil fuels; its penetration was virtually unresisted. The extent to which the availability of oil was the motor of Swedish economic growth is difficult to assess but, being there, it was certainly put to use.

Oil products were initially introduced into Sweden by the international oil companies; for a time they controlled the market absolutely, both as importers and distributors. The Swedish market was small and remote; collusion among the oil companies is always a problem and as a result gasoline prices were some three times world levels. The initial challenge to the companies came not from the State but from the people, in the form of a car owners' co-operative. The co-operative movement in Sweden had been initiated by consumers in the late nineteenth century for the procurement of food; the local consumer co-operatives formed themselves into a national organization in 1899, known as KF, which is now Sweden's largest commercial concern. The farmers quickly followed the consumers, organizing themselves for the common procurement of materials and the marketing of produce. The car owners' co-operative was a later venture, originating from the Taxi Owners' Purchasing Society in Stockholm, then generalizing geographically and extending to private ownership in 1926. The company originally bought its oil products from a Swedish independent oil company then, when that went bankrupt and was bought out by the majors, it began to purchase from the USSR. At the end of the 1930s the USSR stopped selling oil to Europe and the co-operative turned to the Swedish company Nynäs owned by the Johnson family shipping line, which had built its own refinery in Sweden. In 1945 the car owners' co-operative joined with other similar organizations with an interest in oil purchasing to form a new central oil co-operative, the National Swedish Oil Consumers Union, known as OK. The participating interests included KF, the farmers' association and two fishery co-operatives.

After 1945 the use of oil in Sweden increased at a phenomenal rate. War had restricted access to imports of coal, on which Sweden had, in 1940, depended for the largest part of her commercial energy. After the War, coal had continued to be scarce; oil replaced coal in some functions and took over virtually all incremental markets, in particular in manufacturing industry, transport and district heating. There was no resistance; the municipally owned coal-based gas industries recognized the inevitable and went gracefully out of business, replacing themselves with their district heating companies. Only the use of metallurgical coals in iron and steel persisted.

Just after the War the Riksdag debated a proposal to nationalize the oil industry; the proposal was rejected because of the extremely heavy political opposition by the non-Socialist parties, and in part because OK was thought adequately to protect national interests. OK did well out of the buoyant post-war market, especially as its origins helped it in the lucrative gasoline markets, in which it has always kept a very strong market share. At present OK covers 16 per cent of total oil sales including 20 per cent of gasoline and 27 per cent of domestic heating oil.

In 1971 the company began its own refinery, named Scanraff. To benefit from scale the refinery was designed to process 9.3 million tonnes of crude, well above OK's own requirements of 4–5 million tonnes; the extra capacity was intended for operation on behalf of third parties; specifically Texaco had a 20 per cent share in the entire project. The refinery came on stream in 1975 and was a burden for OK until 1978, because of the surplus of oil on the market in Western Europe and the surplus of refining capacity. However, during the second oil crisis of 1979–80, Scanraff turned into a 'golden asset' for OK, because the company was able to arrange crude oil contracts with BNOC, Statoil and Pemex and it managed to make available profits and increase its market share. Without OK's investment in Scanraff, the oil crisis of 1979 could have been a national disaster.

There have been other initiatives in the oil sector. In the 1960s an entrepreneurially inclined group of about ten larger municipalities around Stockholm created a joint oil purchasing company, EFO Oil AB. This company benefited from the low spot prices to obtain cheap supplies for the energy companies of its municipal owners. It now handles about 2 million tonnes of products a year, about half on contract, half on spot. The oil companies attempted to break it up by offering cheap contracts to individual municipalities but they failed.

After the oil crisis in 1973 both the Departments of Trade and Industry began to push ideas for a state oil company. The rationale was to deal with the problems perceived in 1975 and the intention was to offer an alternative channel to oil-producing countries because it was realized that the majors would lose access to OPEC crude. OK was then not thought suitable as an instrument of government policy because of its consumer orientation and first loyalty to members. Nynäs was unsuitable for different reasons; it belonged to the unquoted, family-owned Johnson group. In 1976 the state company Svenska Petroleum (SP) was created, jointly owned by the SSPB and Statsforetag. The declared policy was to buy on easy long-term contracts from producers and lease refining capacity or sell crude on to other oil companies. In fact the initial years coincided with a period in which contract prices were higher than spot prices and the only way that the company could do business was to buy and sell products. In the third quarter of 1978 circumstances had changed sufficiently for the company to sign a long-term contract with Iraq, and later with Iran, Nigeria and Saudi Arabia. When the revolution in Iran disrupted the oil market they were less affected than other companies and they took advantage of the position to expand their market, by taking over supply responsibilities from independents, including EFO. In this they were aided by the imposition of price controls by the Swedish Government in December 1978 which effectively meant that the independents could only have honoured contracts at a loss. At the same time SP acquired equity shares in a BP refinery and Scanraff and arranged processing contracts with other companies. Their total crude supply now is about 6–7 million tonnes/year.

The other Swedish companies, and in particular OK, have not welcomed the appearance of Svenska Petroleum or the intervention of the State in a manner which appears to favour that company. SP's initial dealings on the spot market had a lowering effect on prices at a time when the companies were hard pressed; its acquisition of independent markets under the period of price control are seen as destabilizing.

There are also fears that State money will be used to subsidize further encroachments by SP, especially in the gasoline market. A focus of contention has been an agreement between Norway and Sweden for the exchange of oil and electricity. The agreement was negotiated by the Department of Industry, over the heads of the oil companies, including, it would appear, SP. The Swedes agreed to take at least 2.0 million tonnes of oil in 1983 and 2.5 million tonnes a year thereafter, up to 75 per cent as products according to the decision of Norway. The choice depended in fact on whether the Norwegians would decide to increase the capacity of the Mongstad refinery. This, in the event, they did. In principle the products could be handled either by SP or by OK, but OK is not seeking to purchase more products, at prices which are not apparently advantageous, when it has a gross surplus of refinery capacity of its own. The most likely candidate is SP, especially as the Norwegians want to enter the Swedish market in a more active way establishing a distribution company in Sweden, perhaps jointly owned by SP and Statoil. This adds a new dimension, because SP, up until now, has been excluded from the gasoline market. In a recent government Bill this ban is lifted in circumstances where SP sets up a joint venture with a crude oil producer. There is therefore a strong incentive for SP to collaborate with Statoil. To get these products onto the market SP would have to offer competitive prices and its penetration could only be at the expense of OK and the other oil companies. The temptation to expand at a loss is always present in state oil companies; in 1980 SP lost SK 387 million and losses were even higher in 1981. There seems to be some justification for OK's alarm expressed in the sentiment 'we can compete with other companies, but not with the taxpayers' money'. The original intention of an exchange of oil for electricity fell through, because Norwegian industry thought the electricity price high by Norwegian standards. The Swedish option to take the stated amounts of Norwegian oil at market prices remains unaffected.

SP has a subsidiary role in exploration. It has licences in the Norwegian and United Kingdom sectors of the North Sea, has shown exploration interest in Indonesia, Tunisia and Italy, and hopes to secure acreage offshore Ireland. It also has production interests in the Norwegian Valhall and Tor fields. These initiatives are financed by Government.

Swedish oil refineries have been experiencing the problems of reduced and changing demand familiar to the rest of Europe and at present capacity utilization is around 60 per cent. One of the country's four major refineries, at Nynashamn, will cease fuel production this year, and BP's refinery at Göteborg is next on the list. To cope with changing patterns of demand, a catalytic cracker will be built at Scanraff, scheduled to come on stream in 1985. It will convert 1 mt of heavy oils to the lighter petrol.

The Nuclear Referendum

The event which will ensure for Sweden a niche in international nuclear history is the referendum of March 1980. Nuclear power had been a political issue of sorts in the 1960s, when the Social Democrats had disagreed with other parties on whether to continue with Swedish technology; this in turn became embroiled with a discussion on whether Sweden should make nuclear weapons, an undertaking which would have been facilitated by the Swedish heavy water technology. The arguments about nuclear weapons severely strained the unity of the Social Democratic Party; the eventual settlement reached was not to develop weapons immediately, but to keep the option open.

During this discussion there was never any opposition to nuclear technology *per se*; that mood sprang unexpectedly from almost nothing in the early 1970s. The origins of the popular movement are obscure; there is some evidence that it was contracted from the US; it seems to be continuous with the student movements of 1968 arising from the Vietnam protests. In one view, an important factor was the diversion of effort from Vietnam which for a long time provided an effective outlet for the need to protest. The two earliest leading figures of the opposition were the physicist Hannes Alfven and Birgitta Hambraeus, a Centre party member of the Riksdag. Birgitta Hambraeus introduced the nuclear question into the main stream of politics when, in the autumn 1972 session of the Riksdag, she asked for a moratorium on nuclear construction. At that time Swedish nuclear policy envisaged that twenty-six reactors would be in operation by 1990. In May 1973 the Riksdag adopted a resolution that no more reactors, other than the eleven already agreed, would be permitted until more information was available on need and safety.

Since that time nuclear power has remained a central issue in Swedish politics; it is difficult for the Riksdag to avoid, because each year it has to vote the budget of the SSPB and the Nelsonian policy of a blind eye is scarcely possible. The political parties defined their views. The Communists turned against nuclear power—a curious decision which does not appear to have any ideological base and which is contrary to the views of Soviet, East European and other West European communist parties and yet which is not obviously opportunist either. The opposition had originated within the Centre party, the largest opposition party at the time with 25 per cent of the vote. The Centre party is an agrarian party, right wing, and morally conservative. It has a presence within the co-operatives and is susceptible to ecological ideas. It held the view that it was necessary to maintain an energy balance or ecological balance on earth; the party leader Thorbjorn Falldin claimed that the party's aim was to 'shift from an over-exploitation of limited raw materials and energy resources to a life-style in harmony with Nature's cyclical system'.

The Riksdag wanted a Commission of Enquiry of politicians and technicians. These Parliamentary Commissions are a frequent resort of Swedish Governments and they are an important forum of mediation and compromise; they are normally expected to produce only one alternative. In this case the Commission acted in a rather curious way; it acquired government funds for all parties to use to initiate energy study campaigns within their ranks. The Communist and Centre parties used the funds to mobilize anti-nuclear opinion. Wide public debate followed; it is estimated that some 75,000 people took part in organized discussion groups on the formulation of future energy policy—remarkable, but nothing compared to what was to follow. The Social Democrats were split; they compromised their natural inclinations for growth and industrialization with the need for them to declare their position, by opting for thirteen reactors. They carried this proposal through the Riksdag with the help of the Conservatives. The alliance between the 'growth' parties of left and right against the 'ecology' parties of left and right is a fascinating throwback to the urban and rural coalitions which took up position over railways and electricity across normal political divides.

The Social Democrats then narrowly lost the election in 1976 and the first non-Socialist government in 44 years came to power. There is no doubt that the general political drift was away from Social Democracy and towards the right, but there is equally persuasive statistical evidence to suggest that the Centre party's unremitting attacks against nuclear power in the closing stages of the campaign were responsible for a late swing towards them which carried the day. The right-wing coalition which took over fell immediately into trouble because it could not agree on nuclear power policy. Falldin could not get parliamentary support to close existing reactors or even to prevent the commissioning of Barseback, the especially controversial site near Malmö. As a ploy to remain in government the Centre party promulgated a Stipulation Act to the effect that a reactor would not be allowed to start operating until the owner had proved that the spent fuel would be reprocessed and that the resulting high-level waste would finally be stored in an absolutely safe way, or, alternatively, that non-reprocessed spent fuel could be stored with absolute safety.

Unfortunately, by 1978 two more reactors were ready for commissioning and the Government was forced to interpret the law; the stress finally led to the dissolution of the Government in October, 1978, but before going it declared that the stipulations had been met, the only doubt being whether the necessary geological formations for final disposal of nuclear waste were to be found in Sweden.

In October 1978 a minority Liberal Government took over, with 39 seats out of 349; they set out to carry through a nuclear programme of twelve plants, with the promised support of the Conservatives and Social Democrats. Before the Bill could be voted the whole political environment was changed by the accident at Three Mile Island in Spring 1979. This was taken very seriously in Sweden and followed in great detail by the media. The Social Democrats judged that their sympathetic attitude to nuclear power would be an electoral handicap and therefore, for purely tactical reasons, they proposed a popular referendum in Spring 1980 that would absolve them from taking a stance on the issue in the election campaign of September 1979. When the Social Democrat leader Olof Palme called for the referendum after Three Mile Island he used the occasion to cross to the 'no' side. The Centre party also approved of the motion because it would allow them to remain part of a pro-nuclear government if the people chose that route in a referendum and would thereby remove their particular albatross. Under the Swedish Constitution, referenda are initiated by the Riksdag; there is no peoples' initiative and the result is not binding—although in this case all parties agreed to accept it. The Social Democrats then lost the election and a new three-party coalition Government was formed, Falldin coming back as Prime Minister.

The problem now was to phrase the referendum. The election over, Olaf Palme and the Social Democrats, under pressure from the unions, veered back towards nuclear power. As 45 years earlier for the national grid, the Social Democrats and Conservatives were in agreement on the substance of policy but differed on the question of ownership. This ideological question had not previously bothered the Social Democrats much but at this moment they were very aware of the damage their analogues in Norway had done to themselves by associating with the Conservatives over the Common Market and they therefore felt in need of something to distinguish them from their right-wing allies. Public ownership became closer to their hearts. The referendum contained three lines. Line 1, supported by the Conservatives, proposed using at most the twelve reactors then operating or planned and phasing out all nuclear power in due course. Line 2, supported by the Social Democrats and Liberals, was identical to Line 1 but with an amendment that *inter alia*, energy conservation was vigorously to be pursued, R & D on renewables to be accelerated, and direct electric heating distribution to be banned from new buildings and distribution to be placed in public hands. Line 3, supported by the Centre and Communists, proposed restricting operation to the six plants then working and abandoning all nuclear generation within 10 years.

The debate preceding the referendum was quite extraordinary. It touched almost every Swedish voter and cut across family, political and social alliances; it was bitter and intellectually violent. In the result, Line 1 received 19 per cent of the vote; Line 2, 39.3 per cent; Line 3, 38.6 per cent. The support for Line 3 was remarkable; it was almost certainly only the heavy immediate expense of such a decision which prevented it winning. It is clear from inspection that these numbers could be interpreted in many ways and they were. But such was the aversion to the viciousness of the campaign that popular interest lapsed rapidly.

The coalition parties appear to have accepted the argument that the results show a popular desire for public ownership and have therefore begun negotiations with the private owners of the Oskarhamn plants with the purpose of persuading them to sell a controlling interest to a satisfactory representative of the State; this will probably be Sydkraft, municipally owned and having already a part interest in the plants.

The Centre party, by continuing in the ruling coalition, has lost some sympathy. Other parties have tended to compensate in other areas for their acquiescence on the nuclear issue, but their popular image has suffered. The party argues that the expectations of its supporters were unrealistic and that it continues to exert a marginal effect, e.g. by preventing uranium mining in Sweden and by continuing to restrict electric space heating.

It is chastening to reflect on the great power of popular opinion revealed by this story. By and large, all the established representatives of society had a more favourable attitude to nuclear power than was expressed by any of the Lines of the referendum. Business organizations, industry, the trade unions, the Ministries, the municipal energy companies, the State agencies including the environmental agencies, many politicians and most of the press were in favour. Historically, liberal newspapers have always been more dominant than the representation in the Riksdag would suggest. The glaring exception was Stockholm's leading daily paper, which for several years has mounted a persistent campaign against nuclear power.

On the other side, essentially, were the people represented by new organizations; the women's movement, ecological movements, and peripheral interests of all kinds. From a certain perspective, the referendum has the air of new institutions versus the old.

It is perhaps important to recognize that this direct, popular influence on events is traditionally part of Swedish politics. A striking way to make that point is to quote from a commentary on the parliamentary reforms in the nineteenth century:

The press was overwhelmingly in favour. Pamphlets pro and pamphlets con were distributed far and wide. De Geer in his memoirs tells of the round of meetings held in Stockholm and throughout the country, of the deputations that came to him and the petitions, one with 60,000 signatures, another from the faculty of Uppsala with 39 names. People awakened through their folk movements were concerned as never before with the problems of their society. They were being informed of the issues and were taking part in a broad-based decision-making process.
Franklin D. Scott; *Sweden the Nation's History* (1977).

On another level the referendum can be seen as a clever political manœuvre; it was a means by which the Riksdag, broadly favourable to nuclear power (estimated to be by some two to one), could get a population broadly opposed to that power to accept a nuclear programme which is per capita one of the largest in the world whilst simultaneously appearing to close it down.

Undoubtedly this was in part the aim, but it has been achieved at a high cost. There is no criterion by which to judge for how long the referendum holds. If, by 1995, all the reactors operate well and generate cheap electricity both in Sweden and world-wide then is it likely that Sweden will choose to follow through its decision? Some politicians talk discreetly even now of a new referendum at the end of the 1980s. The uncertainty which this creates for the formulation and implementation of policy in the long term is significant and we shall return to it later.

A striking feature of Swedish energy policy is the heavy emphasis, in cash and politicians' time, put on research and development. The first government R & D programme for energy (excluding nuclear) was set up within a Bill adopted by the Riksdag in 1975 which was intended to define guidelines for energy policy for the period up to 1985. The R & D programme ran for 3 years from 1975/76 to 1977/78 with a budget of SK 366 million; it put strong emphases on energy conservation and, to a lesser extent, renewable energy sources. The general philosophy was catholic, aimed at providing sufficient knowledge to inform later choices of R & D priorities. The Bill also provided for an Energy Research and Development Commission, organized as a committee under the Ministry of Industry. This is a highly political body comprising five members of the Riksdag, an outside industrialist and the Director General of its technical Secretariat; its tasks are to provide information as a basis for long-term R & D planning, to co-operate with the agencies and Commissions spending the money (and to be directly responsible for the Energy Systems Programme) and to monitor and assess progress in various fields.

The second 3 year R & D programme ran from 1978/79 to 1980/81 and was prepared under the Centre party, although introduced by the minority Liberal Government. The Centre party had been reproached with being against all energy options and felt obliged to adopt a more positive style; it therefore became enthusiastic about R & D and this in large part explains the boost in the budget for the second triennium to SK 835 million.

The third programme to run from 1981 to 1982 was prepared after the nuclear referendum and therefore had to be of a nature and magnitude to match the circumstances; the objectives of the programme as clarified by the Energy R & D Commission were to achieve a rapid reduction in the use of oil, to ease the elimination of nuclear power and to promote the creation of an energy system dependent on renewable energy sources. The Commission's proposal, broadly adopted by the Government in its 1981 Energy Bill was for a budget of SK 1,440 million—the biggest R & D programme ever undertaken in Sweden. The sum is large, especially as it does not include any work on thermonuclear fission or nuclear safety. A novel feature of the finance is the intention to find the money not from the general state budget, but as a dedicated tax on oil products.

About 16 per cent of the budget is allocated to researching more efficient processes in industry, especially iron and steel and pulp and paper. Some 4 per cent is allocated to energy use in transport including the design of engines propelled by alcohols. Nearly 20 per cent is directed to continuing work on energy use in buildings including heat pumps, thermal storage and solar applications. But the largest part, over 50 per cent, is for new methods of energy supply aimed at providing the basis for using forest products, energy plantations and wind, for synthesizing methanol, and for cleaning coal of sulphur.

Reaction to the size and content of the programme varies. Among practical men, many of whom will be those who eventually have to make the investments, there is much scepticism. There are also those with lyric expectations. In between there is a margin of industrial interests which, without subscribing to the full range of renewable sources, is prepared to give some of the options a commercial chance.

Methanol has received considerable attention. For some years Volvo and others have been testing conventional cars on a fuel containing 15 per cent methanol with satisfactory results. Special legislation is not required to sell methanol as a transport fuel; the tax legislation exists and defines a level of taxation which makes the fuel a commercial proposition. There are therefore no outstanding negative legislative needs to remove obstacles. The legislative need is for positive measures to compel all cars to be capable of using methanol. This would affect foreign car manufactures. Development of the 15 per cent fuel has been impeded by a new process of thought which would go direct to 100 per cent methanol-fuelled vehicles in priority sectors, thereby achieving higher security.

Supplies of methanol are available from the Norskhydro plant in Norway utilizing methane as feedstock; preliminary purchasing agreements have been made. After demand for methanol has exceeded a threshold of about 500,000 tonnes/yr it becomes economic to make the product in Sweden. Initially feedstocks would be heavy residual fuel oil and coal. Nynäs petroleum which has a refinery designed to handle the heavy crudes appropriate to its asphalt and bitumen interests has designed a plant gasifying fuel oil/coal mixtures and producing methane, methanol and hot water that could be supplied to the Stockholm district heating system. The process is overall 75 per cent efficient and output of the products can be adjusted so as to supply a higher proportion of energy as methanol in the summer when demand for gasoline is high and a higher proportion as heat in the winter.

Several firms are experimenting with methods for producing peat and converting it to forms that can easily be handled (pellets in the first instance). Some peat has been sold on a more or less open market; the qualification arises because Government has subsidized the investments both in production and combustion. OK, for example, seeing its traditional markets threatened and shrinking, is seeking to diversify into sales of other forms of energy and aims eventually to be able to offer a range of peat, biomass, coal, oil, and coal combinations. It has its own peat deposits and preliminary agreements to purchase methanol from Holland.

Peat and methanol are almost conventional options; their use requires only modest extensions of existing technical and organiz-ational abilities. Other possibilities, especially wind and solar, make more novel demands and on the whole support for these appears to be slipping. Wood is intermediate in characteristics between these two groups; the fuel is expensive to harvest and transport; the handling is complicated; the combustion equipment is three or four times as expensive as oil-fired boilers; there is opposition from the pulp and paper industry.

Almost everyone agrees that the Energy R & D Commission exerts a principal influence on energy policy. In one sense there is an obvious explanation for this: policy is crucially constrained by virtually implacable opposition to hydro, nuclear and coal in its primitive applications. Information on alternatives is therefore of paramount importance. No doubt this is a valid explanation. But one should not overlook how revealing of Swedish policy-making is the manner in which the thing is done. In many countries it is usual to promote R & D within controlled state agencies and nationalized industries after a closed process of decision-making; the Swedish approach is to create an independent Commission to specify objectives and for the State to provide funds after which a wide range of institutions can participate. The State having provided the means by which information is generated, it is then available for another wide range of actors to adopt. Not only is this procedure well adapted to the style and nature of Swedish governmental institutions, but it is analogous to other policy areas and in particular to industrial policy in which Sweden has been rather successful. The common element is that the State has acted not by imposing particular choices but by creating an environment conducive to change, in the one case through welfare policy and in the other through R & D.

COAL

Unlike other countries in a similar predicament, Sweden has approached the idea of burning imported coal with great caution. It is planned that by the end of the 1980s about 4–6 million tonnes of coal should be used, mostly in district heating and a little in industry; this is about as much as was burnt in the 1950s. The apparent explanation of this caution is an intense concern with the purity of Swedish inland waters. Swedish lakes and rivers are poorly buffered; small amounts of sulphur oxides formed from the sulphurous impurities in fuel during combustion can have a large effect on the acidity of the waters with devastating consequences for their ecological balance. It is not difficult to demonstrate the recent degeneration of water quality, what is more difficult is unambiguously to explain its origins and confidently to take measures to prevent it. The best available figures suggest that about 50 per cent of the circulation of acidic sulphur compounds comes from precipitation, of which less than 10 per cent arises from emissions of sulphur to the atmosphere in Sweden. If all sulphur could be prevented from escaping the combustion process in Sweden then the influx of sulphur to the water systems would still be 90 per cent of its present extent; the effect on the acidity of the waters would be negligible and the cost could be counted in billions. Swedes well informed on the problem recognize this, but they argue that if they are to persuade the United Kingdom and West Germany, whom they believe responsible for the bulk of airborne sulphur, to take action, then they themselves must show their own commitment. The Swedes have already reduced sulphur emissions by half since 1968. There is a tendency to neglect the 50 per cent of contamination which does not arise from precipitation and which may be more amenable to treatment. One wonders also just how easy it will be to persuade the Government of the United Kingdom in particular to take effective action, given the abstruseness of the problem and the enormous potential for bogging down any debate in erudite cavilling.

In some ways even more remarkable is the absence of any opposition within Sweden to this costly form of environmental protection. There is of course no existing coal-mining or burning sector to lobby for lower standards. The municipal energy companies who will first burn coal have the option of passing costs on to captive customers; they also have access for the time being to government grants to experiment with various means of sulphur removal from coal before or during combustion. The final consumers have no idea as yet of the costs they will eventually incur; even within industry, there is a growing group which have committed resources to the commercialization of coal cleaning processes and to whom lower standards would now be a threat. Moreover – the final irony – much attention was drawn to the problems of using and burning coal during the debate preceding the referendum by those who wished to assert the relative cleanliness of nuclear power; the arguments may not have helped the nuclear cause but they clinched the case against coal. The upshot is that there is virtually no voice to oppose the stringent standards on sulphur emissions from coal burning. The standards for new coal plant are more stringent than for old oil plant. Far from seeking a compromise between environmental priorities and energy policy the Swedes are determined to have both.

The main consequence of these high standards in the medium term is to lessen the competitiveness of district heating; a coal-fired plant is two to three times the capital cost of an oil-fired plant and it is therefore more difficult to make new district heating capacity competitive with individual oil-fired boilers either in the house or in industry. New coal systems are probably cheaper overall than new oil-fired systems, but the status quo is cheaper still. Some large and/or favourably sited municipalities have switched to coal, Västerås is the main example. A slight and temporary restriction on emission standards for small plant is included in the present energy Bill but it is unlikely to change much behaviour and in any case is accompanied by the caveat that higher standards should be achieved in the 1990s. Stricter government intervention is mooted; a committee is working with a draft law to force larger users to switch from oil to solid fuels. More extensive intervention is sometimes seen as an inevitable corollary to any set of equitable and effective energy policies.

Because of these restrictions, coal importers have adopted a low profile. EFD oil, the state mining concern LKAB, the SSPB and Sydcraft have formed the Swedish Coal Consortium to ensure supplies to themselves. The Consortium is vigorously seeking to secure future coal supplies and is negotiating for equity interests with low-sulphur coal producers in Canada and Eastern USA. There are no plans for a large coal importing terminal; instead, the port facilities at Okelosund, Nynashamn and Landskröna will be expanded.

NATURAL GAS

There are substantial obstacles to the use of natural gas in Sweden. There are no indigenous deposits of consequence; there is no infrastructure and no recent experience; the price of imports of gas is now so near, and follows so closely, oil prices that the economic incentive of financial means to build a brand new infrastructure does not exist. Furthermore, the most accessible market is the domestic space heating market in which district heating has already been given a high priority.

It is no doubt to keep the long-term possibilities open that the Riksdag approved, in June 1980, an agreement between the Danish and Swedish Governments which envisaged the distribution of Danish natural gas in Western Skåne from 1985. When fully implemented the project will provide 440 M m^3 per annum. The gas will be imported by the state company Swedegas, a subsidiary of SP, and sold on to Sydgas, a regional utility owned by the municipalities, to distribute. Danish gas is relatively high cost and the Danes are having difficulties in devising a price structure which is attractive to municipalities but does not bankrupt the state purchasing agency. It was originally envisaged that Denmark would absorb all the available gas and the reservations of the municipalities are one reason why supplies are now available for Sweden. Transport of the gas to Skåne can only make it still more costly and it may well be that Swedegas will have to operate at a loss to offer the gas at acceptable prices to municipalities. Legislation permitting local heat planning will probably be needed to ensure the gas is absorbed sufficiently rapidly to make it pay.

The Danish contract opens the option of bringing gas to Sweden from the Norwegian North Sea, since the Danish offshore line is only about 30 km from the Statfjord/Ekofisk/Emden system and a link would be comparatively easy. There are active discussions with the Norwegians on this possibility.

It is also likely that Sweden may import gas from the Soviet Union, which offered to supply gas through Finland by a trans-Baltic pipeline to Gavle in Central Sweden. This line may be linked with the Sydgas system in the South and imports of 1–2 bn m^3 a year of Soviet gas towards the end of the decade are foreseen.

Swedegas and SSPB are engaged in a study of a gas pipeline, running from the North to the South of Sweden, in the hope of importing gas from Norway's recent Arctic offshore discoveries and transporting it to West-Central Europe. Statoil, the Norwegian State Oil Company, has given them details of finds made so far, although it turned down an invitation to participate in the study and Norway has made no commitment to sell gas to Sweden. The trunkline may carry up to 20 bn m^3 a year in the early 1990s.

HYDRO ELECTRICITY

It is said that there exists another 30 Twh of economic hydroelectric production from rivers as yet untouched in Northern Sweden. Opposition to development is strong; recently a small hydro project in the North managed to obtain all necessary legal consents but was still stopped by local opinion. The issue divided the coalition Government and was lost.

A legal framework has been prepared to provide a local tax income from hydro projects to compensate the locality, and proposals exist to extend the construction period so as to provide jobs for local labour over the long term. In time this might ease the problems of making new hydro development acceptable, but it should also be borne in mind that the opposition comes not only, or even mainly, from the thinly populated North but also from people in the South who like to holiday in the North. For the time being there is surplus electricity production; there is no pressing need for new sources and no live conflict.

GOVERNMENT POLICY

Much of the Government policy has been touched on in the preceeding sections; the intention here is to review briefly that material and summarize the content of the Government Bill on Energy Policy, passed in May, 1981. The first major Government statement of intent was presented by the Social Democrats in March 1975 following a lengthy public debate that had revealed reservations about nuclear power. The key aim of that policy was to limit energy growth to 2 per cent a year until 1985 and zero growth thereafter. It authorized thirteen nuclear reactors. The local authorities were made responsible for energy planning; the thermal performance of new buildings was subjected to new regulations essentially halving the energy use of houses compared to those built according to the old, already high, standards.

The three-party coalition in Autumn 1976 created an Energy Commission and assigned it the task of investigating energy policy up until 1990; the announcement was accompanied by a statement of policy by the Centre party Energy Minister on the new administration's 'basic ecological approach' to energy. The Commission reported in Autumn 1978 and presented a variety of options for 1990 including some from which nuclear power had been eliminated at the expense of a substantial dependence on oil. By coincidence, at that point, real politics took over; Falldin resigned, the accident at Three Mile Island happened, and policy was driven by events (mostly nuclear) rather than papers. Immediately after the referendum the Government presented a Bill setting out the fundamental features of its energy policy— these were developed in a lengthy Bill presented to the Riksdag in February 1981.

The energy policy has as its objectives:

1. To create the conditions necessary for economic and social development.
2. To phase out nuclear power in accordance with the decision of the Riksdag.
3. To shift development gradually towards an energy system based on durable, preferably renewable, and indigenous sources of energy with the least possible effect on the environment.

The energy balance envisaged in 1990 is shown in Table 3.2 together with the result for 1979 and the prognosis for 1985. What lies behind these figures will be clear it is hoped from the previous

TABLE 3.2

Total energy balances, Twh, *in* 1979, 1985 *and* 1990

	1979	1985		1990	
		Lower usage	Higher level	Lower usage	Higher level
Oil and oil products	295	229	256	160–140	191–171
Coal	3	12	12	31–45	31–45
Coal and coke for metallurgical uses	18	15	17	17	17
Natural gas	–	0	0	4–9	4–9
Motor alcohols	–	–	–	1–3	1–3
Bark and lyes	36	36	38	42	42
Forest energy, etc.[1]	7	17	17	25–30	25–30
Peat	0	1	1	6–11	6–11
Solar heat[2]	–	0–1	0–1	1–3	1–3
Waste heat[3]	2	3	3	3–4	3–4
Hydroelectric power	60[4]	63	63	65	65
Wind power	–	0	0	0–1	0–1
Nuclear power (electricity)[5]	22	48	48	56	56
Nuclear power (heating)[6]	–	–	–	9	9
Total supplies for energy purposes	443	424	455	428	459
Of which conversion and distribution losses of electricity and in district heating	27	24	25	28	29

TABLE 3.2 (*Contd.*)

Total energy balances, Twh, *in* 1979, 1985 *and* 1990

	1979	1985		1990	
Total final consumption	<u>416</u>	<u>400</u>	<u>430</u>	<u>400</u>	<u>430</u>
Of which bunkering for foreign shipping	10	10	11	11	11
Plus					
Oil and oil products for refinery fuel incl. asphalt, etc.	18	21	21	21	21
Gas and coke works	1	1	1	0	0
Oil for non-energy purposes	11	11	12	12	12
Total supplies	473	457	489	461	492

Notes:
1 Forest waste, wood, chips, energy forest, straw, etc.
2 Added to which heat pumps are used in combination with naturally stored solar energy
3 Incl. burning of refuse
4 61–62 TWh with normal precipitation
5 Incl. the stations' energy consumption (gross production)
6 If heat tap-off from the Forsmark 3 nuclear reactor is not adopted, the electricity production from nuclear power will increase by about 3 Twh. This electricity may possibly be used for operation of heat pumps in Stockholm. The district heating supplies for Greater Stockholm may also be based on coal. The quantity of coal in the figures for 1990 will then increase by about 11 TWh.

discussions. At this point we will consider only some institutional and legislative aspects not previously touched upon.

In the words of the Bill 'a vigorous energy policy aimed at reducing dependence on oil and ensuring the phasing out of nuclear power places strict requirements on an efficient organization'. From 1 July 1978, the appropriate responsibilities of the existing multiplicity of agencies have been brought together into a single energy agency, the National Energy Board. Another institution—the Oil Substitution Fund—is expected to have increasing influence; its task will be to assist with financed measures for oil substitution and energy conservation and the commercialization of technologies with those effects. A special agency for long-term energy research has also been created. For the first 3 year period the need for support is calculated at SK

1,700 million; the support scheme was instituted on 1 January 1981, and is paid for by a tax on oil products.

The State Power Board is assigned a new role in heat supplies; it is envisaged that the Board can assist weaker local authorities to introduce district heating whilst not infringing their responsibilities, for example by participating in joint companies. The intention to use the Board to promote innovation over a wide geographical area through participation is made evident. The Board is also instructed to investigate the conditions for construction of peat-fired plants in South and Central Sweden.

Parts of the costs of substitution will be met by consumers as a result of new legislation which stipulates that large new boilers must be designed so that they can cope with solid fuels and smaller boilers with solid indigenous fuels, without extensive modifications. This law entered into force on 1 January 1982. The cost of this is not given, but it will be great.

A considerable part of the Bill is given over to extraordinarily frank accounts of the possible difficulties with nuclear power and of what is being done to increase safety standards and provide emergency plans to cope with accidents at particular sites.

The State proposes to control and supervise handling and reprocessing of spent fuel and radioactive waste although the operations are to be carried out by a company owned by the power producers. The operations will be financed by a novel method; a levy on all nuclear electric output will be paid into a fund controlled by the supervising agency but from which the nuclear power companies can borrow; the intention is to make it clear that the costs of dealing with spent fuel are being provided for.

COMMENT ON ENERGY BALANCE FOR 1990

The energy balance in Table 3.2 is an official balance which is prepared, as is the Swedish way, in Twh and, more importantly, accounts for primary electricity as the thermal value of the electrical output. This is a common procedure in countries where hydroelectricity has traditionally made a large contribution to energy supply. In other countries, where thermally generated electricity has predominated, primary electricity is accounted for as the notional equivalent of oil that must be burnt to generate that

TABLE 3.3

Revised Energy Balance. Nuclear and Hydro evaluated at Fossil Fuel Input Equivalent. Entries in Twh

	1979	1990	
		Low	High
Fuels	361	298	329
Hydro	180	195	195
Nuclear	66	177	177
Total	607	670	701

amount of electricity. The Swedish balance expressed in this way is shown in Table 3.3.

Presented in this manner the appearance of the Swedish energy balance is significantly different. The low usage scenario for 1990 which in the first instance appeared to represent a 3 per cent drop in energy use compared to 1979, now shows a 10 per cent increase. In the high case, an increase of 3 per cent becomes an increase of 15 per cent. In 1990, nuclear power is seen to account for 25 per cent of primary energy supply. This is nearly as much as the 30 per cent forecast for France under Giscard d'Estaing, generally thought to be an especially dynamic nuclear programme. It is only fair to compare this Swedish energy policy with other European policies on this common basis. It then appears that the expectations of demand control are not quite as astonishing as at first appears, but are still higher than for other countries. The planned increases in primary energy consumption by 1990 in Denmark, France and Italy are 20, 31 and 42 per cent respectively. It is also evident, on this basis, that conventional options, especially nuclear, account for by far the largest part of the planned substitution for oil.

If instead of adjusting the Swedish figures one converts the French energy balance according to the Swedish rules then instead of showing a 26 per cent increase in energy use from 1979 to 1990, France would show only a 3 per cent increase and the nuclear programme, instead of being 30 per cent of the 1990 balance would be 13 per cent. It is poignant, but probably coincidental, that the Swedes choose to present their figures in a way which minimizes the nuclear contribution and the French in a way which maximizes it.

CONCLUSIONS

In the guise of conclusions we shall review the features of the formulation and implementation of Swedish energy policy which are immanent in Swedish institutions.

The Central–Local Dynamic

Inherent in the institutional structure is the separation of the functions of analysis, decision and implementation. Analysis is made by *ad hoc* Commissions and independent agencies, policy is formulated by Ministers and the Riksdag and implemented by agencies and municipalities. The objectives and interests of the participating institutions are not homogeneous. There are of course nuances to be applied to this description, but it is adequate to make the contrast with the closed systems found in other countries, which are built around Ministerial departments in intimate relationship with parastatal agencies.

The dispersion of initiatives and functions has strengths and weaknesses. Three main consequences are the limited means by which the State can operate its policies, the influence which local competence has on the definition of viable choices and the existence of a margin wherein responsibilities are nuclear, disputed, or contradictory.

Restrained as it is in the extent to which it can impose change directly, Government is obliged to influence events indirectly through price signals, taxation, subsidies, legislation and an extensive R & D programme over a broad field. It is impossible in these circumstances to assess the cost and the effectiveness of policies. The costs of inappropriate legislation, of wasted subsidies, distortions induced by taxes, unco-ordinated and even conflicting actions can be large and are intrinsically difficult to measure.

There are signs of irritation within central government at the restrictions on the possibilities of the State. Increasingly interventionist policies may be expected. There is an important distinction between the results of State intervention within an institutional structure like that of France and what might be expected in Sweden. In a closed decision-making system an extension of State powers is likely to lead to more effective and co-ordinated imposition of policies. Within an open system accessible to popular influence the acquisition of extra powers by the State risks leading to unco-ordinated intervention as a reaction of popular sentiment or to gain temporary political advantage.

The high level of competence within municipalities has several consequences. It begins to place responsibility for energy supply locally, thereby obliging communities to face up to the problem of balancing costs and benefits. It provides the opportunity to exploit particular local advantages and circumstances, e.g. peat deposits, access to forest products, urban refuse. It facilitates the provision of central heat supplies, the range of fuels that permits, e.g. solar, wood, refuse, peat, coal, coal-oil mixtures, and all the technical choices that then are possible e.g. cogeneration, incineration, heat pumps from waste water, thermal storage. It aids the implementation of conservation policies in that the local authority is well equipped to detect waste and recommend appropriate action. It facilitates the incorporation of energy into the planning of the built environment. Against these advantages, it must be acknowledged that some municipalities are completely passive and yet because of their important presence they are able to resist the changes instigated by national institutions.

Oil policy shows ambiguities. The creation and rapid expansion of SP is at the expense of other Swedish companies. The first victim has been Nynäs which has had to sell its distribution chain and back out of refining; OK has also been affected. Government intervention through price controls and through government to government deals with Norway appears to have been undertaken outside of any policy defining the function of existing Swedish and international interests. The Swedish oil sector is faced with the need to invest substantially in upgrading capacity in a shrinking market, an abominable task at the best of times but not helped by uncertainty about the role and intentions of the State.

Environmental Factors

There is a tendency outside Sweden to see the high priority given to the environment either as a fad brought on by more money than sense or as a mature reaction against the costs of growth and a guide to others coming behind. But, as in everything else, it is not a recent development but stands in continuity with centuries-old attitudes. The expectation of a right of access to nature and natural products is deeply held; it is to be found in the medieval *allemansrätten* (everyman's right) which gives to all the right to walk, swim, camp and pick berries, flowers, and mushrooms anywhere in Sweden, whoever the landowner may be. It is important to understand the profound origins of the modern concern for the environment in the ancient perception of nature as a common heritage, if one is to appreciate its strength and durability.

The Ambiguity of the Referendum

The ambiguities of the referendum might, with a little imagination, also be seen as a compromise consequential on the balance of power between the centre and the periphery. The referendum was essentially a makeshift reaction to cope with an acute political problem. It has created severe contradictions and uncertainties. Sweden is proceeding with one of the largest per capita nuclear programmes in the world while being publicly committed to scrapping it in due course. She claims a zero growth energy policy, which is ecologically irreproachable; but examination shows that this is the result of an increase in electricity use, based in turn on the massive recourse to nuclear. In human terms the referendum has created a division, all the more serious for being unspoken, between those who believe that nuclear power will eventually be phased out and those, many of whom in one way or another have the responsibility for implementing policy, who believe that the intention will never be put into practice.

This unspoken divide covers great uncertainties. For example: the present surplus of electricity could be sold economically for individual space heating; at present tariffs it would often be cheaper for the consumer than district heating. This policy, reasonable if the option exists of eventually increasing electricity production, is unreasonable if nuclear power is to be eliminated and electricity supplies become difficult and expensive. Another example: if the nuclear programme is to be phased out then electricity production must most probably be replaced by co-generation; the consequences in terms of equipment, the urgency of creating heat networks and eventual fuel supplies will be quite different from the consequences of continuing with the nuclear programme. A third example: the effort put into renewables will vary according to the expectation that they will one day become necessary. The SSPB and Sydkraft are each in charge of a prototype large wind generator which come on stream this year; technically they are the best qualified, but their enthusiasm is likely to be limited. The nature of these underlying uncertainties is best demonstrated by the opinion of a senior technocrat with pro-nuclear leanings, that it would have been better if Line 3 in the referendum had won so that at least the whole population knew where it was and could get on with a genuinely agreed policy.

New Directions of Conflict

The nuclear opposition has won the political battle of the 1970s which culminated in the referendum. It sees its present task as trying to 'win the peace', through a positive programme for a Solar Sweden. The energy supply industry is not convinced that Solar Sweden is necessary, desirable or feasible. The proponents of Solar Sweden are trying to prevent the resurgence of a nuclear option and actively to formulate and cause to be implemented their own alternatives. In both cases they have had some success. Marginal nuclear activities like uranium mining and heat-only reactors have been stopped. Local lobbying has helped with the implementation of government programmes to demonstrate novel technologies like peat and wood burning. What remains to be seen is whether individuals, local lobbies and institutions can win over the hesitant and ambivalent and can succeed in finding the effort and competence to design and sustain their initiatives in sufficient number to be effective, and over the long term.

4
ITALIAN ENERGY POLICY

INTRODUCTION

Italy, like France and Denmark, is vulnerable to interruptions in oil supply, but she enjoys a distinct institutional structure. Study of the Italian response to the oil crisis therefore offers the opportunity to confirm how the transition from oil is determined less by the common technical predicament than by the diversity of the institutional environments. The following sections treat briefly the gross evolution of energy supply to Italy since the War, then examine the separate energy sectors in more detail. The nature of political control through pricing, the co-ordination of activities by planning and by patronage is then discussed.

GROSS EVOLUTION OF ENERGY SUPPLIES

Energy supply in Italy since the War has evolved differently from other European countries; the statistics in Tables 4.1 and 4.2 make this clear. Table 4.1 shows how total energy use in Italy from 1955 to 1980 increased by 355 per cent compared to the increases of 85–155 per cent in West Germany and France, and 30 per cent in the UK. Even in 1955, coal made up only 25 per cent of primary energy use compared to more than 80 per cent in the UK and West

TABLE 4.1

Some comparisons of energy growth in European Countries 1955–1980

	1955			1980			
	(a) Total Energy mtoe	(b) % Coal	(c) % Oil & Nat. Gas	(d) Total Energy mtoe	(e) % Coal	(f) % Oil & Nat. Gas	(g) (d) as % of (a)
West Germany	128	88	9	234	30	64	185
UK	150	85	14	133	37	58	130
France	75	61	28	192	18	65	255
Italy	32	25	44	146	8	85	455

TABLE 4.2

Change in Italian energy supply 1955–1980 (mtoe)

	1955	1973	1976	1980
Source:				
Coal and Lignite	8	8	8	12
Natural Gas	2	14	22	23
Crude Oil	12	105	98	99
Hydro and Geothermal	10	10	9	11
Nuclear	—	1	1	1

Germany, and 60 per cent in France. From Table 4.2 it appears that incremental supplies to Italy since 1955 have been exclusively oil; between 1955 and 1973 hydroelectric, geothermal and coal remained roughly constant; nuclear power made negligible impact, and the use of crude oil grew by 800 per cent.

The reasons for the penetration of oil are straightforward. The supreme status of Italy in the times of Rome and the Renaissance was based on Mediterranean trade; the shift of focus from the Mediterranean, aided by the Anglo-Saxon access to cheap coal on which manufacturing industry depended, left Italy in a backwater. Poverty of energy helped keep Italy behind the levels of development pertaining in most of the rest of Europe. Northern Italy had access to relatively cheap hydroelectric power from the Alps, but it was difficult to transmit that or anything else far South. When oil became available from the Middle East, Italy was a principal beneficiary; the high educational and cultural tradition permitted rapid industrialization and the spread of new infrastructures based on oil. The Suez Canal for a time put Italy back onto a most important trade route for oil; the location of Italy between the Middle East resources and European markets and its suitable coastal sites made it a natural choice as a refining centre for Southern Europe and Germany. The availability within Italy of heavy fuel oil from refineries, (which could only be transported at a proportionally higher cost than light products) was a convenient basis for rapid expansion of electricity. Energy supply in Italy began to take on a structure with respect to oil somewhat similar to the coal-based structure experienced earlier in France and UK, i.e. a symbiotic relationship whereby a single fuel dominated primary supply and supplied the conversion industries. In these circumstances, competition between energy forms is reduced; oil cannot be sold twice and if oil products displace electricity then heavy fuel oil sales fall. The analogous cosy coexistence in coal-producing countries was shattered by the arrival of oil and competition, but it persisted in Italy at least until 1973.

Oil and Gas

At the beginning of the century the principal European nations tried, after their own fashion, to secure oil supplies through a parastatal agency. The British did it first, most discreetly and successfully through the Anglo-Persian Oil Company (eventually to be known as BP); the French set up the Compagnie française des pétroles after the First World War, endowing it with the concessions in Iraq taken from Germany. Italy, under the Fascist regime, tried to emulate the French, but having less influence received no territory. A state owned company AGIP (Azienda Generale Italiana Petroli) was formed in 1926 to engage in petroleum exploration at home and abroad; it had little success at finding oil but it did build up a distribution network for oil products; at the outbreak of war AGIP had a market share of about 25 per cent at which level it remained until the 1973 oil crisis when for one reason or another, more or less directly consequent on state intervention, the share rapidly increased. Even so, the reputation of the company before and after the War was not high; so great was its reputation for patronage as to earn it the nickname 'Azienda Generale Infortunati Politici' (General Enterprise for Politicians in Distress). It was tarred with the brush of Fascist autarky and nearly sold off after the Liberation.

The turning point in the fortunes of the company came in 1949 when large quantities of gas and a little oil were discovered at Cortemaggiore in the Po valley. Signor Enrico Mattei was at the time Northern Commissioner for AGIP and immediately responsible for the resource. In the absence of a government depletion policy, Mattei produced the gas rapidly and sold at prices aligned on thermal parity, thereby appropriating the rent exclusively for AGIP and providing the company with a useful cash flow at a critical stage. Part of the rent went into a rather splendid network of service stations which, along with a considerable exaggeration of the importance of the Cortemaggiore deposits, transformed the image of the company.

Mattei also campaigned for a rationalization of state interests in oil and petrochemicals and for the acquisition by the State of an exclusive right to explore in the Po valley, the most promising prospect in Italy. In 1953, the relevant companies were brought together into ENI (Ente Nazionale Idrocarburi); the company was given an exclusive right to prospect in the Po valley and Mattei was made president.

A principal weakness of ENI was its poor access to supplies of crude oil. Before the War, an independent European oil distributor could buy products freely from independent refineries in Rumania and the USA. After the War these supplies dried up and the national companies were obliged to buy from the internationals with whom they were in competition. AGIP's exclusive supplier was Anglo-Iranian which had surplus crude and a need for outlets and was prepared to offer advantageous prices to AGIP as a way of getting oil into the Italian market.

Under Mattei's leadership, ENI was highly innovative; the company implemented vigorously the idea, not novel in itself, that public enterprise had a function in competitive sectors and challenged the vested interests of private capital at home and abroad. Within Italy, ENI attacked the domination of private interests in chemical fertilizers, man-made fibres, petrochemicals, mechanical and nuclear engineering. Mattei established a new state owned industrial empire and competent technocracy, more aggressive than the elephantine, heavy industry-based IRI. ENI took the lead in progressive reductions of retail gasoline prices and in persuading the Government to lower the high excise taxes. Between 1959 and 1961 prices gross of tax fell by 25 per cent. Mattei supplemented his campaign with allegations of collusion on prices among the majors.

Abroad, ENI signed contracts with the USSR in 1959 and 1961, and with other new producers as they escaped the control of the internationals; it taught non-European oil consumers to seek oil refineries of their own, and it provided the means through specially created engineering subsidiaries; it implemented the idea of joint undertakings with producer governments in which ENI bore the costs of exploration but the host government kept an option to become an equal partner in production if oil were found.

Within Europe, Mattei launched an attack on the retail oligopoly of the oil majors. His intention was to lay pipelines across the Alps to refineries in Bavaria and Switzerland. This threat was too great for the companies to ignore; they countered by bringing forward their own similar projects by several years and undercut Mattei by cross subsidization within their international operations.

ENI was only a catalyst in the inevitable erosion of oil company margins through higher revenues to producers and lower prices to consumers, but that should not detract from the innovative character of the company. Unfortunately, little of this activity made money for ENI; exploration at home and abroad was unsatisfactory; the rent from the Po became proportionally less important; the Alpine pipeline proved inflexible and costly; the ENI group as a whole was bled by the petrochemical war.

After Mattei's death in 1962, ENI became much less aggressive; in particular the policy of cheap gasoline was reversed. At the same time the oil companies became important, secret, contributors to political parties and politicians. Some of the money apparently even went in unauthorized payments to ENI via its gas subsidiary SNAM. In exchange, the oil companies received certain advantages. Amongst these was the 'Suez subsidy' adopted by the Italian Parliament in 1967 to offset added transportation costs arising from the closing of the Suez Canal. In 1971, the manufacturing tax on petroleum products was reduced. Perhaps more significantly than any specific measure, the financial dependence of the parties made it unlikely that agitation against the companies *à la* Mattei would continue. The pressing need for fresh funding for the political parties arose from the nationalization of the electricity suppliers, previously reliable contributors; the parties notified the companies 'as to the level of support they deemed appropriate from the petroleum industry' and the Trade Association (Unione petrolifera) calculated individual assessments based on the amount of oil sold to Ente Nazionale per l'Energia Elettrica (ENEL).

During the late 1960s and early 1970s the relaxation of the downward pressure on prices from ENI's policies was gradually compensated by restrictive price controls.

In 1973 BP and Shell left the country because price control aggravated the technical disadvantage of their poorly structured Italian operations; under political pressure, ENI expanded its activities to compensate. Since then ENI has increasingly been obliged to absorb the effects of the crisis; firstly, by procuring and delivering oil to the Italian market in circumstances where the internationals would not, and secondly by taking over the activities of the heavily indebted private oil company Mach. The attempt to accommodate change almost exclusively by adjustments within ENI was not entirely successful; ENI simply could not find enough oil after the Iranian revolution and after the loss of an important supply contract with Saudi Arabia, through a political scandal. Price control had to be eased to make the Italian market less unattractive to the internationals but the relief was only temporary and the trend was later reversed.

A considerable technical success of ENI is the 2,500 km pipeline built to bring natural gas from the Algerian desert through Tunisia and across the Mediterranean to Sicily and the Italian mainland as far north as Bologna. The technical difficulties of laying pipe in deep water across the Straits of Sicily have been overcome and the project is now complete as far as the Naples area. Gas was scheduled to flow in 1981, building up to 12bn m^3/yr by 1985. However, the opening celebrations planned for November 1981 were postponed, because Italy and Algeria were not able to agree on a price for the gas. Algeria disowned a 1977 agreement, under which the price was to be linked to a basket of competing fuels, and sought parity with the price of a basket of crude oils. Instead of a price of $3.25 per million BTU at the Algerian border, Algeria asked initially for $6.11, and in 1983 was said to be asking for $5.12. SNAM's top offer stood at $3.81 in 1983, and it argued that if pipe-financing charges and royalties to Tunisia were added to the price sought by Algeria, then the gas became uneconomic to use in Italy. Its negotiating position was weakened when France agreed to pay a fob price of $5.12 per million BTU for LNG and accepted parity with a basket of crude oils, although 13.5 per cent of it would be paid directly by the French Government rather than by Gaz de France, because the deal included the award of FFr. 12.5 billion worth of Algerian contracts to French firms. SNAM in turn argued that LNG required far greater investment in Algeria than piped gas. Both Governments became involved in the negotiations and the possibility of the Italian State topping up the Algerian revenue with trade credits and technical co-operation deals was also dicussed.

The strategic consequences aside, the social opportunities

offered by this injection of energy into Southern Italy are great.[1] Whether the opportunities that will arise to help the poorly developed South will be taken is conjectural. In the Italian distribution system, there are two distinct markets. Large industries are supplied directly by the ENI operating company SNAM; domestic users, small industries and workshops are supplied by local networks which buy from SNAM. Industries in the South of adequate size to buy directly from SNAM should have no difficulty in obtaining supplies; there is some doubt whether the smaller consumers will benefit. Because of the short heating season the profitability of small networks in the South is low and the general lack of local expertise is inhibiting. Considerable state support, financially and technically, is needed. In 1981 the Government launched a L1,000 billion scheme to double gas consumption in the Mezzogiorno to 10bn m^3/yr by 1985 and to connect 11 million users in the region, compared to 5 million at present. The European Regional Development Fund is participating in the financing of the scheme.

Before and immediately after the War, electricity supply depended almost exclusively on hydropower and was naturally far more widely available in the North than in the South. For the reasons described earlier, large quantities of heavy fuel oil became available in the 1950s which the oil companies could most conveniently dispose of to the utilities as a fuel for power generation; oil and electricity sales grew together.

At the end of the War, the Italian utilities were mostly owned by private capital, although some had fallen into the IRI conglomerate and constituted an IRI subsidiary—Finelettrica. Most power generation was nationalized over a period from 1963 and responsibility for the electricity supply industry was attributed to the state agency ENEL. The principal motive for this change was political; the Socialists made it a condition of their support for the centre-left coalition; their intention was to destroy the great political power exerted by the private utilities through corruption and through the large financial contributions to the funds of the Liberal and Christian Democrat parties. Edison and the other large utilities were technically efficient and, although there were many small and ineffective companies, the rationalization of the sector could have been achieved in other ways than by nationalization.

A widespread reaction of Italian capital to the creation of ENEL was 'not another ENI'. In the event, ENEL turned out to be rather a weak institution (except with respect to its equipment supplies), mostly because politicians have always been prepared to sacrifice the financial well-being of the enterprise to restrictive but popular price control and an efficient management structure to the requirements of patronage.

Nuclear

After the War, the Italian Government created a public agency with the title Comitato Nazionale per l'Energia Nucleare (CNEN) and gave it the responsibility for promoting applied research on the peaceful applications of nuclear energy. Because of its lack of a solid political power base in military circles, the CNEN has never exerted a comparable influence in Italy to that of the CEA and the UKAEA in France and the UK. When commercial interest was low, CNEN kept things ticking over, but at each commercial revival, the state agency has been easily bypassed. The three essential conflicts which have governed the evolution of the nuclear sector in Italy have been firstly between private and public capital for the control of manufacturing, secondly between ENI and IRI within the public sector, and thirdly between ENEL and the constructors for the architect-engineering functions.

In 1956 Edison, the most powerful of contemporary Italian utilities, made an agreement with Fiat for the construction of a nuclear power station at Trino and in 1957 Fiat signed with Westinghouse a technical co-operation and licence agreement for the PWR. Fiat believed that the nuclear power industry might be nationalized and it built Trino to get a foot in; it should be remembered that there was great enthusiasm for nuclear power at that time. Edison and Westinghouse were both strong in the matter and dominated the design, Fiat did very little. Breda Termomeccanica, a heavy mechanical engineering firm in Milan, owned by another state financial company EFIM, also acquired the PWR licence in 1962 and shortly afterwards came to an agreement with Fiat to manage it together through a complex company structure; a joint company SIGEN (50 per cent each partner) was formed as architect-engineer and general contractor and a second company SOPREN (owned by SIGEN and Westinghouse) was formed for the design in Italy of PWRs.

At much the same time, Italy was chosen by the World Bank (after a run-off against Japan) as a case study of the introduction of nuclear power into an industrialized country lacking indigenous energy resources. Tenders were received from General Electric, Westinghouse, the UK and France in 1958 for a station to be built at Garigliano, to be financed by the World Bank and to be owned by the IRI utility, Finelettrica. GE won the tender with a BWR design. As a consequence of the genesis of this plant, the appropriate IRI plant engineering contractor automatically became a partner of GE and a licensee. This company was AMN, a Genoese power plant designer and constructor with a long tradition in geothermal and fossil fuel systems; the IRI manufacturing subsidiary Ansaldo supplied the turbine and turbogenerator.

ENI, at the instigation of Mattei, succeeded in obtaining the necessary amendment to its statutes, to permit it to enter the field; the company made an agreement with the UK Nuclear Power Group to build a Magnox station at Latina; Mattei's instrument for his intervention was the company Nuovo Pignone, a Florentine foundry and mechanical engineering concern, acquired by ENI in 1954.

After 1958, CNEN contributed to the diversity of effort by its CIRENE project to develop a design for a heavy water reactor.

During the 1960s commercial enthusiasm was muted by widely available heavy fuel oil which was a cheaper source of electricity than was nuclear fuel. Without a military programme, enthusiasm subsided more in Italy than in France or the UK. ENEL, the sole customer for nuclear plant, had enough non-profit-making ventures in its obligations to electrify the South of Italy and rural areas. CNEN kept a low level of industrial activity by financing research projects of various sorts, but the transfer of knowledge to industry as a result was limited because CNEN monopolized the design function, leaving industry simply to manufacture specified components.

The diversity of positions and absence of properly defined responsibilities in the nuclear manufacturing industry persisted throughout the 1960s: in the absence of commercial orders there was no incentive to promote industrial alliances or test capabilities. Within the exclusively state sector, some progress was made: repeated deliberations by the Interministerial Committee for Economic Planning (CIPE) in 1966, 1968 and 1971[2] attributed to

IRI and in particular to Finmeccanica, the holding company within IRI responsible for the co-ordination and control of the activities of the state-owned mechanical engineering enterprises, the duty of developing a design and manufacturing capacity in the field of proven reactors. To ENI was allocated the responsibility for the procurement and processing of nuclear fuels—the operating company AGIP Nucleare was formed at the end of 1968.

On the basis of CNEN's decisions, Finmeccanica began to reorganize its involvement in nuclear and classical thermo-electric engineering. It concentrated its turbine, alternator and transformer manufacturing capability, and eventually acquired Breda from EFIM through the swap of an armaments firm. This was a vital acquisition; not only had Breda a high reputation for the manufacture of pressure vessels for export to the US and West Germany and a manufacturing capability of six vessels a year, but it also had 50 per cent of the PWR licence through its holdings in SIGEN and SOPREN.

In the meantime, ENEL opened tenders for an 850 MW(e) plant at Caorso. This provoked a serious conflict over the responsibility for the architect-engineering. The construction industry argued that it needed to acquire the overall experience essential to make a realistic attempt at exports; opinion in ENEL was seriously divided, but a strong faction maintained that the utility must preserve its traditional right to specify in detail the design of plant for its system. At Caorso the industry won and the invitation to tender was for turnkey plant. There were several tenders: from the Westinghouse-Fiat-Breda consortium for PWR; from Finmeccanica for BWR; from ENI, in association with private capital, for a gas reactor and a heavy water design. The order was apparently given to Finmeccanica (AMN and Ansaldo) on commercial grounds, but it reinforced Finmeccanica's efforts at straightening out its design and manufacturing capabilities and consolidated the state companies' pre-eminence in the field. Construction and commissioning of the plant were plagued with problems for a long period, but the station has recently been performing well.

In 1973 ENEL invited bids for another turnkey station and an option. To be able to tender on a turnkey basis, the Fiat-Breda joint company SIGEN founded the consortium Elettro-nucleare Italiana (EI) in conjunction with the private Milanese firms Franco

Tosi (turbines) and Ercole Marelli (generators). EI won the tender, but ENEL was persuaded by political pressure to share the contracts and so in 1974 made the option a firm order. The political imperative arose from the transfer of the naval shipyards from Genoa to Trieste; Genoa had been promised compensating work in nuclear manufacture at Ansaldo. In 1977 Finmeccanica obtained a site at Montalto di Castro and began civil works; EI was less fortunate and was alloted a site at Molise where public opposition was sufficiently strong to prevent development. These really rather accidental factors conspired to confirm Finmeccanica's position as the only organization with real experience in the nuclear sector. EI's unfortunate loss at Molise coincided with a hardening of opinion, especially within CNEN for reasons of safety, that Italy could only afford a single design of reactor. The PWR was preferred. At that stage, Finmeccanica had 100 per cent of the BWR licence, 60 per cent of the CANDU licence and 50 per cent of the PWR licence; it wanted a controlling share in PWR construction. Fiat, the leading private partner in EI, was in any case reluctant to expose itself to the commercial risks of full responsibility and preferred in many ways to be able to manufacture components under risk-free conditions, thereby making money whilst maintaining prestige. In early 1980, after months of negotiations Fiat relinquished to Finmeccanica a controlling share of SOPREN and SIGEN. In return Fiat obtained a favourable agreement in the aviation manufacturing sector. The conflict between private and public capital appears to have passed a critical threshhold. In principle, Tosi and Marelli, the other private partners in EI, will get orders for the balance of plant, and indeed ENEL has traditionally distributed orders among its suppliers in order to maintain competition; Ansaldo is capable of 3GW/yr of turbo-alternators, Tosi and Marelli together about the same. In practice, the next likely move from Finmeccanica will be to try to concentrate manufacture of the balance of plant at Ansaldo; this is especially probable if orders are short. Finally, in late 1980, Nuovo Pignone of the ENI group and Fiat agreed to rationalize design and manufacture of a range of components used in the nuclear fuel cycle, and in 1981 CNEN and AGIP Nucleare set up a joint company to deal with nuclear waste management, decontamination, and decommissioning. These steps completed the nuclear industry rationalization programme.

The story is instructive; it reveals how the dominating feature in the evolution of the nuclear structure has been the need for the State to absorb the commercial risk and the way in which it has done so. In the Italian case, it has been through Finmeccanica's relative immunity from the restrictive financial disciplines of the private sector; as a consequence, nuclear construction has finished up in the state sector. This is in contrast to France, where the State has borne the risk by guaranteed contracts to a privately owned concern.

The conflict between ENEL and the constructors also appears to be potentially resolvable. ENEL has invited bids for four new nuclear steam supply systems and some other parts of the nuclear islands; this departure from the turnkey concept is a compromise between the needs of ENEL and industry; it allows industry to acquire experience in the overall design of the nuclear island which is the essential requirement to sustain pretensions to export, whilst allowing ENEL room to design power plant adapted to its precise requirements.

In short, there is reason to believe that Italian industry has the design and manufacturing capability to make a significant effort in nuclear energy. Bedevilled by conflicts during the 1960s and 1970s, the organization of activity was poor. Slowly, Finmeccanica has succeeded in establishing its control over manufacture; other limits of responsibility have been defined.

Nuclear Siting

Nuclear siting is governed in principle by a specific law. Basically, ENEL selects a site; if the region in which the site is located disagrees, then it must propose two others; if neither is acceptable to ENEL then Parliament decides. The law unambiguously attributes to the State the power to impose sites; in practice, Parliament has never been asked to decide because the parties have considered the local political damage unacceptable. It very nearly came to the test over the site at Molise, but the Minister backed down at the last moment.

There seems to be some attempt developing to use the regional Councils as a means of mediating between national interests expressed by the State or state enterprises and local concerns expressed through the municipalities. Puglia is an interesting case. In early 1980 the regional government agreed in principle to host nuclear stations in the region and a year later signed an agreement for the siting of a 2 GW nuclear station and initiated a site selection process. Local unions protested against the nature of the selection process itself, while continuing to favour the siting of a nuclear station in Puglia. In late 1981 the regional government reduced to two a list of three potential sites, but early in 1982, 10,000 people demonstrated against siting a nuclear station in Avetrana, which is the most likely of the sites selected. Because of a local political crisis, Puglia has not met a government-imposed deadline on three regions for designating sites for 2 GW nuclear power stations on their territory by June 1982. The other two regions, Lombardy and Piedmont, have chosen sites long favoured by planners in ENEL and CNEN. The consent of the municipality or commune which covers the sites has still to be obtained.

In general, opposition to nuclear power in Italy is becoming less intense. Prolonged electricity blackouts during the 1980-81 winter have influenced the major political parties, especially the Socialists, to have a more favourable position on the nuclear issue. At the local level, people are prepared to accept nuclear power, partly to assist regional economic development and partly to obtain other concessions from the central government in return for meeting a national need. Opposition tends to concentrate on the level of compensation and other special arrangements rather than on nuclear power as an issue. This factor was exemplified in October 1981 when the head of the regional government in Puglia declared that the region did not want a nuclear station any more, after a row with the Minister for State Holdings over the future of a fibre plant in the region. The Government is preparing a Bill which will give communes near a nuclear station about 1.5 per cent of the building cost and about 1 per cent of the income from the electricity generated.

Coal

Traditionally, coal has not been an important source of energy in Italy; indigenous supplies have been lacking; no widespread distribution of imports has even been attempted, although coking coal has been imported for the steel industry. What organization did exist was very quickly displaced by the oil companies. Only after 1973 was reluctant consideration given to importing coal as an energy source. There are several difficulties.

Italian law requires that all power stations should be constructed to burn two fuels; convenience has ensured that this law has been universally met by designs to burn oil and gas. Conversion to coal burning, according to ENEL, is expensive and suitable only for coastal plant. The costs of providing and operating transport to inland sites are excessive. Consistent with its opinion, ENEL has done little to convert plant. This lethargy contrasts remarkably with the rapid substitution of coal for oil by the privately owned Danish utilities, initially in a similar predicament.

In November 1979, the Minister for State Holdings created a Commission for Coal which included the presidents of ENI, ENEL and Finsider (the state steel company). The aim was to agree coal use targets up to 1990 and to delegate responsibilities between the interested bodies. There was little problem in agreeing quantitative objectives. Finsider expected to maintain its 9-10 Mt/yr consumption in the future. ENEL proposed to increase its coal burn rapidly from 2 Mt in 1978 and 3.7 Mt in 1979 to 25 Mt in 1990. The intention was to burn this in converted oil plant and three planned new coal-fired stations, which still lacked sites. With 4-5 Mt going to other industry, the agreed estimate for 1990 was 40 Mt.

Negotiations on the division of responsibilities were protracted because ENI and ENEL would not compromise. Initially ENEL, ENI, the private oil companies, and IRI, had all made plans to establish a presence in coal importing. IRI had proposed the construction of a coal slurry line from Poland to Trieste which was regarded with justified scepticism by the other actors. The major international oil companies were counting on their experience and massive investments in coal, at a time when ENI had no contracts, no ports and no transport. ENI, having been clearly allocated, by CIPE, the role of state energy company, believes it should be the sole state importer of coal. ENEL does not wish to be tied to a single supplier and wishes to procure its own supplies. In an attempt at reconciliation, the 1981 Energy Plan proposed that ENEL was to make its own long-term contracts with producers, while ENI was to explore abroad and buy resources and production capacity as a basis for a secure national supply and should provide a growing proportion of ENEL's needs at world market prices.

ENI has increased its coal activities considerably in the past few years. In 1981, AGIP Carbone was formed, owned 55 per cent by ENI and 22.5 per cent each by ENI's subsidiaries AGIP and SNAM, to co-ordinate all the coal activities of the ENI group, including exploration, development of new production, and coal-handling infrastructure both in Italy and abroad, and coal gasification and liquefaction. ENI has interests in mining ventures in British Columbia in Canada, the United States, South Africa, and Australia, and in 1981 signed an agreement worth $1.1 billion with Occidental Petroleum to form a new company, Enoxy, which will link chemical operations of ENI in Italy with coal-mining operations of Occidental in the US. ENI is also going ahead with plans to build a 15 Mt/yr coal terminal in Trieste, capable of taking 150,000 dwt vessels. A new company, Terminal Trieste, has been formed by AGIP Carbone, Finport (the port's financing company), and a group of regional industrial concerns, to develop and run the terminal, and the project has been approved by the Trieste Port Authority. Some of the coal handled will be delivered to Austria and West Germany. The energy plan envisages two more large terminals at Vado Ligure near Genoa and at Gioia Tauro in Calabria.

Conservation

Policy for the efficient use of energy in Italy is almost nil. There have been several attempts of which the most celebrated was the Niccolazi plan named after the ephemeral Minister for industry who introduced it. The plan was designed to achieve the 5 per cent saving in oil consumption agreed by Italy as an obligation within the IEA: it was based on papers from ENI and ENEL, although formally it originated from the Ministry. It relied heavily on reductions in oil consumption through substitution of coal in electricity supply; those aspects which aimed at saving energy concentrated on behavioural objectives of low cost and lower credibility, e.g. restrictions on the temperature and timing of space heating, suspension of road traffic on certain days, control of office hours and illuminated advertising, etc. No political consensus could be found to support the plan, no politician would accept being compromised by so many irksome and implausible constraints.

An interesting example of the difficulties and the ingenuity of Italian politicians is a series of attempts to legislate on conservation in the winter of 1979/80. The Government introduced three successive decree laws providing limitations on the use of central heating; these were thrown out by Parliament one after the other, but since a decree law is in force for the first 60 days from its promulgation, at the end of which period it should be confirmed by the Assembly, the effect was to maintain the legislation in existence. The following winter the Government introduced restrictions on space heating. The country was divided into six zones where space heating during the winter was allowed for only 6-14 hours a day, depending on the latitude. The practical effects of the legislation have been small.

Generally, one would not expect conservation by legislation to have much future in Italy. A principal aspect of Italian political life is the alienation of the individual and the central government; created over many years of unrepresentative rule and exacerbated in the twentieth century by the abuse of Parliament; the lack of legitimacy in the State finds expression in a range of activities from terrorism to tax evasion. It is difficult to imagine that legislation to influence behavioural aspects of energy use would be respected.

Although the energy plans call for incentives to energy conservation, substantial state involvement is ruled out by the reluctance to place any greater load on public expenditure already overwhelmed by a costly and ineffective bureaucracy and the debts of state industries originating from price control and inefficiency. The form of public expenditure preferred by politicians is that which by its creation of jobs or benefits to a specific community can be adapted to the service of patronage. Subsidies to energy conservation are too unselective to lend themselves to this purpose and therefore lack political support.

Cogeneration

Municipal electric utilities, especially in Northern Italy, have embarked on major combined heat and power programmes. The first scheme was developed by the local authority in Brescia, after the initial opposition of ENEL to cogeneration. Two units have been completed and the final one will come on stream in 1984, when the scheme will serve 100,000 people. The most ambitious project has been initiated in Milan. This is the world's biggest district heating scheme and will serve 3.5 million people when completed in 1992. It is designed to use waste heat from power stations and industry in the Lombardy region. The project will cost L2,300 billion and save 800,000 toe a year. Other towns that have schemes planned or under construction are Reggio, Verona, and the Torrino Sud district of Rome. ENI has signed an agreement with the regional government of Piedmont to assist in drawing up an energy plan for the region, including identification of the most suitable cogeneration projects and urban areas for district heating projects.

An important mechanism by which Government influences real events and which may or may not be operated in a fashion consistent with stated policy is price control. It is an especially important phenomenon in Italy and has greatly influenced the structure of the Italian energy industries.

Oil Product Prices

Up until 1977 Italy operated a controlled system for the prices of all oil products. The general idea was to set prices at a level which covered costs; the principal complaint of the companies was the delay between changed circumstances and the appearance of decrees updating prices. Price control was a contributory factor to the departure of BP and Shell in 1973, but in those cases it was superimposed on unsatisfactorily structured presences.

In November 1977 the Interministerial Committee for Prices (CIP) devised a new system within which some prices are set by the administration and others are set by industry and notified to the administration (supervised prices).[3] Initially, supervised prices applied to naptha, jet fuel and other minor products. Shortly afterwards heavy fuel oil was included.

Administered prices were essentially set to cover overall costs by the following procedure. The secretariat to CIP calculated the total costs of the industry according to a specified formula; industry notified the CIP of its prices for supervised products. CIP on this basis calculated the revenue from administered and supervised products; if revenue fell below costs, then prices of administered products were adjusted. The necessary adjustment had to be allocated among products; the law proposed that this be done in such a way as to maintain Italian prices close to relative world prices.[4] However, the law also contains a note to the effect that CIP can do what it likes in this respect if it thinks it necessary and in practice CIP inevitably allocated the increases according to a balance of reasons made up of domestic politics (how much will the car owner stand) and supply considerations (a chronic shortage of gas oil). At the beginning of the system there were six or seven increases for gas oil, but none for gasoline.

The costs of the industry are calculated from an average crude cost plus transport, refining and distribution costs assessed as specified in the law. Refining costs are calculated with respect to a notional refining campaign proposed by CIP including amortization of capital and operating costs.

The system incorporates two principal distortions:

1.   There is no way of apportioning costs among products in such a way as to ensure that prices reflect the economic reality of the Italian petroleum refining industry in the context of the international capital structure and world markets;

2.   It shelters companies with access to low cost crude. e.g. from Saudi Arabia, but it gives no incentive to companies with high cost crude, including, as it happens, ENI. Prices are based on average crude costs and there is no reason for a supplier to put high marginal cost crude onto the Italian market.

The new system reduced the delays in passing on costs; adjustment was made annually for the amortization of capital and refinery operation, monthly for crude oil and transport, weekly for exchange rates. Prices were adjusted if the change exceeded 2 per cent.

Before long the system came under strain; from October 1977 to July 1979 there were seven decrees for the revision of prices downwards. Gas oil became short despite concentration of price increases on that product; the reason was that demand in Italy could not be matched with refinery output and prices were not high enough to justify imports. The Government tried to persuade companies to produce 'heavy gas oil' by widening the technical limits of the gas oil stream from the refinery. The companies would not do so because that would have reduced the heavy fuel oil output, which was a supervised product on which they made a good profit.

An additional consequence of CIP pricing policy was to cut the margins of the independent refiners and distributors who had relied on the spot market for supplies. This happened because the cost of crude used in the calculation was averaged over all companies and was well below spot market prices.

The system collapsed when the whole of Italy's crude oil supply was jeopardized by ENI's loss of a contract with Saudi Arabia; the prospect of shortages in 1980 required that the Italian market be made acceptable to the international companies; prices were accordingly raised above the cost plus formula. The situation was formalized at the beginning of 1980 when CIP presented a new method which compared the ex refinery revenue, calculated much as before, with ex refinery revenue in other European countries. Comparison is made every 6 months and discrepancies accommodated in the administered prices according to the discretion of CIP.

The Government, however, has not promptly applied the agreed formula. Product price rises were consistently delayed throughout 1981, and it did not allow adequate increases to cover the effect of the rise of the dollar against the lira on the cost of imported oil. The Government was prepared to resist protests from the oil companies for as long as possible, in order to reduce inflationary pressures and limit increases in wages, which are inflation-linked. The losses of the oil companies in 1981 exceeded L2,000 billion and Amoco Italy announced that it was seeking a buyer for its operations in Italy after heavy losses. ENI was forced to increase its market share to over 50 per cent, after the private oil companies started cutting unprofitable operations, and thereby increased its share of the loss. The Government finally gave into pressures from the oil companies and raised the price of the oil products in 1982 to over L1,000 a litre. Most importantly, from August the price of gas oil was transferred to the category of supervised prices. The oil companies believed that this measure would reduce the problems caused by delays in applying the price formula.

The Italian system of price control has been described in detail because it demonstrates the difficulties inherent in the endeavour and the often unexpected effects that can follow. The value of the process should be assessed against the objectives of the decree establishing the regime.[5]

1. To protect consumers and prevent speculation.
2. To assure adequate supplies in the short and long term by ensuring adequate returns to the companies.

    3. To maintain an adequate number of operators.
    4. To rationalize the refining and distribution system so as
       best to meet the needs of the country and improve
       economic efficiency.

The system up to 1979 apparently provided Italy with on
average the lowest net of tax oil prices in Europe. Part of objective 1
may be said to have been achieved. Speculation has certainly not
been avoided; hoarding of products (especially gas oil) before
expected price increases has been a frequent source of scandal.

One might argue that low prices are not proper signals of
long-term scarcity, but there is in fact no contradiction. It is prices
gross of tax which signal the viability of conservation and
substitutes; there is no reason not to have high taxes and price
control.

The difficulty of providing secure supplies (objective 2) at low
cost has been visible in the chronic near-shortages which beset
Italy and which were an essential part of the brinkmanship politics
between CIP and the oil companies. When security became the
priority then the whole methodology had to be revised. In one
sense this demonstrates the inadequacy of an instrument that has
to be completely revised to reflect a shift of emphasis among
priorities, but in another it reveals considerable flexibility and
adaptability within the bureaucracy. CIP is one of the few islands
of competence in the generally weak Italian administration.

Diversity of operators (objective 3) is also in conflict with low
cost; since 1973, ENI has steadily increased its market share at the
expense of the internationals. At the margin this has been done at
a loss. Whether this is a conscious policy decision or excessive
adherence to a policy of low net of tax prices is not clear.

There is no evidence of any thought being given to the objective
to rationalize the physical structure of the industry. Indeed price
control has created an artificial set of signals. Allowing relative
freedom to heavy fuel oil prices while restricting light products has
caused the costs of changes in crude oil prices to be passed on
disproportionately to heavy fuel oil users, mainly ENEL and
industry. The distortion may also impede investment in upgrading
capacity and other structural alterations.

On the whole the policy does seem to provide low prices at some
expense. While the bureaucracy remains flexible enough to adapt

to changing circumstances, the policy can be considered one of the more successful aspects of Italian energy policy.

Electricity

Electricity prices contain two elements. There is a tariff aimed at recovering costs excluding increases in fuel oil prices that have occurred since 1973; the revenue from this goes to ENEL. Fuel price increases from 1973 are expressed as a thermal surcharge; the revenues from this go into a fund from which they are distributed to all producers, in proportion to their thermal production. On top of this are discounts to various classes of consumers; the most important is the discount to domestic consumption. This was originally intended to protect the poor, but it now applies to 95 per cent of customers and 65 per cent of domestic sales. The loss of revenue to ENEL because of the discounts was about equal to its total loss in 1981, and discounts to domestic users accounted for over 50 per cent of the total.

The consequences of this for energy policy are diastrous. The tariff reflects historic costs, even before discounts, and does not therefore signal replacement costs, nor does it permit the finance of expansion. This deficiency is exacerbated by the domestic tariff and ENEL's extensive obligations to undertake uprofitable expansion in rural areas and the South. ENEL has as a result a most unsound financial structure; balance has only been achieved by a continuous resort to bond issues and consequently an accumulating obligation to repay interest. Because of the delays in approving basic tariff and fuel premium increases and in paying a capital injection by the Government, ENEL lost over L2,000 billion in 1981 and was heading for a similar loss in 1982. At one time it had stopped paying its suppliers and contractors on construction sites and Esso had stopped fuel deliveries as a result, although the delay in its payments to suppliers then dropped from 6 to 3–4 months.

The political opposition to a change in electricity pricing policy is considerable; the highest electricity consumption per capita is in the South; trade unions argue that the domestic tariff is a necessary, if partial, compensation to the poor for tax evasion by the rich.

It is interesting to compare the consequences of electricity and oil pricing policy. ENEL has suffered greatly because there has been almost no limit to the extent to which politicians have been able to preserve low prices at the expense of the state agency and in the long run of its creditors. The drain on ENEL is almost certainly a cause of its rather low innovative capacity.

ENI has not been a victim of this particular political syndrome because there is a limit to the rigour of price control beyond which the international companies would leave. It is true that ENI is given political missions; if Esso does not want to sell in a certain place then ENI must, but there are compensations. ENI has a disproportionate share of the licences for the profitable motorway outlets and the lucrative contracts for other state agencies, such as Alitalia. On balance, ENI has, in this respect, been protected from the cupidity of its political masters and permitted to preserve a relatively sound financial structure.

Planning

Economic planning in Italy was another concession demanded by the Socialists when they entered government, along with the creation of the regions and the nationalization of electricity supply. The notion had been in debate for at least 10 years and enjoyed broad political support from the left wing of the Christian Democrats and the Republicans, but the supporters did not have quite the same expectations from the process. The Socialists saw it as an essential part of the transition to a socialist economy, as a means of redressing substantial imbalances in the economy, and as the essential element in the relationship between central government and the regions. The favourably disposed faction of the Christian Democrat party saw planning as a means of making incremental reforms to facilitate the functioning of capitalism. This underlying divergence of expectations impeded the formulation of a programme of precise objectives which could command broad support.

All participants at the time envisaged that planning should regulate growth rather than create it. They thought to influence the distribution of wealth; the sectorial distribution between industry and agriculture; the geographical distribution between North and South and the social distribution between private and public enterprise. It was the time of cheap oil and the *miracolo italiano*, the creation of wealth seemed less pressing than its regulation. At the beginning of the 1970s, planners became aware of basic changes appearing in the Italian economy and revised their views. Priority was given to microeconomic action to improve those aspects of the economic structure which were thought to obstruct growth. This was the first acknowledgement that planning should or could serve to assist the creation rather than the regulation of growth. The oil crisis of 1973/4 stimulated the creation of the first specific 'National Energy Plan', this again was an innovation which specified in some detail the development of a principal sector of the economy over a long period of time.

In none of these functions has planning in Italy had any significant effect. The procedure of planning has been inhibited by decisional slowness, political conservatism and the technical weakness of the Italian bureaucracy. The Ministry of the Budget and Economic Planning (BEP) has not been considered a strong department; it has failed to mobilize support among the unions and industry. The trade unions have interpreted planning, at least under Christian Democrat control, as a disguised incomes policy. The state companies IRI and ENI paid lip service to plannning objectives and assisted in their preparation, but discarded the duty of implementing them if it proved unfavourable.

The public enterprises were well disposed to planning if it meant lending support to their own ambitions, but not if it constituted a threat to their traditional lines of influence. Private firms never felt any loyalty to the choices of planning. Both public and private firms took advantage of the absence of statutory powers to enforce the plan.

Other departments of the civil service have not taken the BEP seriously. Endemic conflict persisted between the technocratic and often left-wing perspective of the planners and the traditional bureaucratic centre-right civil service trained in jurisprudence (better to be legally sound than effective). There was an inevitable conflict with the Treasury.

Although the principle of planning is widely accepted in Italy, in practice its influence has been small. Even as an attempt to bind the public sector to a coherent set of goals it has failed as will become clear in the following analysis of the energy plans. Underlying reasons are the discrepancy in objectives which has impeded broad support for specific initiatives, the rapid disappearance of the Socialists from government, and the total lack of support from the party bureaucracies with their own well-established ideas on who should get what and how.

Preparation

The principal institutions involved in planning are the Ministry of the Budget and Economic Planning, and the Interministerial Committee for Economic Planning (CIPE). The initiative for planning lies with government; Parliament does not choose the objectives, but must eventually approve the plan. The Regions are consulted, but central government tries to confine them to a role in implementation; on this conception, CIPE formulates broad criteria for regional development and the Regions then organize their affairs within these parameters. Application of the plan depends exclusively on sustained political will, not a common quality in Italian public life.

Energy Planning

The first National Energy Plan was presented in August 1975; an updated version was approved by Parliament in Autumn 1977 and by CIPE in December 1977. It is a lengthy document:[6] the principal objectives were:

1. Total primary energy consumption in 1985 to be 199.5 mtoe, representing 4.3 per cent per annum growth from 1976.
2. Dependence on oil imports to be reduced from 66 per cent in 1976 to 63 per cent in 1985, mainly by an increase in nuclear, which source contributes 10.0 mtoe by 1985.
3. Net oil imports to increase in volume from 91 mtoe to 126 mtoe in 1985.

The plan having been approved by CIPE, the next step should have been for government to acquire the powers to implement specific actions. To aid energy efficiency in industry it was proposed to use an existing law on aid to industrial restructuring.[7] Authority to specify maximum room temperatures, insulation standards and design of heating systems was obtained in principle in April 1976,[8] but implementing regulations were issued only in February 1978. Authority to impose nuclear sites on local authorities was provided by a law in 1975,[9] but the use of this legislation has been minimal.

It is perhaps easier to understand why there has been so little progress if it is appreciated that the plan is created essentially from papers drafted by CNEN, ENEL and ENI. In energy planning, in contrast to economic planning, it is not that the state enterprises refuse to accept the objectives of the politicians, but that the politicians fail to support the objectives of the technical agencies. In this respect the Italian plan has a quite different significance from the French plan in which the aspirations of the technical agencies are co-ordinated, heightened or reduced according to the requirements of a clearly specified political framework. Energy planning in Italy adds nothing to the sum of the corporate plans of the state enterprises.

New energy plans were announced by the Industry Minister, Signor Giovanni Marcora, in mid-1981, and were approved by CIPE by the end of 1981; a very short time by Italian standards. The plans cover investments of L87,000 billion in the decade to 1990, the biggest sum ever spent on a single sector. The main aim of the plan is to hold Italy's oil consumption at its present level of around 100 Mt/yr and thus reduce oil's contribution to total energy requirements from around two-thirds at present to around one-half by 1990, by increasing the contributions of coal, nuclear, and natural gas. Few observers, however, take the latest programme at face value.

Corporate Planning

The individual corporate plans of the industry have also to be approved by CIPE, again the process seems to bear little relationship to reality. At the beginning of 1980 ENEL presented to CIPE a 10 year plan; it provided for 27,000 MW(e) of new power stations, of which 10,000 MW(e) would be nuclear and the remainder mostly coal-fired; some oil plant would be converted with the cumulative effect of reducing the dependence on oil in the fuel burn from 62 per cent in 1978 to 42 per cent in 1990; in absolute terms the oil burn was expected to increase as plant under construction was commissioned. The cost of the first 5 years was estimated at $25.5 billion. The plan was quite unrealistic; ENEL has done little to convert existing oil plant or to provide the coal infrastructure. There is no sign of an acceptable procedure for siting nuclear plant, or coal plant for that matter. The cost of the investment programme is disproportionate to the resources of

ENEL, already heavily indebted. Despite all this, CIPE approved the plan without demur.

Bureaucracies

During most of this century, Italy has been without a civil service of competence and integrity. The Ministries are staffed by careerist lawyers from the South, ill-paid and ill-equipped to handle technical or political demands. There are islands of competence which keep the system ticking over. The National Assembly has only a presentational function; the decisions which pass through it are negotiated outside by shifting coalitions of deputies reacting to pressures from the party bosses and the leaders of various factions. Many decisions of the Assembly are delegated to parliamentary Commissions within which the same bargaining takes place, but with the added refinement that the members are few enough for the media to follow in detail the shifting balances in the weeks preceding an important decision.

The absence of a competent civil service means that there can be no approximately detached appreciation and arbitration of the demands of pressure groups. Italy is not unique in its organized lobbies, but in its lack of balance. Cynics allege that the politicians permit a bare minimum of competence in essential aspects of the civil service thereby preventing the entire system of patronage from crumbling around them, and allowing them to continue to enjoy its benefits.

State enterprise has a dual role in this scheme; on the one hand it is a client or pressure group seeking to promote its own interests, but on the other it is an instrument of the State, capable of being used to further party objectives. Positions of influence in the state enterprises are therefore subject to competition among parties and party factions. The most remarkable manifestation of this is the negotiation for the Presidents and Boards of the principal enterprises.

Every 5 years, appointments for these posts are made by the decrees of the Minister for State Holdings (ENI, IRI), and the Minister for Industry (ENEL, CNEN); the law requires that the Parliament give an opinion through the competent parliamentary committees. The process of nomination is widely known as 'spartazione' (the division of booty). The appointments due at the end of 1978 were delayed many months by blocked political negotiations—essentially a Socialist bid to take over ENI, a well-known piece of Christian Democrat property. The Socialists had agreed a candidate with the then Minister for State Holdings, Signor Bisaglia, but this meant replacing the existing President Signor Sette, against his will. Signor Sette being an old friend of Signor Aldo Moro, this operation was difficult. As a compromise, Bisaglia accepted the sacrifice of one of his own candidates, either for ENEL or IRI, in favour of Sette; the latter would not take ENEL, but was prepared to settle for IRI. The elaboration of this and other compromises necessitated a long series of 'decisive' Ministerial meetings. Eventually, Signor Giorgia Mazzanti, with allegiance to a particular Socialist faction, was appointed as President; several ENI Board positions went unfilled for over a year as the political infighting continued.

Shortly after Mazzanti was appointed, he was brought down by a rival faction of his own party who created a scandal out of a payment of commission on an oil contract with Saudi Arabia to unknown intermediaries (generally believed to be Saudi Arabian). Mazzanti was cleared by a Commission of Inquiry, but was obliged to resign; the Saudis, alarmed at the scandal, cancelled the contract. The revealed willingness of politicians to sacrifice matters of substantial national interest to intra-party manœuvring is indeed remarkable. The subsequent appointment of Signor Egidio Egidi to the Presidency had not been ratified before he also resigned for reasons relating to party political disputes.

Egidi was replaced by Signor Alberto Grandi, a technocrat associated with the Christian Democrat party. In February 1982 he also was asked to resign, ostensibly because the Government wanted to appoint new men to govern the State's relationship with ENI under a new system. However, the real reason was that the coalition government had agreed to replace him with a Socialist, in order to change the balance in state sector jobs between the major government parties, and ENI's Socialist vice-chairman Signor Leonardo di Donna was the main candidate. Grandi had also committed a tactical error by pushing the Government too hard into approving ENI's finalized contract to join the Siberian gas pipeline, a controversial deal risking the upset of the delicate balance in Spadolini's coalition. Grandi refused to resign and had to be forced out of office. After this controversy it was decided to appoint Signor Enrico Gandolfi as a special commissioner to replace the Board for 6 months.

Things were much the same at ENEL. The Board had been due for change for 3 years and the uncertainty caused by this situation prevented any major decision being taken. The source of the tangle here was the Communist party (PCI). The President and three other posts had been 'allocated' to the Christian Democrats; one post was reserved for a Republican; the Socialists wanted the vice-presidency, and there should also be a representative from each of the three opposition parties. The Liberals (PLI) and the Social Democrats (PSDI) would go along with the scheme, but the Government was blocked by a fear that the PCI would refuse a post as a tactic in their campaign against 'Ripartazione'; it would then be difficult to place the PLI or PSDI on the board which would present problems. Moreover, ENEL was engaged in delicate negotiations with local authorities for power station sites and it was essential to have a wide political representation legitimacy with communes or regions which were not governed by the DC-PSI-PRI-based national majority.

For the moment ENI and ENEL seem almost helpless victims of the struggle for patronage. But the tail continues to wag the dog. Enrico Mattei, the first president of ENI, consistently managed to manipulate the parties for his purposes. He achieved this by maintaining influence in all parties and factions and through an astute building of consensus for his actions; he has assisted by the financial benefits the company enjoyed at that time. Under Mattei, there were apparently few political appointees in the usual sense; loyalty to Mattei was the prime quality. This was an extraordinary change from the discredited AGIP on which Mattei built; when Mattei died, his successors were unable to maintain a positive balance of influence in the state-parastatal dialogue. The present situation is more complex; ENI, the financial holding company, is very much a politically sensitive body and attempts to influence the operating companies to act in accordance with political objectives, compounded in part of social objectives, in part of political patronage. The management of the operating companies, AGIP especially, are comparatively lightly colonized and have a mentality far closer to the private companies. They resent political interference through ENI and at the present time are benefiting from ENI's problems to launch an attempt to establish their presence on ENI's board. To a non-Italian, the present structure does indeed appear dangerous. Mediation between political and technical needs occurs not between state enterprise (AGIP) and a clearly governmental body (CIPE), but within an institution (ENI) controlled politically by lines that are, to say the least, obscure.

One of Mattei's objectives was to use the resources of ENI to build up an alternative bureaucracy as a substitute for a competent government capability in industrial policy and as a countervailing power to Italian big business. To some extent he was successful; the bureaucratic effort in energy planning comes from ENI, ENEL, CNEN, but this effort simply enhances the role of the parastatals as clients; it cannot supply the mediating role of a competent civil service.

The deleterious consequences of this dependence of Byzantine political bargaining are fairly clear. Delays and the sacrifice of national to factional interests are inevitable—the recent history of ENI is an illustration of this. The strengths of the system are less obvious, but they do exist. The trade-offs implicit in such inside dealings can be a reasonable way of allocating the costs and benefits of change. The painfully slow negotiation of a rational structure for the nuclear industry is one example. Another could conceivably arise in nuclear siting; Italy faces the same problem as most other countries in reconciling the national need for nuclear power with local objections. An attempt to impose sites was given legal form but the party bureaucracies refused to be compromised by any application of the law. The present trend is to use the Regions to mediate. Local communes and central government are too distant to do deals and in any case the municipalities have no great trust in Rome. Regions can deal with the State and in turn know what communes might be bought off and how. This process could conceivably lead to a relatively stable siting policy, because the mechanism ensures a reasonable degree of satisfaction on both sides. It is possible that the stability inherent in some, if not all, such deals is a contribution to the stability which must perforce underlie the Italian economy, given the fact that it has done relatively well in spite of the structural problems and the lack of an efficient central administration.

In the same fashion, an eventual deal on coal imports is possible. There is some hope, therefore, that slowly Italy will adjust to supply substitution, the costs and benefits to transition being allocated by arcane political compromise. It is less likely that Italy will adjust on the demand side. It is impractical to buy off millions of individual consumers; energy conservation legislation is unlikely to be effective. Political bargaining is no substitute for correct pricing signals and a perceived legitimacy of imposed restrictions, properly applied and maintained by competent bodies, as energy conservation is practised in, for instance, Denmark,

REFERENCES

1. SNAM, *Il Metano Oggi-Informatzioni sulla metanizzazione del Mezzogiorno* 1979.
2. CNEN, *Serie Documentazioni, Delibere del Cipe sulla actività del settore nucleare* 1978.
3. *Proveddimento*, CIP, No. 43/1977.
4. Ibid.
5. Ibid.
6. 'Programma Energetico Nazionale', reproduced in *Notizario*, CNEN, March 1978.
7. Law 675, August 1977.
8. Law 373, April 1976.
9. Law 393, August 1975.

5
WEST GERMAN ENERGY POLICY

One might expect that West Germany would be the most difficult of countries in which to demonstrate how the history of its institutions has constrained modern technical choice. The political history of that part of Europe is marked by frequent and extreme change; in little over one hundred years it has gone from fragmentation and diversity, through unification, centralization, partition and federation. To identify continuity in something as peripheral as energy policy is daunting. It is odd then to discover the remarkably consistent evolution of the institutions of energy supply in West Germany. The process divides into three phases.

The first phase proceeded through the settlement of conflicts of interest in and around the coalfields; from it emerged local industrial structures with well-demarcated internal responsibilities, geographically and operationally. The greatest and most perfect was located on the Ruhr. Ownership of the structural elements was highly interdependent; the field of interdependence extending well beyond the energy industries as they are narowly conceived. Behaviour was constrained by horizontal trusts, vertical integration, territorial agreements, and interlocking shareholdings. The principal architects were the great capitalist families, the commercial banks, and, to some extent, the Prussian State. Competition was not eliminated but damped down. Almost all energy came from coal; the electricity utilities and gas utilities were owned or had reached agreements with the mine owners; their relationships were symbiotic rather than competitive.

In the second phase the utilities began to compete for territory well beyond the limits of their home coalfield regions. The result of this differential expansion based on commercial advantage, alliance and entrepreneurial skills was confirmed again by negotiated territorial agreements. In this second phase the utility structure came clearly to be dominated by the Ruhr. Competition was essentially for territory; the integrity of the energy sector, arising from the physical interdependence of the coal, electricity and gas industries, was still not threatened.

The third phase was characterized by the absorption of new

primary energy forms—oil, natural gas, nuclear energy; the ancient interdependence of the sector was eroded. Oil and nuclear competed with coal for power generation; natural gas competed with coal as a fuel for gas utilities; oil competed with gas and electricity in end uses; the competition between gas and electricity in end use now had implications upstream which earlier it did not possess. The form of the existing institutional structure was a crucial determinant of the adjustment to these new options. It affected the global rate of adjustment (i.e. the backing out of coal) and the relative success with which the new options were absorbed industrially (high for natural gas and nuclear, low for oil). In turn the new options had their own influence on the hierarchy of dominance within the institutional structure.

EARLY INDUSTRIAL HISTORY

A convenient start to an account of Germany's energy institutions is the creation by Prussia, beginning in 1828, of a series of customs unions (*Zollvereine*), including, significantly, the Ruhr. In 1834 the German *Zollverein* was formed and later extended under the stimulus of expanding infrastructures. Lacking the political coherence and stability conducive to the development of an industrial economy, the exigencies of such an economy became the means of stability itself. The capacity of the Prussian civil service for innovation in economic and industrial life ran ahead of the diplomatic and military achievements of Bismarck and Moltke. The removal of administrative barriers to trade within the customs union was paralleled by removal of physical obstacles. Canals and railways made transport of goods feasible over long distances. The potent combination of administrative and technical innovation caused the manufacture of goods to concentrate in the most advantaged areas and especially on the coalfields of the Ruhr.

Many of the great mines and the companies which ran them were founded in the years immediately following the formation of the German *Zollverein*. Curiously they have preserved an identity up to the present and their names are still part of the institutional fabric of energy policy. The Gelsenkirchener Bergwerks AG (GBAG), which came to be the biggest mining concern on the continent, was founded in 1873 to manage two mines, lying near the village of Gelsenkirchen, which had been opened in 1845.

Coming late to the Industrial Revolution, Germany was able to draw on the technological experience of others. Entrepreneurs from the UK were common imitators of new projects; another of the famous collieries, Hibernia, was founded by an Irishman from Dublin, William Thomas Mulvany.

From the coal of the Ruhr come three important products: steel, electricity and chemicals. There also come the celebrated cartels.

THE SYNDICALIZATION OF THE RUHR

Studies of the monopolistic combinations of the Ruhr were for many years a favourite topic for the doctoral theses of German scholars, (with the Americans not far behind). The fascination which cartels have for students of economics did not begin with OPEC.

Coal has been mined in the Ruhr since the Middle Ages, but was of no industrial significance until about the beginning of the nineteenth century. Rigid control of production by the Prussian State initially gave no incentive and little possibility of monopolistic combination; this control was largely removed in 1851 and there followed considerable speculation ending in a crash in 1858/9.[1] Thereafter prices continued to fluctuate and became especially unstable in the 1870s during and after the Franco-Prussian War. Producers, in seeking relief from these unsatisfactory conditions, tried several different schemes for stabilizing the industry. The three fundamental devices in use were agreements to limit production, arrangements not to sell below agreed prices and formation of associations to sell the output of a group of producers. These projects experienced the difficulties which one might expect; agreements, whatever their nature, were violated when it appeared to be in an individual interest so to do.

It was not until 1893 that producers succeeded in founding an organization which controlled enough of the output of the region to have a perceptible stabilizing effect on prices. The cartel succeeded in bringing in 87 per cent of the production of the region of the Rhine-Westphalia; it established a double organization comprising a selling company with the title Rheinisch-Westfälische Kohlen-Syndicat and an association bound by legally enforceable agreements to restrict output, regulate prices and divide the market. Regulation of the industry proceeded through a contract between the mine operators association and the selling Syndicate. Subject to specific exceptions, the entire output of the mines of members had to be delivered to the Syndicate for sale; the only exception of significance was that of coal used for 'own consumption'. The Syndicate sold part of its products directly to large customers, such as steel plants, gasworks and railways, and part to dealers, who were forbidden to sell on to other direct customers of the Syndicate.

The Syndicate had enormous trouble in controlling production. One term in the agreement allowed an increase in the quota of a member of 400 tons per day for each new shaft house; these apparently then sprang out of the ground like mushrooms, there being no legally binding requirement that the shaft be capable of producing the extra output, despite the owner obtaining an extension to his production allowance.

The existence of the Syndicate promoted integration of the steel industry. While a few of the parties to the original agreement in 1893 had been steel companies which produced a part of their own coal and coke requirements, the steel industry had for the most part relied upon fuel purchased in the market. The hardening of coal prices and the generally less favourable terms of purchase which the Syndicate was able to exact, naturally caused the steel companies to seek to free themselves from their dependence. Some steel companies attempted to buy coal-mines from members of the Syndicate and then free at least that part of the output intended for their own consumption. In this they were partly successful, but generally it turned out to be easier for the steel companies to open new mines. The Syndicate soon found that it controlled a decreasing share of coal output in the region.

The steel companies were not alone in their efforts to free themselves from the Syndicate. Other large consumers set about acquiring their own mines, either as individuals or in groups. The chemical, gas and electricity industries were among them; they were joined by cities such as Cologne and Frankfurt. Smaller industries and domestic consumers formed co-operative purchasing associations which later combined into great regional co-operatives. The wholesalers of coal also organized themselves to co-operate in the purchase of coal, its transport and storage. These groups had conflicting objectives; the wholesalers evidently had a common interest with producers in stable output and prices, and the management boards generally had representatives from the Syndicate.

The organizational effect of the Syndicate was far reaching; in order to protect themselves against its economic control and arbitrary regulation, consumers of all sizes took action which eventually helped stabilize the structure, albeit that the distribution of power within that structure shifted.

The main shift of power was to the steel industry; as the industry opened new mines, the Syndicate lost control of output and was obliged to seek to take in the steel companies as new members. This they achieved, but only by means of concessions which were advantageous to the steel companies and accelerated the process of integration.

The Coal Syndicate was also challenged by the State. The functions of marketing and regulation of production and pricing which the Prussian State had taken to itself in the first half of the nineteenth century and then abandoned to a free market had been reassembled and put under the control of a cartel of producers. The State had also almost disappeared from the scene as an operator. With the formation of the Syndicate the State itself felt threatened as a consumer. It reacted like industry and in 1903 tried to buy up the shares of Hibernia; it was beaten off by the Board which increased the capitalization of the company and formed a trust to hold the new shares. The State accordingly took the same course as others, bought new acreage and opened new mines.

The Syndicate did make an effort to buy up all promising acreage but markets are difficult to corner at the best of times and it could not prevent outsiders of all sorts gaining access to new mines. The Syndicate was about to fall apart when the German State stepped in. In 1917 it was seen as an indispensable prerequisite of war that the coal industry be stabilized. The Government issued a decree permitting State Governments to organize compulsory syndicates on the main coalfields if a free syndicate did not control at least 97 per cent of production. This gave the Prussian State considerable leverage on the Ruhr Syndicate because Prussia controlled more than 3 per cent of the production in the Ruhr; the Syndicate needed the state owned companies to join to avoid being formed into a compulsory state directed syndicate. The eventual compromise was that the State joined, but on favourable terms including acquisition of the Hibernia mine.

As a consequence of the decree, syndicates patterned after the Westphalia model were formed in each of the bituminous and lignite-producing districts of Germany. These syndicates, created and put into operation at the instigation of the Government, gave the nucleus of a structure which at any time could be used to regulate the industry as the Government thought fit. The post-war Government of Germany did indeed attempt to socialize the industry through the Imperial Coal Union—a sort of syndicate of syndicates, but the scheme was not a success and was soon abandoned. The Ministry of Industry remained vested with the authority to organize syndicates by decree.

The essential structure of the coal industry itself was by this time determined. The economic conjuncture would change; there would be good times and bad. The exercise of government control would come and go (as above) and come again under the Nationalist Socialist Government but with little practical effect. The changes of significance for the 'industrial sociology' of the sector were occurring outside the coal industry itself in gas and electricity supply, steel and chemicals.

OTHER CARTELS

The Ruhr Coal Syndicate had its parallels in all other sectors. The steel industry was founded in 1924 to regulate crude steel production according to the state of the market; all principal producers belonged. Further associations were created later for various products, bars, plate, wire, tubes, etc. The associations were controlled by half a dozen trusts. These trusts, by virtue of the acquisitive process already described, were also responsible for the greater part of coal production.

The most powerful of all the trusts, and the one of most significance for later energy policy was Vereinigte Stahlwerke. At the end of 1924 and the beginning of 1925, following the stabilization of the German currency, a deep recession persisted. The response of seven of the main Ruhr coal and steel companies was to coalesce their activities in a single enormous trust. In 1926, Vereinigte Stahlwerke was founded; among the participants were GBAG and the steel firms of Thyssen and Phoenix. The subsequent rationalization of services to and amongst these companies gave an interesting stimulus to the development of gas and electricity utilities, as will be seen later.

The coal tar wastes of the Ruhr steel industry gave sustenance to the chemical industry. When an Englishman, Perkins, discovered a means of making aniline dyes from coal tars the German chemical companies recognized the industrial potential. By the turn of the century they were the biggest producers of synthetic dyes in the world. In 1916 the main companies came together in a cartel, or 'community of interest' (*Interessengemeinschaft*); the aim was to reduce competition by sharing the profits of the dye businesses. In 1926 the component companies of the cartel reformed themselves into a single corporation, but retained the name of the 1916 cartel—IG Farben, even though the enterprise was no longer strictly an *Interessengemeinschaft*. By the mid-1930s the company was the largest chemical company in the world.

In the electrical industry two large cartels were formed each dominated by a pioneer of the industry. The Siemens-Schubert group, headed by Werner Siemens and the Allgemeine Elektrizi-täts Gesellschaft (AEG), headed by Emil Rathenau. These two companies were important not only for their control of electrical manufacture, but also, as is described later, because of their contributions to the stimulation and organization of electricity supply.

The brown coal or lignite industry is important in Germany; it developed somewhat differently from hard coal. The fierce competition which was once the characteristic of the coal trade and which lead to the cartellization of the industry by survival of the fittest was less pronounced in the brown coal trade. Brown coal is cheap to produce but expensive to transport because of its low calorific value and density. The transport costs impeded competition. Nor was brown coal of any value in steel production. Although periodic efforts were made to cartellize the industry, and associations were created for the purpose, it was not really until brown coal was recognized as a favourable fuel for power generation that the industry came to the fore.

THE DEVELOPMENT OF ELECTRICITY SUPPLY

The trusts and cartels in coal, steel, chemicals and electrical plant were designed to suppress competition among suppliers of goods.

Gas and electricity supply are not subject to the same forces. The dedicated and expensive infrastructure for delivery owned by the supplying company imposes its own limits on competition. Utilities compete for territory and low cost sources of primary energy; accommodation of the ambitions of different actors cannot be achieved by the cartels favoured by producers of simple goods.

Electricity supply began in heavy industry as a means of supplying motive power and in towns for lighting buildings. The generator was often driven by a gas motor fuelled by blast furnace gas or gas from the local gas works. By the turn of the century most large towns had a small public power station and a municipal distribution company. In the coal-mining areas there rapidly developed regional supply companies delivering to the municipalities the surplus electricity production of the mines. Their histories illustrate how the public and private interests in their development were variously accommodated.

In 1898 the company that would eventually dominate Germany utilities was founded: Rheinisch-Westfälisches Elektrizitätswerk (RWE). Curiously, it was originally a daughter company of a Frankfurt utility—an unusual example of South to North colonization. The company built its first power station in 1899/1900 supplied with steam from a mine owned by Hugo Stinnes—one of the great Ruhr industrialists. This form of energy was suggested by Stinnes as a means of getting around the Syndicate's restrictions on coal sales. Stinnes and August Thyssen rapidly acquired a majority of the shares of the company and undertook a programme of gas and electricity supply from their mines to municipal distributors. The towns of the region were alarmed; they feared being at the consuming end of a monopoly controlled by private capital and they were concerned for the future of their corporate gas works. Against the commercial power of RWE the municipalities had a subtle weapon—the granting of wayleaves without which the emergent utility could scarcely prosper. A compromise was needed; it took the form of co-determination of RWE's activities, the territories of RWE and the municipalities were delineated. The municipalities took part of the share capital of the company and eventually became majority owners.

RWE then came into conflict with the great mining companies when the latter began to build high voltage lines between their various collieries for the purpose of pooling the companies' internal resources. There was a danger to RWE that by this means the mines could extend their sales to municipal distributors. This dispute was settled by a new form of collusion; the mines agreed not to build out their high voltage nets and in return RWE contracted to take their power; sometimes they ceded their existing transmission lines to RWE. The arrangement was satisfactory to both sides; the mines were able to use poor quality and unsaleable coal in their own power stations along with coke oven gas and various other wastes; RWE gained control over the strategic element of the system—the high voltage grid.

The second utility of the Ruhr was the Vereinigte Elektrizitäts-werke Westfalen (VEW). This company arose out of the Elektrizi-tätswerk Westfalen founded in 1906 by the town of Bochum. It contracted, in the year of its foundation, to take power from the Hibernia colliery up to a maximum of 4 MW for the duration of 45 years.[2] A second company (WVE) was formed in 1908 with the participation of the town of Dortmund and some of the bigger mining companies, including GBAG; supply contracts were signed with its coal-mining shareholders. The company also undertook the distribution of gas from its coal-mining to its municipal shareholders. In 1925 the present VEW was formed through the merger of WVE with Elektrizitätswerk Westfalen; the merged company soon after bought extensively into coal-mining. In this respect it differed significantly from RWE, which contracted much of its power supply.

Progress outside the coal-mining areas was constrained by the absence of cheap local fuel. Municipal distribution companies could generate electricity from imported coal, but there were not the same possibilities of rapid expansion. Municipal electrification was encouraged in a practical manner by the electrical plant manufacturing cartels, AEG and Siemens. These companies operated a few supply undertakings themselves, e.g. the AEG in Berlin and Siemens in Hanover, until they were bought out by the municipalities or States. More usually they promoted electrifica-tion at home and abroad by providing finance through affiliated agencies. Evidently, a condition of financial help was that the orders should come back to the parent manufacturer.

In Bavaria water power formed the basis for the state-initiated unification of supply. The Bayernwerke AG was founded in 1920 to co-ordinate existing supplies, finance new water power schemes and create organizations for the generation and supply in bulk of electricity. It promoted the formation of new supply companies, including the Mittlere Isar AG. with the task of building power stations at points along the River Isar. The power from these projects was delivered to the Bayernwerke; also feeding into the network was the Amperwerke AG in Munich. Bayernwerke built and owned a transmission system over Southern Germany second only to that of RWE in Westphalia.

The largest utility in Germany in the period before the Great War was Electrowerke AG, operating in Central Germany, deriving its output from extensive deposits of lignite and selling most of its power to Berlin. The Prussian State came late to the feast; her ambitions for economic advancement entailed the electrification of relatively thinly populated territory. To acquire the necessary means she bought into existing suppliers and in 1923 established new companies whose shares belonged entirely to the Prussian State. She even took a participation in RWE using money acquired from the Federation as compensation for territory lost in the Treaty of Versailles. The wholly-owned interests were later (1927) consolidated into the Preussische Elektrizitäts-Aktiengesellschaft, generally known as Preussenelektra; the objective of the company was to promote electrification over Central and Eastern Germany. In 1929 the Prussian State consolidated all its coal and electricity interests into a Berlin holding company, VEBA (Vereinigte Elektrizitäts-und Bergwerks-Aktiengesellschaft); Preussenelektra and the Hibernia mine were among the assets transferred.

As the supply companies expanded they began to run out of territory and competition between the companies for access to peripheral fuel deposits and markets became acute. One of the fiercest commercial disputes between nominally public bodies was waged over the Brunswick brown coal deposits at the junction of the spheres of influence of RWE, Electrowerke and the interests of the Prussian State. These disputes were settled by commercial manœuvring and confirmed by agreement.

The basic assets of the players in terms of access to fuel, power stations and territory were essentially determined by the end of the 1920s. The question arose as how best to arrange that the electricity supply industry continue to develop through a process of interconnection and collaboration. The Government of the

Republic prepared a scheme for central control by a state institution; it received support from AEG predicated on the belief that only a super-state organization could adequately design a system for the Republic as a whole and extract maximum benefit from economies of scale and favourable sites near cheap sources of energy. AEG was an exception, most of industry argued for a solution whereby private ownership was continued within a framework of state supervision. This was the character of the legislation eventually passed in 1935. The law (the *Energiewirtschaftgesetz*)[3] regulates the behaviour of the constituents of the public electricity supply, defined as all undertakings regardless of their legal form and ownership which supply electricity to others. The statute obliges utilities to supply electricity with a high degree of reliability, in sufficient quantities and as cheaply as possible. Tariff rates are supervised by State and Federal Ministers. Utilities which did not comply with these obligations could be prevented from operating a public service. The crucial questions of investment in generating capacity and transmission lines were left to the companies.

The advantages of arrangements among companies are evident; interconnection serves to reduce the intrinsic problems of matching supply and demand; if load peaks occur at different times on different systems then interconnection reduces the capacity required on the combined systems. Interconnection also reduces the amount of installed capacity which each partner need install to cover for the breakdown of some of his plant. Moreover, when the consequences of breakdown are less serious, then utilities feel able to build plant in larger unit size with a consequent fall in unit cost.

Inevitably, collaboration among utilities did not end at helping each other out in times of difficulty; it progressed to the construction of extended transmission systems which could carry large volumes of electricity from one part of the country to another according to the cost advantages defined by time of day or intrinsic geographical advantage. Through the construction of this network, the natural autarchy of the supply companies was finally overcome; the full consequences took a long time to develop and did not fully materialize until well after the Second World War.

Perhaps the most important link in the German system was that constructed from the brown coal power stations of RWE on the left-hand bank of the Rhine down to the hydro stations of Bayernwerke in the Bavarian Alps.

Within the Ruhr itself the relationships between the mines and the utilities continued to evolve. In 1937 the mining companies came together to form their own production company, the Steinkohlen Elektrizitäts AG (STEAG). The concept of the foundation was to pool the resources of the mining communities in order to obtain the most profitable use and in order better to balance the commercial clout of the utilities. The enterprise soon built two large power stations for the direct sale of power to large aluminium and chemical factories.

The continuous agglomeration of the iron and steel industry was another factor shaping the relationship between mine-mouth power stations and utilities. The bringing together of geographically diverse units into a single company naturally encouraged the idea of rationalizing gas and electricity services between different units by building privately owned infrastructures. The clear evidence, in the years after the Great War, that the most rapidly growing market for coal was in power generation, reinforced the arguments for the mining companies to move further into production and transmission. Gelsenkirchener Bergswerks AG, the giant mining company incorporated into Vereinigte Stahlwerke, would not consent to participate in a high voltage network. The lukewarm support from GBAG obliged the mining companies to lower their sights. A compromise was reached where the companies collaborated with the utilities RWE and VEW in the planning of a transmission network appropriate to the needs of the mines and of other consumers. Associated with this they signed agreements with the utilities for the delivery of power and contracts for the use of the network in supply-consuming sites distant from producers. The control of the utilities over the strategically crucial transmission system was confirmed.

The expansion of the utilities, and especially RWE, out of the Ruhr area combined with the natural advantage of the Ruhr in power generation enhanced the existing dominance of the utility structure by the members from the Ruhr and North West. By 1962 about 11 bn kWh of electricity were exported from the power stations of North Rhine Westphalia and 4 bn kWh from those of the North West coast, to other regions of Germany.[4]

The collaboration between utilities which replaced competition for supply territories then yielded to a new form of competition in bulk supply. This is the general condition which has prevailed since, exacerbated by the demands on organizational capacity later to be made by nuclear power.

THE DEVELOPMENT OF GAS SUPPLY

The first public gas works in Germany were begun in 1826 in Berlin and Hanover, using gas derived from coal processed in the city. In the subsequent 50 or 60 years most of the large towns acquired enterprises based on the same principle; these were sometimes privately, sometimes municipally owned. The privately owned companies were mostly taken over during the wave of municipalisation which swept Germany after the turn of the century.

During this period the gas industry had no especial significance within the 'social structure' of the energy industries; it was a coal consumer like others. The first change to this state of affairs came in 1897 when a nearby colliery took over the supply of gas to the town of Kastrop.[5] In 1903 'Thyssenische Gas -und Wasserwerke' was founded with the purpose of arranging the supply of surplus gas from the Thyssen coke ovens to municipal distributors. At about the same time Thyssen bought into RWE and that company also began to supply gas from Thyssen collieries.

The technical development which gave the gas industry its special character was the demonstration of long-distance gas transmission. The first pipeline was constructed to take gas from the Thyssen colliery at Hamborn to the town of Barmen. It was 40 km long and worked at a pressure of 2.5 atmospheres. In the subsequent years, especially following the end of the Great War, similar pipelines came into operation on all the important German coalfields; in the Ruhr, the Saar, in Silesia, and the known coalfields of Central Germany. The ability to carry gas over significant distances had a dramatic effect on the industry because it made available the enormous, unused gas reserves of the German coke ovens. Not only did this make it possible greatly to expand the size of the industry but it transformed the industrial structure from one based on local production of gas, to one based on purchase of long-distance gas and the elaboration of interconnected networks based on the coal-mining regions. The tendency was given a decisive boost in the late 1920s and early 1930s when it became possible to produce thin-walled, high integrity steel pipes cheaply and join them easily by welding. It is a splendid example of the effect of technical change on the structure of an industry.

The immediate 'sociological' effect of long-distance transmission was to bring utilities into territorial conflict. Frontiers were established by agreement; the first and most important was signed in 1912 between the Thyssen company and the by now municipalized RWE which divided up the Ruhr.

In a curious contrast to the attitude which had originally brought about the municipalization of RWE, in 1926 the gas interests of the enterprise were transferred to a private company in which the majority of the mining companies of the Rhine-Westphalia Coal Syndicate participated. The company, Aktiengesellschaft für Kohlenverwertung, had the function of undertaking for its participants all chemical processing of coal in addition to the construction of a gas distribution network. In 1928 the company was renamed Ruhrgas AG. Almost the first act of the company was to produce a long-range plan to supply virtually the whole of Germany with gas from the Ruhr.[6] It might not seem that there is much of interest in a fifty-five-year-old plan; but there is. For two reasons, it is worth describing in a little detail.

The planned system was comprised of three arteries starting from the heart; that is to say the Ruhr. One went to the North East to Hanover where it split into a northern branch to Hamburg and Kiel, and an easterly branch to Magdeburg and Berlin. The second artery went eastwards to Kassel, Dresden and Breslau; the third went south to Cologne and Frankfurt where it divided, one part continuing south to Mannheim, Karlsruhe and Stuttgart, the other going on to Munich through Nuremberg.

Ruhrgas envisaged that at a later date the system should be strengthened by a ring travelling anti-clockwise from the Saar to Hamburg via Nuremberg and Berlin. The network could then also be fed with gas from the Saar and at the extremity of the eastern artery with gas from the Silesian fields.

The interest of this plan is firstly, that it reveals the 'colonialist' perspective which lay behind the creation of Ruhrgas; secondly because, in spirit at least, Ruhrgas would eventually pull it off; albeit the path to the desired end would be in several ways more involved than that envisaged and the partition of Germany would reduce the scale of the concept.

What actually happened can be divided into five phases, two of which will be described now and three later. The first phase followed the lines of the long-term plan; the great volumes of gas produced by the coke ovens and used for the most part for heating the coke ovens or for power generation could instead be transferred to more profitable markets. The network was built out rapidly and by 1939 had reached Hanover in the North East and Frankfurt in the South. Active also, but less expansionist, were Thyssen gas to the west of the Ruhr, VEW to the east and Westfälische Ferngas around Dortmund. Outside the Ruhr the main growth was from the Saar, initiated by the Saarferngas AG.

As RWE profited from the integration of the coal and steel companies, so did Ruhrgas. The bringing together of coke ovens and steel mills made possible the use of blast furnace gas to heat the coke ovens, releasing the coke oven gas, previously used for that purpose, to be delivered to the metal working plants.[7] A carrier was needed. Shortly after the formation of Ruhrgas, the company signed an agreement with the new agglomeration of Vereinigte Stahlwerke, for the transport of gas. (Vereinigte Stahlwerke had taken 21.4 per cent of the initial share capital of Ruhrgas). The agreement was for Ruhrgas to transmit large volumes of gas (1 mn m^3 daily) between the associated companies of the steel trust. The transmission pipelines amortized by this activity could then be used to deliver incremental gas to third parties.

The second phase of development began towards the end of the 1930s as the surplus of gas from the coke ovens proved unequal to growing demand. It coincided with the destruction of much of the gas transmission network by bombing and a lapse in expansion. It was not before the early 1950s that the network was restored to its pre-war state. There was still a lack of gas. A large plant for production of gas from hard coal was built by Ruhrgas at Darsten, but the costs of this specially prepared gas were far higher than that of the coke oven surplus. The territory of the gas transporters appeared limited by the high cost of incremental supplies and the high cost of transport over ever increasing distances.

This brings us to the end of the period of coal-based intimacy among energy supplies. The relationships of the Ruhr utilities to the coal and steel complexes of their home base were broadly defined; territorial acquisition had been limited in the case of electricity by running out of territory and in the case of gas by running out of incremental supplies. The dominance of the Ruhr was established, but was not overwhelming. The whole structure was faced by, or would soon face, the absorption of three new primary energy sources: oil, natural gas and nuclear power. The mutual influence of the choice among these technologies and the institutional relationship of energy supplies will be examined later in this chapter.

THE PENETRATION OF OIL

The traditional German energy supply structure has never absorbed the oil industry properly; the reasons for this are many.

Before the Great War, the Deutsche Bank had acquired a 25 per cent share of the capital of the Turkish Petroleum Company; 50 per cent of the capital was held by the Anglo-Persian Oil Company. The Turkish Company enjoyed substantial concessions in Iraq. There appears to have been no sense of national strategy behind the acquisition; the Bank considered its expenditure a sound commercial investment. Before German entrepreneurs had a chance to exploit the acquisition in any industrial sense, it was taken by the French as a spoil of war; the shares were transferred to France in the Treaty of San Remo in 1920.

Germany had, during the Great War, experienced the crucial military significance of secure oil. The defection of Rumania from the German side, the destruction of their oilfields by the Allies and the blockade of product imports compounded Germany's natural deficiency. Already, in 1916, the German scientist Bergius had successfully demonstrated, on a laboratory scale, a process to make light oil products from coal and thereby technically give Germany self-sufficiency. After the War the process was acquired by the IG Farben cartel and demonstrated on a commercial scale; the cost of the synthetic fuel produced was some seven times the world price of refinery gasoline. Further progress awaited the autarkic economic policies of the Nazi Government.[8] In 1933 IG Farben negotiated with the Government, price and sales agreements for synthetic gasoline and accordingly brought up the output of their plant to 350,000 tonnes per annum. The process was taken up by the Ruhr coal companies. In 1935 the Hibernia company converted one of its old nitrogen plants at Scholven to the hydrogenation of coal (225,000) tonnes per annum. A year later Gelsenberg Benzin AG was founded by GBAG and began work on a 400,000 tonne per annum plant in Gelsenkirchen. Finally a third large mining company, Mathias Stinnes, formed a subsidiary, Ruhröl, to construct and operate a 130,000 tonne per annum plant. With smaller plants here and there, in 1943 the Ruhr was producing more than 800,000 tonnes of oil a year from coal. The two large hydrogenation plants were the origins of the later oil refining interests of the VEBA and Gelsenberg companies.

The oil-from-coal programme was matched by determined prospection for fluid hydrocarbons in Germany. During the 1920s, German firms with state help found and produced considerable reserves. In 1930 Germany was producing 175,000 tonnes per year and by 1940 this had been forced up, by wartime conditions and to the detriment of the reservoirs, to more than 1 million tonnes per year. Crude oil and products were also imported; the former being refined at sites on the North coast, the latter coming in mainly from the US.

During the Second World War any installation connected with oil supply was a prime target, damage to the hydrogenation plants in the Ruhr and the coastal refineries was severe. After the War the industry reverted substantially to its original form. The refineries on the coast were rebuilt and extended. The three large hydrogenation plants in the Ruhr were originally scheduled by the occupying powers to be dismantled and removed; their operation was at first prohibited. When this intention was reversed and the ban lifted, the plants were converted to function on crude oil; the nature of the process was such that they produced only gasoline.

The West German market at the time was characterized by its small size and the predominance of light products for internal combustion engines (diesel and gasoline). Both these characteristics were to change rapidly; from 1955 to 1965 the consumption of oil products increased from 4.5 to 83.6 million tonnes—an almost twentyfold increase—a quite staggering expansion. The product mix made almost as dramatic a shift from 58 per cent diesel and gasoline in 1955 to 25 per cent in 1965.

Both these features were a consequence of the slow absorption

by West Germany of the new energy source; this fact is important
and worth detailing. Table 5.1 shows refining capacity and inland
demand in the four principal European markets in 1950.[9]

TABLE 5.1

Refining capacity and inland demand in the principal European markets in 1950

	Refining Capacity (in tonnes)	Inland Demand (in tonnes)
France	15.7	9.2
Italy	5.9	5.2
UK	11.5	15.3
West Germany	6.0	4.5

West German consumption was actually below that of Italy, a
country scarcely industrialized throughout most of its extent.
Throughout the 1950s demand for oil products in West Germany
went up eightfold and then in the following decade quadrupled
again, making West Germany the largest market in Europe by
1970. Table 5.2 shows some comparisons with other European
countries.

TABLE 5.2

Consumption of oil in some European countries

	1955 mt (%)	1960 mt (%)	1970 mt (%)
France	21 (28)	28 (31)	94 (74)
Italy	12 (37)	24 (50)	87 (73)
UK	28 (15)	50 (27)	102 (45)
West Germany	12 (9)	34 (23)	129 (53)

This extremely high growth rate was not always welcome. The
Federal Government attempted to protect both domestic oil
production and domestic coal; it introduced a protective tariff on
the import of crude oil and abandoned it only with reluctance in
1964 as part of the move towards an EEC common external tariff
structure. There had also been tax preferences for crude oil

processing in the hydrogenation plants of the Ruhr, and a special tax on heating oil. The government also made an interesting attempt in 1958/59 to get the West German coal and oil firms to organize a cartel with the international oil companies for the purpose of controlling the penetration of oil. When this failed the West German Government tried to persuade the oil companies to enter into a voluntary agreement to restrict the penetration of heavy and light fuel oils to certain annual rates. The results of this Canute-inspired policy are evident from Table 5.2.

Apart from these interventions the West German oil market remained free in the sense that there was no restriction on entry of firms and there was no control of prices or attempt to influence investment. Nor was there any real attempt to prevent the take-over of foreign firms by American companies.

The result of this open access and introverted domestic perspective was that the international oil industry rapidly took over the supply to, and production of oil in, West Germany. The process culminated in 1966 when Texaco bought out the last West German oil company of any significance, Deutsche Erdöl. The remaining West German presence was oriented to refining and in particular to the chemical industry. The main participants were VEBA, Wintershall (a subsidiary of the giant chemical company BASF), Union Rheinische Braunkohlen Kraftstoff (possessing a refinery near Cologne designed for the provision of feedstock for petrochemical manufacture), and Saarbergwerke (a publicly owned company operating the mines of the Saar also designed to provide petrochemical feedstock).

But, 'the king is dead, long live the king'; 3 years after Texaco had taken over the last significant West German producer, the Federal Government inspired the launch of a new national oil company based on some of the Ruhr's classic concerns: VEBA, Gelsenberg, BASF and RWE. However, that is to run ahead with the story. One should first look at another crucial dimension of the development of the oil industry in post-war Germany: the shift in emphasis of the economic geography brought about by the changing distribution of crude oil availability.

In 1950, 83 per cent of the imports of crude oil into West Germany came from the Middle East and the rest mostly from Venezuela. All were delivered to the North Sea ports. As consumption rose, it made increasing economic sense to attempt to deliver crude oil to inland refineries rather than to transport products from the coast to inland markets. This tendency was reinforced by the shift in market share towards heating oil, a product less able to stand high transportation cost than motor fuels which had no easy substitute and therefore little competition.

Pipelines were built first from the North Sea ports to the refineries in the Ruhr domain. The first such line ran from Wilhelmshaven, the second from Rotterdam. This innovation gave the Ruhr the opportunity to establish its traditional dominance and it grabbed the chance, rapidly acquiring the largest installed refinery capacity in West Germany. Whereas in 1950 the North possessed 65 per cent of refining capacity and the Ruhr 35 per cent, by 1960 the North had 41 per cent and the Ruhr 59 per cent. In neither year was there any refining capacity in any other part of the country.

Crude oil imports still came predominantly from the Middle East. Both the concentration of refining in the North and West and the concentration of sources of imports were to be eroded by the discovery of oil in North Africa.

These deposits, discovered in the 1960s, could be landed at low cost on the Mediterranean coast. The German market offered open access to companies not represented up until then. The pickings for those who could deliver crude to Southern Germany would be good. The charismatic Mattei of the Italian company ENI was a prime mover in the affair, enjoying the extra motive of stealing a march on the majors; his concept was to feed a refinery in Ingolstadt with a pipeline from Genoa. The task proved somewhat beyond the resources of the company. Goaded commercially, and in their self-esteem, the major oil companies brought forward their own plans and built lines from Marseilles and Trieste. Mattei's line, though initiated first, was completed last and lost ENI a fortune.[10]

The building of refineries which accompanied the pipelines had brought the geographical distribution of capacity into balance by 1970. Concurrently the origin of crude oil imports into West Germany altered. Imports from North Africa rapidly came to dominate the supplies, reaching a peak of 58 million tonnes in 1970, 59 per cent of the total; Libya alone provided 41 million tonnes (41 per cent). In the early 1970s production cuts in Libya, coinciding with continual increase in West German consumption,

obliged renewed recourse to the Middle East; since 1979 oil from
the North Sea has become increasingly significant. In 1980 the
four foremost suppliers were Saudi Arabia (24.6 Mt., 25.1 per
cent), Libya (14.9 Mt., 15.3 per cent), UK (14.7 Mt., 15 per cent),
Nigeria (10.9 Mt., 11.2 per cent).[11]
We now return to the attempt to build a new national oil
company on the rocks bequeathed to modern Germany by the
Ruhr and the State of Prussia. In the late 1960s concern with
security of supply caused the Federal Government to encourage
the formation of a German exploration company. The Government sought to obtain the collaboration of all the German
companies of any substance which had succeeded in absorbing
some aspect of the oil industry; this minor miracle was achieved by
the promise of large subsidies to exploration abroad. In 1969 the
company was duly formed and baptised DEMINEX (Deutsche
Erdölversorgungsgesellschaft), the original participants and their
shareholdings are shown in Table 5.3.

TABLE 5.3

Original shareholders in DEMINEX

	%
Gelsenberg AG	18.5
VEBA-Chemie AG	18.5
Wintershall AG	18.5
Union Rheinische Braunkohlen Kraftstoff AG	13.5
Deutsche Schachtbau GmbH	10.0
Saarbergwerke AG	9.0
Preussag AG	7.0
Deilman AG	5.0

It is worth resuming the pedigrees of these companies. VEBA
AG had been founded in 1929 to manage the interests of the State
of Prussia in coal and electricity, including the Hibernia mine and
the utility Preussenelektra. In 1965, in accordance with government policy to diversify the ownership of large companies, VEBA
sold 56 per cent of its shares to the public. It is now the largest
company in West Germany, the largest shareholder in Ruhrkohle
and the second largest producer of electricity after RWE. Its oil
interests began with the hydrogenation plant at Scholven begun
in 1935. Gelsenberg was a daughter of Gelsenkirchener Bergwerks

formed pre-war to manage a hydrogenation plant; it emerged as one of the successor companies of Vereinigte Stahlwerke in the largely unsuccessful process of decartellization undertaken by the occupying powers after the War; it was almost bought up by an international oil company during that period when most German oil interests were acquired by foreign concerns, but was rescued by RWE, who took over 48 per cent of the shares. Wintershall AG was a wholly owned subsidiary of the chemical giant BASF. Union Rheinische Braunkohlen Kraftstoff AG was owned 75 per cent by RWE and 25 per cent by Hoechst (a principal steel concern); Saarbergwerke was the state owner manager of the Saar mines that had been diversified into refining; Preussag is short for Preussische Elektrizitäts AG which had a minor interest in gas production and a modest presence in coal and power generation in North Germany; Deilman and Deutsche Schachtbau were the remaining two German owned producers of small quantities of hydrocarbons. Gelsenberg and Wintershall controlled a small volume of oil production in Libya.

Between 1969 and 1974 DEMINEX received DM 575 million in subsidies for exploration. The subsidies took the form of a loan of 75 per cent of the total cost of exploration; there was no obligation to repay the loan if oil was not discovered. If exploration led to commercial production then a nominal return of DM 3 per tonne was to be paid back to the Government. If DEMINEX bought into a proven field the Government provided 30 per cent of the purchase rights. The subsidies have been extended in several follow up programmes covering the years 1975–78 (worth DM 800 million), 1979–81 (worth DM 600 million) and 1982–86 (worth DM 600 million). Despite these generous terms the high cost of entry into the oil industry was to prevent DEMINEX from making a profit until 1982.

This preference to DEMINEX was apparently uncontentious. The established producing companies in West Germany knew that they were treated lightly, suffering only a 22 per cent royalty on production. The subsidies to DEMINEX were seen as a form of balancing. In parenthesis it is interesting to ask why the royalties were kept so low. The implied agreement is that if the big companies are left with the rent from domestic production then in return they will take it on themselves to supply West Germany in times of crisis. Evidently even free market philosophy needs a little insurance.

The initial success of DEMINEX could only be described as modest. In the early 1970s the Government began to feel increasingly exposed to turbulent world oil markets and sought to strengthen the German presence by concentrating responsibility on VEBA. Before settling on VEBA the Government made serious efforts to persuade RWE to take on the task through their Braunkohlen subsidiary; RWE did not see itself in this role.

In support of its objectives the Government forced a take-over by VEBA of Gelsenberg. According to Grayson this initiative was agreed in May 1973 between the Economics Minister at the time, Hans Fridericks, and the head of VEBA, without consultation with Gelsenberg.[12] In November the Cartel Office was notified of the merger, which in January it declined to approve. The objections of the Cartel office were overruled by decree of the Government. The Government had acquired the 48 per cent share holding in Gelsenberg held by RWE and some others, bringing its proportion to 51.3 per cent; these shares it gave to VEBA in May 1974. VEBA continued to consolidate its holding and by 1975 owned 96 per cent of the capital.

The Government's intervention in the process was decisive. It was the initiator and the political proponent; it set aside the Cartel Office; it acted as go-between in the share transfer and it supported the merger financially. The net cost to the Government in the share dealings was estimated at DM 140 million.[13]

Following the merger VEBA acquired the shareholdings of Preussag AG and Deutsche Schachtbau; RWE's subsidiary acquired the holdings of Deilman. DEMINEX was then owned by the four German refiners and controlled by VEBA. The basic objective of the Government's manœuvring was to improve the security of supply to, and the co-ordination of, the 20 per cent of refining capacity lying in German hands.

The new arrangement was disappointing. In the conditions of the time no oil company in Germany could avoid heavy losses unless it possessed indigenous oil and gas production (i.e. Shell and Esso). The free market structure depressed market prices; excess capacity world-wide drove the rent on refining capacity down close to zero.

Accordingly the Federal Government agreed in 1978 to an arrangement between BP and VEBA whereby BP took over large parts of the Gelsenberg refining and marketing operations plus VEBA's 25 per cent share of Ruhrgas in return for a DM 800 million cash payment and a 20 year crude contract with the BP group of 3 million tonnes per year. The Cartel Office again blocked the merger and was again overridden by the Economics Ministry.

Despite this effort the returns have been low. The petroleum sector remains VEBA's biggest problem, because of oversupply and low demand. Moreover its product balance is sadly out of tune with market conditions. It is persuaded by government subsidies to burn coal in its power stations in preference to its own heavy fuel oil and therefore has to find an outlet for this by upgrading it to light products. It plans one big downstream investment in a hydro cracker for this purpose. All the other available funds are to be directed upstream to improving oil supply and in particular to extending its own production. It has problems in financing that exploration despite public subsidies through DEMINEX and cross subsidization internally by profits from electricity supply. If it cannot finance upstream activities then it will shrink on the West German market. The West German Government is well aware of this but has no apparent intention of providing further help. The nominal, and *a fortiori* the real, value of the DEMINEX subsidies has been decreasing and the stronger commitment to free market philosophy within the Ministry of Economics is not likely to be sympathetic to renewed support.

The impression is that the West German Government did not match the effort put into the creation of a national oil company with due consideration of the difficulties of sustaining it in one of the most competitive oil markets in the world. The contradiction in policies is profound.

THE PENETRATION OF NATURAL GAS

I stated earlier that the development of the gas industry was divided into five phases. The first two were the period of rapid expansion centred on the coalfields and based on readily available supplies of coke oven gas, and the period of relative stagnation as sales were limited by costs of transport and incremental supplies. The industry was jerked temporarily from this static conjuncture by the shift during the 1950s in the economic geography of oil refining. New sources of gas, in novel locations, became available from the processing of by-products from oil refining. This third phase of development was not to last long, but it was of some importance sociologically, because it opened opportunities to new suppliers and brought new participants. Bavaria was able for the first time to build up a high pressure gas transmission system through the activities of two companies Bayerisches Ferngas and Ferngas Nordbayern; the former company was founded by the city of Munich and other nearby towns. The latter company was owned by Saarferngas; it permitted these two coalfield-based producers to extend their influence east from Frankfurt, where their territories coincided, into North Bavaria.

Ruhrgas also took a considerable part of another new supply company, Gas Union, serving Frankfurt and areas east and north respectively of the territories of Ruhrgas and Ferngas Nordbayern. Although this extension of gas supplies by volume and territory was made possible by the new inland oil refineries and the development of high pressure processes for cracking petroleum, it did not cause the oil industry to become a participant in gas transport. In most places the relevant services were offered by the existing transporters who thereby extended their influence. The change had little effect on the character of the relationships among transporters. The system, although bigger than before, was still made up of a set of regional networks, connected more or less together but with little exchange of gas between areas. In part this arose from rivalry among companies, in part it arose from the technical fact that the gases from coke ovens and petroleum cracking processes were not easily made substitutable.

Natural gas by contrast worked wonders for the industry's internal relations. Methane is more easily transported over long distances than is coke oven gas. In part this is because it usually comes out of the ground at a pressure suitable for transmission and does not require to be pressurized at a considerable cost. But mainly its advantage lies in its high calorific value, so that for the delivery of an equivalent heating capacity the piping and compressors required in the case of natural gas are smaller than those needed for coke oven gas. The use of natural gas also brought, for the first time, oil industry capital into the transmission network.

This fourth phase of development began with the discoveries by Shell and Esso of natural gas in Northern Germany. The oil companies, through their subsidiary, Gewerkschaften und Elwerath Brigitta Betriebstührunggeselschaft, constructed a pipeline to deliver gas from the fields to large users in Bremen, Hanover and Hamburg and also to Ruhrgas for onward sale.

The incorporation of natural gas into the network forced close collaboration onto the companies; the heavy investments in transmission capacity had to be fully utilized to be profitable; it would have been absurd to duplicate such constructions. A good example of this collaboration is the finance of the line, built in the late 1960s, to carry gas from the Northern German fields and the Netherlands, south to Bavaria. It comprised a branch from the Dutch frontier down the left bank of the Rhine, crossing at Cologne to join at Bergisch Gladbach an easterly branch collecting gas from the North German fields. The combined line then went on south to Frankfurt. The western branch from the Dutch frontier to the junction was financed by Ruhrgas and Thyssen gas. One section of the eastern branch was financed by Gewerkschaften Brigitta; the second section down to the junction with the western branch was financed by Ruhrgas. The section from the junction south to Musselheim was financed two-thirds by Ruhrgas and one-third by another company owned jointly by Shell and Esso. Further sections south from Musselheim brought in finance from Gasversorgung Süddeutschland and Gas Union.

The consequences of this were fundamental. Physically the line bound and overlaid the networks of Ruhrgas, Thyssen gas, Gas Union and Gasversorgung Süddeutschland. Institutionally it obliged the companies to collaborate in the forecasting of market requirements, in planning of the transmission network, in purchasing and in finance. In this procedure Ruhrgas was, without doubt, *primus inter pares*. This principle of dominated collaboration henceforth was to guide and inform the West German gas industry.

The arrival of natural gas did not displace manufactured gas. In the mid-1960s the production of manufactured gas was around 20–25 bn m^3 and it has remained at approximately that volume ever since. The increase in demand since that time has been met exclusively by natural gas. There is still a transmission network for manufactured gas, but sales are confined for the most part to large industrial consumers.

The fifth, and so far last, phase of the story is the transition of Ruhrgas from the state of *primus inter pares* in West Germany to the West German representative internationally. This transition also involves the extension on an international basis of the process of collaboration on purchasing, planning and finance. In this role Ruhrgas has struck deals with the USSR for delivery of gas to the Czechoslovak border (1973), with Norway for delivery of gas to the coast at Emden (1978), and with the USSR for delivery of gas in the 1980s.

The last of these contracts with the Soviet Union has provoked controversy within West Germany and with the US. Under the agreement Ruhrgas will receive 10.5 bn m^3 of natural gas per year at the Czechoslovak border, starting in 1985. The gas will be produced in West Siberia and transported through a 5,500 km pipeline. When the gas is flowing at the contracted quantities, the USSR will provide some 30 per cent of West German natural gas consumption. Only a part of the delivered gas will be used in West Germany. The pipeline is designed to carry 40 bn m^3 a year of gas; at least six West European countries will share the remainder.

During the negotiations Ruhrgas has represented entirely the interests of other participating West German gas carriers and has led the West European consortium. The participation of other countries was necessary to share the risks and achieve economies of scale, but the initiator and sustainer of the project has all along been Ruhrgas.

THE PENETRATION OF NUCLEAR POWER

The seminal event in the history of the West German nuclear power programme was Chancellor Adenauer's pledge to forgo the production of nuclear weapons on West German soil in exchange for the consent of France to West German membership of the Western European Union and NATO and to the termination of the Occupation Statute. This was the outcome of a grand compromise between the insistence by France that the production of arms by West Germany be strictly controlled and the plans of the US that West Germany be militarized.

There reigned in West Germany at that time a belief that the country was not keeping abreast of technology; the catch phrase was 'a technology gap'. There had been some erratic and limited development of nuclear power during the War but thereafter West Germany had made no consistent and extensive effort in the rapidly advancing subject of nuclear physics. The Government accordingly created a Ministry of Atomic Questions to institute research and development in the subject.

The strategic objective of Government was to use the process of acquisition of nuclear expertise as a motor for the entire West German manufacturing industry. The demands of nuclear power in matters such as electronics, material and quality control were seen as vital to modern manufactures. Research and development of nuclear technology would oblige the acquisition and dissemination of these capacities. Within the nuclear sector itself the Government was seeking through its financial support of R & D to create a nuclear technology with a West German stamp; in particular, one which would be independent of foreign suppliers of components or services. Enrichment of uranium was closed to West Germany; she might not be permitted to develop breeders. The Government was therefore disposed towards the concept of the heavy water reactor, using natural uranium, and the organic moderated reactor. The great and uncontrolled expenditure of government money led to considerable competition among manufacturers to develop various reactor lines and to pick up government funds. At one time seven reactor lines were under study; more per capita than any other country in the world. Most manufacturers attempted to enter with foreign concepts; Siemens was more creative and entered its own heavy water design; for this reason and as a result of its close links with Government, Siemens received most of the money. The reactor was developed in the Karlsruhe nuclear research centre founded by the Ministry of Atomic Questions in 1956 with this particular objective. Siemens's contribution was limited to half the cost of the reactor, costs of the centre were financed by the State.

AEG and Siemens also had access to nuclear technology through their traditional links with the principal US companies. For many years the German companies had taken US licences and there had been joint attempts at some cartellization of international markets. AEG possessed a licence from GE for the manufacture of BWRs and Siemens had a Westinghouse licence for PWRs.

The overriding concern of the electricity utilities in nuclear matters was economy; nuclear power needed to compete with other fuel sources. Under West German Law the utilities had complete autonomy over investment, subject to licensing procedures. Not surprisingly the running was made by RWE. Unimpressed by what was offered domestically they chose to build the conceptually cheapest reactor design: the BWR. The company's first effort, a 15 MW reactor at Kohl, came into operation in 1961.

The commissioning of this plant marked the end of the West German attempt to develop a first generation domestic design. Orders thereafter were for light water reactors and were placed equally between AEG and Siemens. In 1969 the two companies agreed to combine their turbine generator interests in a joint company, Kraftwerk Union, KWU. The rationale was the belief that 1,300 MW or larger turbines would in future be required to match the optimal economic size of nuclear reactors. Faced with the need to make heavy investments and recognizing the risks of misjudgement or overenthusiastic competition, the companies chose to pool their resources. At Mulheim they built the first factory designed for series production of large turbine generators; a factory capable of producing six units a year.

A few years later both companies had progressed so far with the technology of nuclear power that they were able to terminate their US licences and offer West German light water designs. Taking the logic of the turbine generator merger one step forward, the companies agreed also to bring their separate nuclear contracting operations into KWU. AEG then ran into grave financial problems exacerbated by the falling popularity of BWRs and by its existing commitments to an extensive programme of construction. In 1976, Siemens, which ever since the 1970s had been the financially more conservative of the two companies, took over full control of KWU and responsibility for completing AEG's construction programme. This left Siemens as the sole supplier of nuclear plant—the preferred generating tool of the utilities.

This fundamental change in the structure of the heavy manufacturing industry and therefore its relationship to the utilities would seem only to be to KWU's advantage. Immediately following the take-over this appeared to be the case. In the first energy programme published in 1973 the Federal Government had anticipated that installed nuclear capacity would reach 45,000 MW or more in the mid-1980s; this was a large market. In fact popular opposition killed the construction programme stone dead. Since June 1977 no construction permit has been granted. To be efficient KWU needs between four and six orders a year. There are three reasons why it is not suffering as much as this bleak comparison implies; first, Siemens's super-conservative financial attiutude— they have only invested where they could guarantee a return which would at least cover their outlay. Second, Siemens does not manufacture complete plants—it provides an architect-engineering service. The share of the value of a power station which it buys in from outside contractors is 70–80 per cent; for the 700 or so smaller companies collaborating in the construction of a nuclear power station the absence of orders from Siemens must be absorbed by profits from other areas in which they operate. Third, Siemens provides utilities with extended services and prepares licensing procedures. As the procedures become steadily more complicated they generate a steady flow of income and work for the design teams which are KWU's principal nuclear commitment. The main difficulty is the turbine plant at Mulheim, but that is not intrinsically a nuclear venture.

The utilities in general, and RWE in particular, were unhappy about the coalition between AEG and Siemens. The existence, or appearance, of competition is taken as a basic requirement. RWE therefore invited Brown-Boveri of Switzerland into the West German market with the offer of an order for a plant at Mulheim-Karlich. Brown-Boveri accepted, tendering a US, PWR design in collaboration with Babcock and Wilcox. It is generally thought that the constructor will lose money on the project because of delays.

The decision to invite Brown-Boveri into the market was made at a time when RWE was more optimistic about the future level of orders than it is now. The company was then preoccupied with maintaining competition and keeping up pressure on KWU; its preoccupation today is rather whether KWU will not go under, leaving RWE without a nuclear supplier. If RWE had known how the market was to evolve, it would probably not have brought in Brown-Boveri.

Nuclear power also made demands on the organizational capacity of the utilities and forced them into tighter collaboration. The characteristics of nuclear power confirmed RWE as the unchallenged leader of the electrical community. Only RWE is really large enough to build nuclear plant alone. As a rule of thumb an individual grid can support units of 5–7 per cent of its total capacity. RWE's grid is the biggest; it therefore has the opportunity to install the largest plant and to act alone. This appears to have been a fundamental part of RWE's nuclear philosophy; by building bigger plant it could manage lower costs, lower prices for electricity, attract further load and advance its position among the West German utilities. This reasoning resulted in the order for two 1,300 MW PWRs at Biblis on the Rhine near Frankfurt which came into service in 1975 and 1977. These stations were built under easier licensing and economic conditions than those which now pertain and they generate for RWE an enormous rent of some DM 1 million per day.

It was this preoccupation with economies of scale which made RWE review its judgement between the merits of BWR and PWR lines. It had started with BWRs because the absence of an intermediate cooling loop appeared to offer an efficient design. The company then realized that scaling-up would be more difficult with BWRs than PWRs because of the problems with the neutron distribution in the core; moreover it seemed unlikely that 1,300 MW turbines could be built for active steam because of the impossibility of making them adequately leak-tight.

The other West German utilities could not benefit from these economies of scale to anything like the same extent. Generally they sought collaboration e.g. Nordwest Deutsche Kraftwerk (NWK) and Hamburgische Elektrizitätswerke (HEW) collaborated in a PWR at Stade and a BWR at Brunsbuttelkoog; Bayernwerke and Isar-Amperwerke built a BWR together at Ohu. NWK is the largest subsidiary of Preussenelektra, in turn part of the VEBA group; it generates power from stations on the North West German coast mostly fired by coal. HEW is also a North German utility originating from Hamburg.

The utilities entered into this process of collaboration in finance and construction with some reluctance; when companies eventually have to compete to sell power the last thing they want is joint production. The greater ease and speed with which RWE could absorb nuclear generation has confirmed its position as a centre of wealth and technocratic ability at the centre of the utility structure. This pattern of RWE-dominated, uneasy, collaboration is repeated in the institutions of the fuel cycle.

The chemical companies which showed an interest in entering the fuel cycle processes in the early days of nuclear power soon became disenchanted by the distance of the speculative profits and they left. The utilities have been obliged, either by need or by government pressure, to fill the gap.

The main point of interest is the way they have allocated responsibilities among themselves and the amount of stick and carrot that has been deemed necessary by the Government.

Fuel supply

West Germany has few natural deposits of uranium of commercial value; small domestic mines exist and are worked, but they are insignificant in comparison with the needs of the country's power stations. Consequently West Germany is dependent on foreign supplies; based on long-term contracts for forward delivery, it is more or less sure that supplies for the mid-1980s will come 50 per cent from South Africa and Namibia and 30 per cent from Canada. As with oil the Federal Government has made subsidies available for prospecting and exploration; it has also agreed to share with companies the risks which arise from the usual obligation placed on participants in joint ventures for exploration and production, to take delivery of part of the production. The aim is to ensure that 60 per cent of West German requirements for uranium come from own production or mines with West German participation. That is a long way off.

Five West German companies are active in mining projects for natural uranium, but the principals are two companies controlled by RWE and STEAG (in which RWE also has an indirect, but influential stake). Urangesellschaft was formed in 1967 and is owned equally by STEAG, Metallgesellschaft AG and VEBA; it is currently engaged in prospecting and exploration in Australia, Canada, USA, Brazil, Colombia, Indonesia, Niger and Germany. Uranerzbergbau formed in 1968, is owned 74 per cent by Rheinische-Braunkohlenwerke (a wholly owned subsidiary of RWE) and 26 per cent by Deilmann AG, a family owned concern with diverse interests; the company owns a 49 per cent share of a mine in Canada producing some 2,000 tonnes of uranium a year; it is also prospecting in Canada and the US. Saarbergwerk also has a subsidiary prospecting in Canada and elsewhere.

Enrichment

Research and development on techniques for enriching uranium had continued post-war on a modest scale in the research institute at Karlsruhe and Jülich. In 1968 the Governments of West Germany, the Netherlands and the UK agreed jointly to enter commercial markets with the centrifuge technique. This was formalized in the agreement of Almeno in 1970; two companies were established, CENTEC for design and construction of gas centrifuge plant, URENCO for their operation. The one-third West German presence in CENTEC was held jointly by MAN and Interatom (a wholly owned subsidiary of KWU). The West German part of URENCO is held by Uranit, whose share is distributed among Nukem (40 per cent), Preussenelektra (40 per cent) and Hoechst (20 per cent). Nukem in turn belongs to RWE (45 per cent), Degussa (25 per cent), Metallgesellschaft (10 per cent), RTZ (10 per cent). The West German utilities control the company through Preussenelektra and RWE. The participating companies in URENCO have plants operating in Almeno (NL) and Capenhurst (UK). There is a plant under construction in West Germany in North Rhine Westphalia which should be commissioned in 1983 and reach an output of 400 tonnes of SWU per year by 1987. Ownership of the specific plants is not equally spread among the partners. Uranit has 49 per cent of the Almelo plant, 2 per cent of the Capenhurst plant and 96 per cent of the plant at Gronau.

The natural inclination of the West German utilities to control the upstream end of the nuclear fuel cycle has been strengthened by their experiences with France and the US. At present the only contracts of enrichment that can be placed are at Pierrelatte in France at tariffs which the utilities find economically horrifying. An even more potent incentive for independence was the decision by President Carter to use the dependence of European countries on US enrichment as a political weapon. Contracts with German utilities were broken. As one executive remarked 'Does price matter in these circumstances? We have learnt a lesson; what we don't have in the country is not safe'.

Fuel Fabrication

West Germany began the manufacture of fuel elements at an early stage in the development of her nuclear industry. There was no special political problem as there was with enrichment and the process comprised the kind of precision, high quality controlled operations at which West German manufacturing industry excels.

The leading company is Nukem, which has holdings in individual fuel fabrication companies as follows:

1. Reaktor-Brennelement Union (RBU), owned 60 per cent by KWU, 40 per cent by Nukem, which fabricates fuel elements for LWR and natural uranium reactors.
2. Alkem, owned 60 per cent by KWU, 40 per cent by Nukem, which fabricates plutonium bearing fuel elements for LWRs and fast breeders.
3. Hobeg, wholly owned by Nukem, which fabricates pebble fuel elements for high temperature reactors, and is of no commercial significance.

The fabrication of fuel elements is one of the more profitable parts of the nuclear industry; the relationship between the nuclear reactor and the fuel elements has been likened to that of the apocryphal recommendation for success in marketing shavers; to give away the razor and sell the blades. RWE is well aware of this and despite its presence through Nukem it consciously introduced Esso into the West German market for the purpose of balancing KWU, just as it invited in Brown-Boveri to give leverage on KWU for reactor costs. Exxon Nuclear has a fabrication plant for LWR elements in Lingen.

Reprocessing and Waste Disposal

The activities involved in storing, handling, processing and disposing of spent fuel elements after they are discharged from the reactor tend to be seen in Germany as a unity described by the word *Entsorgung*. *Entsorgung* has become the crux of a German nuclear policy.

Well before the matter attracted the political attention it now enjoys, the West German Government had financed the construction of a demonstration reprocessing plant at Karlsruhe, with a nominal capacity of 40 tonnes of uranium oxide fuel per year. The decision to construct the plant was made in 1966 and it has been in operation since 1971. The plant was built according to the usual principles of West German R & D; it was constructed by private industry, under government contract, at a government financed research centre. The research centre did not participate in the project as a contractual partner, but their R & D programmes were adapted to meet the needs of the project and the results of

the programmes where given freely to the project partners.
The objectives of the demonstration project were:

1. To familiarize German industry with the problems of
   constructing a reprocessing facility.
2. To gain operational experience for the later construction
   of a commercial facility.
3. To further the development of reprocessing technology.

At this time it was envisaged that reprocessing could be made a
commercially attractive proposition and would find a natural niche
in the market. In order to construct and operate a commercial
plant, the Kernbrennstoff-Wiederaufarbeitungs-Gesellschaft
(KEWA) was formed in 1971. The capital of the company was
held in equal proportions by Bayer, Farbwerke Hoechst, Gelsenberg and Nukem. These were the companies which had participated in the Karlsruhe demonstration plant. It is interesting to see
the representation of the great West German chemists.

It rapidly became clear that reprocessing as a separate operation
was not commercially attractive; the value of the recovered
products did not cover the costs of the operation. The chemists,
whose interest obviously lay in making this unitary operation
profitable, were not willing to proceed. Viewed in the context of
the nuclear industry as a whole it was essential to demonstrate an
acceptable means of dealing with the problem of *Entsorgung*.

From a legal perspective the question centred on the responsibility for *Entsorgung*. Accordingly in August 1976 the West
German Government passed an amendment to the Atomic Law
which decreed that the operators of nuclear power plants are
responsible for *Entsorgung*. Ultimate storage of radioactive waste
was excepted and responsibility for this rests with the Federal
Government. The costs of *Entsorgung* have to be added to
electricity prices.

To allocate responsibilities is of course all very well, to ensure
action is another matter. To concentrate the minds of the utilities
the Federal Government and States decreed in a special order that
licences for nuclear power stations would only be given if the
companies applying to build or operate them could give adequate
evidence of secure and safe *Entsorgung* of the spent fuel elements.

To discharge their joint responsibilities the Federal Government
and the utilities developed the *Entsorgungskonzept*. This was a

national fuel cycle centre to which all spent fuel cycle elements would be sent, where all processing facilities would be located and where all wastes would be kept. The twelve West German utilities with interests in nuclear plant formed a joint company as a legal instrument for the discharge of their obligations; the company is known as the Deutsche Gesellschaft für Wiederaufarbeitung von Kernbrennstoffen (DWK); the shares are held in approximate proportion to the present and future interests of the utilities in nuclear power plant. The principals are shown in Table 5.4.

TABLE 5.4

Principal participants in national fuel cycle centre

		%
	Rheinisch Westfälisches Elektrizitätswerk (RWE)	31
VEBA	Nordwestdeutsche Kraftwerke (NWK)	11
	Preussenelektra	11
	Bayernwerke	10

The Federal Government entrusted its responsibility for final disposal to the Physikalisch-Tecknische Bundesanstalt, the West German Bureau of Standards, who intend eventually to contract the construction and operation of final waste storage to private companies.

The favourite locations for a site were on the salt deposits in Lower Saxony. The Federal Government proposed to test three sites. In February 1977 the State Government rejected all three and proposed a new location at Gorleben. DWK accordingly bought a 1,360 acre site adequate for the six separate, co-located plants involved in the *Entsorgungskonzept*. The Bureau of Standards began deep drilling in August 1979 to test the geological and hydrological characteristics of the salt-dome.

Inevitably, Gorleben became the centre of attraction of the anti-nuclear movement. Reprocessing is intrinsically the politically most vulnerable part of the nuclear cycle, but the making, by the Federal Government, of power plant operation conditional on *Entsorgung* had given to the Gorleben project an extra symbolic significance.

Faced with the mounting political opposition to its decision to host the *Entsorgungskonzept*, the State Government of Lower

Saxony decided to hold a hearing, outside the usual licensing procedure as legally prescribed. The lack of local support for the centre was evident at the hearing; the State Government attempted to get itself off the hook by a masterly worded declaration that although the reprocessing project was feasible and safe it should be discontinued because it could not succeed politically (May 1979).

This change of heart by the State Government of Lower Saxony was a blow to the Federal Government and the utilities. Under West German law the Federal Government has no powers to impose even military sites on the States. The Federal Government recognized that the only way out of the 'put-it-somewhere-else' syndrome (if there was one) was to involve all State Governments in a joint study. This it did; the negotiations ended in a revised concept for waste management which replaced the integrated reprocessing cycle.[14] This version was presented in a joint decision of the heads of the Federal and State Governments in September 1979.

The basic elements of the decision are:

1. To permit the interim storage of spent fuel, including compact storage in power stations.
2. To examine waste management techniques other than reprocessing.
3. To continue evaluation of Gorleben.
4. To continue development of reprocessing, with especial regard to safety.

The revised concept is a compromise between the technically preferred centralization of waste management and the unwillingness of individual States to take the local political rap. The Federal Government managed to rescue the final disposal site at Gorleben. The State Governments of North Rhine Westphalia and Lower Saxony offered to provide sites at Ahaus and Gorleben, respectively, for interim storage of fuel elements away from the reactor; the fuel will be stored above ground; in transport casks with air cooling.

The State of Hesse also took up its share of the political burden. The Hessian parliament voted to co-operate with the Federal Government to find solutions to the problems of locating a reprocessing plant, in particular in Hesse. This decision reflected the pro-nuclear views of leading politicians in the State, in particular of the Premier, Holger Boerner; conversion of the parliamentary support in principle into a practical project has not been easy.

DWK announced that their first choice for the plant would be at Wethen, 20 km from Kassel. But local opinion has not followed its leaders; a protest group, formed with the exclusive objective of fighting the installation, took 41 per cent of the vote in the elections of Spring 1981. The State Government then rejected the site; supposedly on the grounds that geological tests had shown a slight risk of subsidence. DDK has now selected two other possible sites; the State Government is thinking about them.

The discrepancy between the amount of irradiated fuel which will be produced by West German nuclear plant and the facilities available to cope with it is serious. If installed nuclear capacity were to grow to 35,000 MW by the year 2000 then the cumulative volume of irradiated fuel arising would be some 15,000 tonnes. Some of this can be processed through the existing contracts with COGEMA in France for 2,300 tonnes of reprocessing up to 1985. These contracts are most unfavourable to the utilities and contain clauses which no free purchaser of a service would want to sign. The purchaser must agree to take the fuel back if COGEMA finds it cannot cope, must accept to take back the plutonium and waste in any form COGEMA chooses and must pay any excess costs arising. The terms of these contracts made a considerable impression on the West German utilities and persuaded them to make more strenuous and sustained efforts than before to get reprocessing accepted in West Germany. In the words of a senior executive, 'We have learnt what it means to be dependent'.

There are further uncertainties with respect to the French Socialist Government. The CFDT, the socialist trade union, has tried hard to prevent reprocessing on foreign account. There was a genuine worry in West Germany that the Socialist Government would revoke existing contracts, which they did not, and there is still concern that COGEMA may not be allowed to review them when they expire in 1985.

West Germany has noticed the symbiosis between her position (money for reprocessing, but no site) and the position of the US (site, but no money); she has begun discussions with the US Government about the idea that she should contribute funds to the commercialization of existing reprocessing facilities at Barnwell and in return benefit from the services created. There are many difficulties. In the US it is not possible to separate plutonium from irradiated fuel outside military control; the US would be unlikely to accept the final disposal of the waste, although she would probably accept intermediate storage. On the West German side, the approach is in any case half-hearted because she is convinced that agreements with other countries are no substitute for her own facilities. This applies especially strongly in the case of the US, whose record on oil and enriched uranium inspires no confidence in West Germany's Ministries.

However one looks at it, it is hard to argue that there are as yet adequate facilities for waste management on which licensing of power plant is conditional. Nor could one argue with confidence that progress towards the provision of these facilities will rapidly be made.

Fast reactor

The fast reactor has long been a favoured technology of the Federal Government. The programme originated in the Karlsruhe nuclear research centre. After work on the heavy water research reactor had come to an end the design teams needed new projects; the fact reactor was chosen. In contrast to the customary arrangement for nuclear research and development the design and engineering work was carried out by the centre's own design teams, not industry. The work was paid for by Federal Government funds. The programme never commanded broad support from the utilities. In 1967, when the Federal Government attempted to launch a 300 MW liquid metal cooled prototype in collaboration with Belgium and the Netherlands, only RWE of the West German utilities would participate. The plant, at Kalkar, was to be owned and operated by a joint subsidiary of RWE along with Dutch and Belgian utilities, RWE holding 70 per cent of the capital. The vendor was a consortium of KWU and Belgian and Dutch manufacturers. The utilities' contribution to finance was limited to 8 per cent of the construction costs, the remainder was paid by the Governments: West Germany 62 per cent; Holland 15 per cent; Belgium 15 per cent. Civil engineering works began in 1973 after long delays occasioned by licensing problems and design changes. Further delays with interim licences were experienced in construction.· When contracts were signed in 1972 the total costs were estimated at DM 1,500 million, already three times the 1967 estimates.[15] By 1981 estimates of total expenditure exceeded DM 5,000 million.

The Federal Ministry refused to agree to provide the DM 1,100 million required from it to complete the project; it set about persuading other German utilities to participate. The Ministry aimed at bringing the utility contribution up to about 30 per cent. Little co-operation was forthcoming, for two reasons. The other German utilities had always seen Kalkar as a monument to RWE, built by RWE because no other utility could afford to do it; they enjoyed seeing RWE in difficulties and saw no reason to fall over themselves to help out. The other problem was that the Bundestag had reserved a right of veto over the permission to operate Kalkar once completed. Perhaps understandably the utilities were un-enthusiastic about investment, the return from which was subject to political whim. The utilities agreed to pay the bulk of the remaining costs provided that the Bundestag withdrew its veto over Kalkar. A Parliamentary Commission recommended that the veto power be lifted and the Bundestag complied. In the meantime the Federal Government provided bridging finance; it also accepted that the utilities be permitted to recover their expenditure through an increase in tariffs for electricity. It is worthy of note that the Federal Government's effort to persuade the utilities to come in on the funding of Kalkar led to one of the rare political interventions by the public authorities in the running of utility affairs. The State Governments holding shares in the utilities in Southern Germany, including Bayernwerke, overruled the decision by the executive boards of the companies not to comply with the Federal Government's request.

The interests of RWE in fast reactors do not rest exclusively in Kalkar. RWE also has a 16 per cent shareholding in NERSA, the joint German-Italian-French utility company which owns and will operate Super-Phénix. This participation, and the decision on Kalkar, were not taken on the basis of detailed economic analyses of the fast breeder reactor (FBR) as a generator of electricity. They were predicated rather on grand strategic arguments. Projections of the future purchases by Germany on the world uranium market come to about 10 per cent of the whole; no one can imagine that Germany could confidently plan to get that; she has to prepare to live on less. Against this line of reasoning stands the fairly unattractive economic present, not so much concerning the capital cost of the reactor as its fuel cycle cost. Kalkar will cost some six to seven times as much as an LWR of similar generating capacity. Built again it might be twice the LWR equivalent; that is already difficult to make pay. Over time the margin could probably come down to something less than 50 per cent. More intractable are the fuel cycle costs. To be of economic size a fuel fabrication or reprocessing plant should probably service 10 GW of fast reactor plant, maybe 20 GW. At the moment there are more fuel fabricators than there are fast reactors, but there are no sound reprocessing plants. This is unlikely to change over fifteen or twenty years.

THE ADJUSTMENT OF THE COAL INDUSTRY

British and American troops occupied the Ruhr in April 1945. Great damage had been done to every form of economic asset. Production of coal had dropped to the level of 50 years before. The mines were put by the occupying powers under direct military control; the Ruhr Coal Syndicate was dissolved after 52 years of life. Responsibility for production, transport and allocation of coal was transferred again to German administration in 1947, with the formation of the Deutsche Kohlenbergbau-Leitung (DKBL); the Allies retained rights of intervention in its activities. The Allies envisaged that the DKBL would be an instrument of their programme of decartellization. In fact the leading personalities of the Ruhr had struggled hard to preserve in the DKBL the essential apparatus of the preceding Sales Syndicate. Not unnaturally the management of the DKBL saw it as their task to frustrate Allied attempts to experiment with the structure of the industry.

The Allied plan for decartellization of the Ruhr foresaw the creation of ten new coal-selling concerns and the separation of iron and steel interests. Limited initial progress towards the second objective was quickly reversed and the pattern of ownership reverted to its original form; by the mid-1950s more than half the coal-mining output of the Ruhr was controlled by the steel companies. In the matter of sales organizations there was a little more formal change from the pre-war structure.

By the time the DKBL was dissolved, in 1953, the management

had prepared the groundwork for a new common sales organization in the historical tradition.[16] That they were not able to obtain
the consent of the Allied powers to this is probably due to the
concurrent efforts to found the European Coal and Steel Community, based, however inappropriately given the character of the
sector, on the idea of competition.

The Allied High Commission was able to oblige the industry to
group itself into six independent, separate sales offices. German
attempts to leave the restructuring of the industry to the High
Authority of the European Coal and Steel Community (ECSC)
were vain despite the rather sound argument that meanwhile the
general Allied policy of decartellization had been overtaken by
events. The historic structure was not, in practice, much damaged
because the six sales organizations were co-ordinated by a single
company: the Gemeinschaftsorganisation Ruhrkohle GmbH
(GEORG); this appears to have functioned as a fairly effective
cartel. It was left to the ECSC to deal the last formal blow to a
Ruhr Syndicate when in 1956 it liquidated GEORG and condensed
the sales companies to three, without a strong co-ordinating
body. The practical consequence of this was limited. Who needs a
cartel when they have a telephone?

The pace of the recovery of the coal-mining industry after the
War was remarkable given the technical problems and the
simultaneous preoccupation of management with frustrating the
process of decartellization. By 1952, under the management of
DKBL, production in the Ruhr fields was back to 90 per cent of
the 1938 level. Moreover many of the mines had been re-equipped
and mechanized. The important commercial change in the
industry was the marked shift from sales of raw coal to sales of coal
products. From 1936 to 1954 consumption of raw coal had declined
by 9 per cent, but consumption in the form of coke had risen by 25
per cent, as gas by 27 per cent, as liquid products (Benzol etc.)
by 57 per cent and as electricity by 181 per cent.[17] This was
encouraging for the industry for it permitted them to add value to
their product. New processes seemed to ensure that this trend
would continue. Nowhere in Europe was the shock to the coal
industry as great as in West Germany when in the late 1950s the
substitution of coal by oil in massive volumes began.

The German economy had not taken to oil as early as others.
Germany industry and the banks tended to the view that fortunes

were made on the Ruhr coalfields not by wandering around the world prospecting for oil. Having only a short coastline, much of Germany was difficult of access and moderately protected from oil. The tremendous success of German chemists and industrialists in finding some way of making from coal almost anything that was needed had been reinforced by almost 10 years of economic autarky.

Rapid economic growth post-war disguised the penetration of oil; markets exceeded the available coal; long-term import contracts were made with producers outside Western Europe. Production of coal reached a peak in 1956, at 151 million tonnes (including the Saar which was still then in French hands). Output thereafter fell rapidly and almost without restraint to 112 million tonnes in 1967.The State and Federal Governments made some attempt to resist this decline by voluntary agreement with oil companies to restrict sales, and with utilities to burn coal; by subsidies to coking coal and by taxes on heating oil. But the effort was half-hearted. The economy was growing rapidly; there were plenty of jobs for displaced miners. Many firms located their factories on the Ruhr with its low cost services and available labour. The main task of the Government appeared as assisting with retraining and adoption of people and reorganization of companies.

The slight recession of the mid-1960s brought matters to a head. Redundant miners could no longer easily be re-employed. Increasing commercial losses caused the mine owners, in large part the steel industry, to seek government help. In 1968 the Government passed the Coal Adoption Law; this was the first formal attempt at a policy for coal. The law provided for the Ruhr coalfields to be incorporated into a single private company Ruhrkohle AG (RAG). The capital of the company was financed by a government loan repayable over 20 years; two large share-holders in the new company were VEBA with 14.1 per cent and Gelsenberg with 13.1 per cent. In the subsequent musical chairs around these two companies the RAG holdings were consolidated into VEBA, which is now the largest shareholder with 27.2 per cent of the capital.

The somewhat more cheerful economic conjuncture in 1967 and 1968 actually permitted a slight increase in coal use which continued up to 1970 when the downward trend set in once more.

The events around 1973 did more harm to coal through the induced economic recession than they benefited it through the sudden advantage in price compared to oil. The principal efforts to stabilize demand for coal were an equalization levy to subsidize coal burning in electricity supply and the introduction of a restriction on imports from third countries of about 5 million tonnes per year. The equalization levy was a tax, the proceeds of which were paid to electricity producers in proportion to their consumption of coal to compensate them for the additional costs involved. An advantage of the manœuvre in German eyes was that it left unchanged, in manner if not matter, the market mechanism between mine and utility.

This *ad hoc* arrangement provided little long-term unity for the mines; it scarcely gave confidence in the profitability of future investment. Later attempts to stabilize coal consumption for power generation have concentrated on long-term contracts between the mines and the utilities. These are described in more detail later; they have been reasonably successful, in part because of problems with nuclear licensing and in part because of the concurrent quota on imports of coal from outside the Community. A symbol of the recovery was the opening of the first new coal-mine in 17 years, in October 1981 on the Ruhr. The mine is planned in conjunction with a mine-mouth power station.

The brown coal or lignite industry has nothing like the same problems; the resource can be produced cheaply. Production rose sharply after the oil crisis; 108 million tonnes in 1970, 123 million tonnes in 1975; in 1979 output exceeded 130 million tonnes. The dominant producer is Rheinische Braunkohlenwerke, the shares of which, thanks to wise decisions between the Wars, are held almost totally by RWE. The output is mostly used for power generation in RWE power stations.

THE PRESENT STATE OF AFFAIRS

The preceding sections treat of the historic evolution of energy policy in West Germany and in particular with the development of relations among participating institutions. The following sections deal with some of the more interesting aspects of the present situation.

RELATIONSHIPS AMONG UTILITIES

The electrical sector is characterized by what might be described as 'two dimensional pluralism'; two dimensional because not only are there many participants but they are also very different in nature. They differ from each other in size and function, in legal form and ownership and in their economic structure. There are three industrial groups: the public power utilities, industry generating for its own purpose, and the national railways. The public supply generates about 80 per cent of gross production with industry generating 18 per cent and the railways 2 per cent. Within the public supply, each individual company is entirely responsible for meeting its demand commitment according to the framework of the law; the principal relevant statute is the *Energiewirtschaftgesetz.*[18]

There are about 1,000 electricity undertakings in West Germany today, compared to the 3,000 which existed 20 years ago. By function the companies fall into three groups: the owners of the large power stations and transmission lines; the regional distributors, who may also have production capacity; and the local distributors. Each of these three groups has its own separate trade association. Most of them are also members of an association of public suppliers of electricity—the Vereinigung Deutscher Elektrizitätswerke (VDEW). By size the companies range from RWE, which generates 40 per cent of the electricity sold in West Germany, down to a municipal distributor with a domain of a few tens of square kilometres. The VDEW has reliable statistics on 680 of these companies, representing more than 99 per cent of total final deliveries. [19] Of these 680 companies, 46 produce, but do not distribute; 356 distribute, but do not produce; 278 produce and distribute.

The West German utilities differ also in corporate structure and ownership; it is customary to distinguish between:

1. Public ownership, in which 95 per cent or more of the capital is held by the Federal or State Government, cities or other local authorities.
2. Mixed ownership, where the share of public authorities of the capital lies between 15 percent and 25 per cent.
3. Private ownership, where 75 per cent or more of the capital is private.

Typically the publicly owned companies are municipal distribution companies supplying many small customers in highly built up areas. The privately owned companies account only for a few per cent of sales; they are generally found in thinly populated areas. The principal companies tend to be mixed enterprises. RWE is slightly unusual; it is in mixed ownership but although the majority of capital is privately owned, a majority of the votes are in the hands of cities and counties (not the Federal or State Governments); this arises because the shares dating from its inception carry disproportionately high voting rights.

A few statistics clarify the picture; those shown in Table 5.5 are for 1979.[20]

TABLE 5.5

Ownership of electricity utilities in FRG

	Public ownership	Mixed ownership	Private ownership	Total
Enterprises *with Production*				
Number of Companies	169	61.0	94	324
Capacity (GW)	15.7	54.1	1.8	71.6
Production (TWh)	50.6	244.1	4.0	298.6
Enterprises *with Distribution*				
Number of Companies	424	81	129	634
Area of territory (in 1000s of km²)	50.9	173.2	21.4	245.5
Sales to consumers (TWh)	93.8	183.3	9.8	286.9

Superimposed on the diversity of ownership is a diversity of legal form. The predominant form is the joint stock company (*Aktiengesellschaft*); companies of this form account for 83 per cent of final deliveries. The next most frequent form is the private company with limited liability (*GmbH*), 11 per cent of final deliveries. The third category is the *Eigenbetrieb* with 6 per cent of final deliveries; this is a peculiar legal form, limited to publicly owned companies, of historical interest, but little modern significance. The point of all this discussion is that although the industry is largely owned by public authorities of various sorts, it has predominantly the form of private enterprises, and indeed the companies are almost all run as private companies; this is especially true of the large producers where the public ownership is distributed among so many authorities of such conflicting interests that there is no opportunity for them to exercise any politically motivated influence. By and large the interests of the public authorities are identical to that of any other shareholder, i.e. that the dividends are good. It is almost unknown for municipalities to collaborate to exert political control. In times of recession especially, the dividends from RWE are an important contribution to municipal budgets. Generally also, and for RWE in particular, the municipal owners are of different party persuasion and that more or less does away with any possible coherent view.

Although public ownership may not have any effect on the way a company perceives itself and on the policies it adopts, it occasionally has an influence on the way in which the local community sees the enterprise. In Hamburg, for example, the Hamburgische Elektrizitätswerke is almost entirely owned by the city of Hamburg; the company has a share of the controversial nuclear power station at Brokdorf. Public ownership in this case has enabled nuclear opponents to put pressure on local politicians to exercise political control over the decision.

The third source of diversity within the utility structure is the different way in which the various utilities are imbedded in the economy at large. RWE is integrated backwards in coal and especially lignite; it owns almost all the shares of Rheinische Braunkohlenwerke, which produces some 110 million tonnes of lignite annually and delivers most of it to RWE's power stations. RWE is also tied into petrochemicals through Union Rheinische Braunkohlen Kraftstoff and therefore has incentives to find higher value added application for its power station fuel as petrochemical feedstock. It is integrated backwards into the uranium fuel cycle.

RWE also has an indirect stake (30 per cent of 25 per cent) in the second largest electricity supply company in Germany, i.e. Vereinigte Elektrizitätswerke Westfalen (VEW), which generated 10 per cent of West German electricity sales in 1979. Its position is different from RWE; it originated from mining companies selling power surplus to their own needs and it still has links with coal producers. The company's electricity production is based almost entirely on conventional thermal plant and it has only ever had one small nuclear power station—at Lingen, a BWR which has since been closed down. (It was shut down for repair after 9 years operation and the licensing authority took the opportunity to require such extensive retro fitting, without guarantee of permitting future operation, that VEW decided to decommission the nuclear section and run the steam turbine from a gas turbine and boiler).

The VEBA subsidiaries, Preussenelektra, NWK, Nordwest-deutsche Kraftwerke and VKR, VEBA Kraftwerke Ruhr, are different again. NWK generates its power from plants on the North West German coastal regions and has excellent access to imports of coal; it is the largest importer of coal in the West German electrical sector; the plants at Kiel and Hamburg work on coal from Poland, the USSR and South Africa. At the same time VEBA is the largest shareholder in Rurhkohle (27 per cent). Preussenelektra and NWK account respectively for 7.1 per cent and 7.4 per cent of final sales. VKR originates from Hibernia AG; it was founded in 1970 to take over the power-supply activities of that ancient company; its plant operates mostly on West German hard coal. The company possesses no transmission lines; but sells on to RWE, VEW and the other VEBA subsidiaries. The value of the combined electricity sales of the VEBA electricity companies in 1979 were some DM 3.5 billion; the value of group sales was DM 42 billion. Electricity generation for VEBA is in a sense a sideline, although a highly profitable one. The company evidently does not have the same conception of appropriate policies as would a company whose activity centred on electricity supply.

The fifth largest utility is Bayernwerke with 6.5 per cent of production. Originating from limited water power resources, the company was obliged to expand using other means; river borne coal, heavy fuel oil residues from refineries, and natural gas from local deposits and imports of USSR gas, for which the company is well located. Bayernwerke serves an area deficient in easily available sources of fuel for power generation. Nuclear power, independent of local fuel sources, is especially attractive. Unable to initiate nuclear power in isolations, Bayernwerke collaborated initially with RWE; that collaboration continues, although Bayernwerke now also has under construction its own 1,300 MW plant at Grafenrheinfeld on the Main.

Another utility with a pronounced character of its own is STEAG, which comprises the old pit-head power stations of the Ruhr coal-mines. STEAG maintained an independent existence when Ruhrkohle was formed in 1968. STEAG is 69 per cent owned by Ruhrkohle and is its largest customer for coal; its power stations have a capacity of more than 3,000 MW and deliver to the national electricity supply mainly through the system of RWE.

The behaviour of utilities is also conditioned by their profitability. RWE enjoys large rents from its lignite and its nuclear plants, especially Biblis A and B. Other utilities are in some difficulties, especially those burning natural gas. VEW has been especially badly hit; in the 1960s it made some good contracts with the Netherlands for direct imports of natural gas to its power stations; the Dutch recently revoked the price agreements in the contracts. Bayernwerke is also financially embarrassed by the price of the gas it buys from the USSR.

What is the consequence of this 'two dimensional pluralistic structure'? It presents itself to the outside observer as an uneasy balance determined by the intrinsic particularism of the actors and the extrinsic constraints on its exercise. Along the economic dimension, behaviour varies from simple monopoly to fierce competition, passing through a grey area of oligopolistic positions.

Monopoly behaviour is characteristic of the distributors who have concessions to supply granted by the public authorities. A system of price control operates, but in the case of a municipally owned distributor, the shareholders grant the concessions, give the wayleaves and control the prices. Not surprisingly profits are good and in many towns the utility will cross-subsidize public transport, which has to suffer competition from the private car and is more difficult to make pay.

At the other end of the range there is strong competition within the production function. This competition is for sales and, nowadays, for licences. Competition for sales can be expressed either by the electricity going to the consumer, or the consumer going to the electricity. A producer with capacity coming on line will go around regional and local distributors seeking outlets; when it has arranged sales it must then sign contracts with the owners of intervening transmission lines. So, for example, VEW recently contracted with RWE to use the latter's transmission lines to deliver power to distributors in South Germany. The owners of the transmission lines must allow their use on reasonable terms. There is difficulty when large industry wants to use the grid for transmitting between its own sites. That practice is not subject to legislation regulating the public supply, and the utilities can be difficult.

Competition can also be expressed through the relocation of industry to minimize power costs. Sales to large consumers are made under contract, not by published state controlled tariff; the difference in the cost of electricity from one location to another can easily be enough in a German context to decide the location of a factory, especially for heavy industry. There are numerous examples: when DOW chemicals decided to build a magnesium plant for Volkswagen body-shells it went around the country looking for the cheapest power; the intention of RWE's planned 1,300 MW reactor Biblis C was to deliver cheap power to the chemical plants of Hoechst. Industry plays off one utility against another to lower their prices. One consequence is that RWE does not need to expand territorially in order to attract new load. Differential power costs are likely to exacerbate the tendency for heavy industry to locate in the Ruhr and North, light industry elsewhere. Often indeed it is not so much the power station which excites the opposition of local communities; it is the industrializa-tion which tends to follow. West German utilities and industrialists are sensitive to this issue to a surprising degree; two firms have actually moved out of West Germany, to France and Canada, to get cheaper power and there is a real concern that heavy industry, especially base chemicals and non-ferrous metals, could leave the country.

Reflecting the changing preoccupations of the modern utility there is also substantial competition for licences to construct. Obtaining construction licences for any plant, coal or nuclear, is problematic in West Germany today. VEW has begun licensing procedures for two plants although it needs only one. In and around Recklinghausen there are nine licence applications for more than 6,000 MW of plant; RWE, VKR, STEAG and others are all trying to catch a site, push the process through and find a buyer at the end of the day.

The grey area of mistrust, and suspicions that oligopolistic positions are being exploited, arises mainly in the relationships between the large producers and some substantial clients. Complaints by heavy industry that they were prevented by collusion from receiving proper credit for surplus power generated from combined heat and power schemes were mollified by a government inspired voluntary agreement by the producers to offer more favourable terms. Voluntary agreements are a favourite feature of the West German free market which will deserve a later section to themselves. By and large, industrialists are believed to be satisfied with the new terms. Municipal distributors are less content; there is an increasing tendency for them to seek autonomy, although often they are unwilling in the event to bear the additional costs that autonomy incurs. Some municipalities have made medium voltage interconnections between their systems to reduce somewhat their combined reliance on the great producers. The cities of Cologne, Düsseldorf and Duisburg had a plan to construct their own high voltage grid so as to benefit from the economies of scale which would be available if they built their own large power plant. The plan has died but it indicates a new attitude of mind. The city of Cologne is still considering replacing part of the current presently bought from RWE under a concessionary agreement, by its own production. There was a period when large urban power stations were thought of as environment-unfriendly; they are now viewed with more favour because of their association with district heating, a technology which has a good image. The big utilities now tend to be seen as unfriendly and it is judged politically desirable for a town to control its own electricity supply even at some extra cost. How long this backlash of municipalities will last is hard to say; it will probably depend on how successful cities are in introducing district heating and cogeneration into their distribution territories.

The balance between intrinsic particularism and extrinsic constraints can also be seen in a spectrum of political behaviour ranging from dominance to representation. It is astounding to an outsider to see the extent to which utilities accept their diverse interests being represented by one body, and that the arrangement works so smoothly. One thinks of the contracts between the utilities and the coal-mining industry agreeing to burn large and specified volumes of domestic coal into the distant future. The details of these contracts are sketched later, for the moment their interest lies in the capacity which they reveal for utilities to act together. The legal context of the agreement comprises at one level an agreement between VDEW and the coal producers association, plus an agreement between the coal producers association and the industrial generators of electricity who sell to the grid. The implementation of this agreement involves separate contracts between the utilities and the producers, the details of which are not yet completely settled.

The utilities did not like signing the agreement, but they realized that if they did not comply there would be legislation. Despite the conflicts of interest, this relatively subtle threat was sufficient to persuade the utilities to reach agreement among themselves. It is probable that this process of representation depends on the dominance of RWE. Once the terms, and in particular the price conditions, were acceptable to RWE it was able to deliver an agreement within VDEW.

RWE's dominance is most clearly evident in the nuclear domain; it has the largest capital stake of the utilities within the nuclear fuel cycle and has an influence at almost every stage; it is the leading actor in co-ordinating the activities. It was RWE which decided to attempt to standardize reactor design and thereby cut costs, improve performance and simplify licensing procedures. It was RWE which promoted the formation, in 1974, of working groups composed from the main utilities and reactor suppliers to argue the specifications for the standard reactors. And when in mid-1976 the decision was taken to put the idea into practice by instituting licensing procedures for three similar 1,300 MW plants, two of them, Vaknum and Biblis C, were applications by RWE, the other was from VEW for a plant at Hamm.

The dominance of RWE is still increasing, although over the last 4 years it has presented a lower profile. The Cartel Office fought RWE in several cases when RWE tried to buy up distribution companies. The office lost but RWE was made aware that it was under political scrutiny. In 1977 the Cartel Office successfully prevented RWE from buying Gelsenberg's holding in Gesellschaft für Energiebeteilung (GFE); RWE already held 46 per cent of GFE, the purchase would have given it complete control. The attraction of GFE to RWE and the nervousness of the Cartel Office, arose from GFE's 25 per cent share in STEAG. The acquisition would have given RWE a substantial influence within that producer. RWE was also prevented from absorbing VEW when the latter ran into serious financial problems after the Dutch revoked their contracts for natural gas. The fusion was prevented partly by the Cartel Office, but also by RWE's shareholders who had no enthusiasm for the purchase of a loss-making company.

Other utilities appear to accept this dominance, if ungraciously. Their real fear, shared by RWE, is not of RWE, but of socialization by the State. To some extent they are protected from this by RWE itself which by its sheer size and competence can ensure that the sector as a whole responds to the demands made on it.

The working of particularism within constraints explains some of the economic and political behaviour of the utilities. Much the most interesting relationship occurs at the interaction of the two areas; the political economy of the great investments in electricity production and transmission. The relationship between utilities affects the operation of the existing investment, the choice of new productive investments and innovation in the available means of production. In other words the relationships affect how the investment is used, extended and improved.

Collaboration in the operation of the power system is apparently limited, at all levels. The management of the local distribution companies have a certain entrepreneurial flair, but operate in a limited perspective; they concentrate on the immediate problems of supplying their area rather than on equilibrating costs among distributors. The complex systems of contracts between suppliers can also restrict flexibility. For example, there is a tendency for the boundaries of municipal authorities to expand and for the cities to acquire jurisdiction over surrounding areas. When this happens the municipal electricity distribution may attempt to supply the surrounding area, but may well be frustrated by existing contracts between the old distributor and the regional supply company. This can have a real dimension because it can end up in large price differentials on either side of a street within a single municipality.

Optimal operation of generating capacity is similarly restricted. There is little attempt to equilibrate marginal costs nation-wide. Grid interconnections are used to prevent complete loss of load in either participating domain, but not generally to give optimal scheduling of plant. This is consistent in a way with the idea of competition. If utilities co-operated perfectly to equilibrate marginal costs among themselves then it would not be possible for them to compete for sales; the offers to supply any market would be identical. Competition depends on less than perfect co-operation.

When it comes to co-ordination of new investment in production and transmission, the plans are co-ordinated within a select group of those utilities which own the public system of high voltage transmission lines. The members of this group compare their investment intentions and discuss whether or not there is free capacity in transmission or production. The idea is not to have centralized planning, but for the participants to have to inform each other of their plans so that decisions are made on the basis of as good information as possible. How effective this is, is difficult to judge. It is scarcely possible that this procedure will lead to the overall lowest cost provision of generation and transmission. But there are positive elements. The autonomy of the utilities leads them to give greater attention to the maximization of local resources than might a national body, e.g. coal in the mining regions, water power in the South. Also the integration of utilities vertically rather than horizontally has a stabilizing effect on fuel choice. The holdings which utilities have in coal-mining must affect their views of costs. When mining is separated from electricity generation, as in the UK, then the power producer will not perceive that a high proportion of the costs of mining coal are irretrievable; he will perceive prices that are set to recover such costs. The imperfection of prices as measures of costs will be somewhat reduced, at least in this respect, when the power station has an interest in the mine. In the long-run it could be that the power station will look elsewhere, but in the short-run the transition would be slower. It is impossible to prove this hypothesis; so many factors determine choice of primary fuel, but the theoretical case is plausible and anecdotally there is some evidence for the effect.

The operation of the utilities as private companies also affects their perception of risk; with the present licensing arrangements for nuclear plant and the high degree of public opposition the return from any investment in nuclear plant is problematic. The cash flow profile for an investment in a nuclear power station is weighted towards initial capital expenditure and the return is sensitive to delays in construction or operation. It is not easy for a utility to defend to its shareholders an investment of DM 2–3 billion for a 1,300 MW power station not knowing when, or if, it will be allowed to operate it. A nationalized utility would be aware of the same possibility but less acutely.

The future structure of an industry depends on innovation. How does the pluralist structure affect innovation? It may have reduced the rate at which nuclear power was taken up by the smaller producers. A more interesting question is whether it had any effect on the reactor lines which were developed. The unquestioned responsibility of the utilities for the choice of commercial plant undoubtedly brought about the rapid demise of the various West German nuclear reactor lines and established the LWR as the preferred line of development at an early stage. The fragmented structure of the industry was no impediment to an early and decisive choice in this instance. The utilities are often of different minds, but this can be a distinct advantage; whereas different currents of thoughts in one institution can engender internal strife, tergiversation, delay and eventual whimsical and compromising action, the same currents in different institutions permit different views to be experimented with and broaden the base of subsequent choice. RWE, for example, plumped for the BWR as the design for its first reactor; other utilities gave their support to the PWR, which later became the predominant type in RWE's own stock.

The advantages of pluralism for innovation at the downstream end are more evident. It allows many flowers to bloom. RWE undertakes the kind of promotion which could be expected from a utility conscious of the need to maximize the load on its productive capacity; it is active in research and development of bivalent heat pumps and has offered inducements to the first 1,000 users on its distribution systems, in the form of shared investment costs and reduced tariffs. RWE tends to be cautious about the potential of heat pumps and envisages that only a part of electric heating should have that form. The immediate problem is that heat pumps are not cost effective; fashion and government subsidies led to a big push in 1979 but sales fell off dramatically after the reservoir of those with surplus money was exhausted. There is now a considerable excess capacity for manufacturing heat pumps and a minor industrial problem.

An advantage of separating the distribution function from producers is that it gives incentives to explore the possibilities of more efficient planning of electricity supply along with district heating and gas, as part of the whole process of physical

development. This concept of regional energy planning is much
mooted in West Germany and described later in detail. It is not a
subject to which production oriented utilities willingly devote
effort. RWE has gone into some trial projects, but it freely admits
that it does so in order not to be blamed; it is less than half-hearted
participation. The thrust for this kind of innovation comes from
smaller municipal utilities whose primary vision of the world is
defined by the economic geography of a town rather than by the
exigencies of a national power system.

One last area of innovation deserves mention. RWE is deeply
involved through its brown coal subsidiary in research and
development on the gasification of coal, especially brown coal; it
owns more than 90 per cent of the large brown coal deposits
between Aachen and Cologne and its aim is to develop the means
of adding the greatest value to the raw material. Its preferred
strategy is to replace its brown coal-fired power plant with nuclear
and gasify the coal. The implementation of the strategy is delayed
because nuclear plant is delayed, but a commercial-scale gasification plant is already under construction. The plant will provide
synthesis gas for petrochemical feedstocks. The rather different
strategic views of different utilities lead therefore to the curious
position in which some utilities are buying natural gas to make
electricity while RWE is aiming to switch its lignite into feedstock
for a gasification plant. It is extremely interesting that an industrial
structure which permits such diverse relationships between companies in different sectors can have so significant an effect on the
innovative process as to make a utility a centre of research on coal
gasification.

The relationships within the gas industry are different; there is
less competition and more dominance. Competition among
companies is less because the marginal sources of supply are
imports from the North Sea or the USSR; these supplies can only
be obtained by the companies acting within consortia; they
therefore have the same costs and can scarcely compete for
downstream markets. Because there is no competition the
dominant position of Ruhrgas cannot be threatened.

The purchasing, transmission and distribution of gas to the
individual customers takes place as shown in Figure 5.1.

The existence of domestic producers does not much affect the
relationships between these components. Those companies fortunate

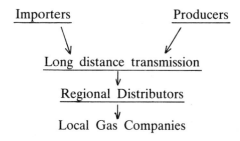

Fig. 5.1. Structure of the gas industry in FRG

enough to have domestic gas make good money in the favourable West German fiscal regime. The relationship between the components is determined by the obligation to import to maintain the size of the sector or to expand it.

In 1979, seven companies imported natural gas in the quantities shown in Table 5.6.

TABLE 5.6

Imports of natural gas by company

	br m^3
Ruhrgas	24.7
Thyssen gas	5.0
VEW	4.9
Energieversorgung Weser-Ems	1.4
3 others	4.7
Total	40.7

The importers use some of this gas for their own purposes (e.g. VEW) and sell some on to long-distance gas transporters and regional supply companies; the first four companies listed in Table 5.6 are also themselves long-distance transporters. Whether they arrange the transport to the regional distributor or whether they sell on to another transporter depends on who owns the intervening transmission system. It is clear that the similarity of marginal costs of supply and the well-characterized, inflexible infrastructure for distribution pose severe limitations on competition between any elements of the structure.

The way in which imports, domestic production and storage capacity are deployed to meet final demand does need to be optimized. This is done via carefully structured contracts between producers, transporters and distributors. The seasonal load variations tend to be followed by domestic production and Dutch imports. There is little flexibility in the Norwegian and USSR contracts, a little more with the Netherlands. With the domestic producers there are closer relations, also the lower commitment infrastructure allows output to be modulated without so great an economic penalty as is entailed in dropping the throughput of a line ending in the northern basin of the North Sea or Western Siberia.

The lack of opportunity to compete for supplies at the margin means that the majority of transporters have little to lose in letting Ruhrgas negotiate with suppliers for them, either as a direct representative or indirectly.

THE REGIONAL ENERGY SUPPLY CONCEPT

The ideas of district heating and the more advanced 'regional energy supply concept' (Regionale Energieversorgungskonzept) have acquired a considerable following in West Germany during the early 1980s. Among the advantages attributed to it are:

1. It substitutes for oil because in West Germany much domestic heating and hot water is provided from heating oil.
2. It increases markets for domestic coal.
3. It increases the number of energy carriers and, especially when produced in combined heat and power plants, it increases flexibility.

For opponents of nuclear power it reduces the need for electricity and therefore nuclear power stations. There is accordingly a wide consensus that these ideas should be encouraged.

About 8 per cent of the space heating and hot water in West Germany comes from district heating. Occasional attempts to push district heating by utilities have not been successful, even when cross subsidized by electricity sales. The infrastructure costs are high and there are all sorts of organizational difficulties. One oft-quoted exception to the generally bleak scene is the town of

Flensburg near the Danish border. Between 1970 and 1981 about 80 per cent of the town was converted by willing choice to district heating; virtually full connection is planned for 1985. This outcome was achieved in part through a decision of the town council not to distribute gas in the town; moreover the heating works benefit from imports of competitively priced coal from nearby Poland.

The Federal and State Governments have given massive financial support to encourage district heating. Between 1977 and 1981 grants of DM 730 million were given in a joint Federal-State programme in subsidies of up to 35 per cent to the capital cost of a district heating plant; investment incentives through tax allowances in the same period are estimated to have been worth DM 600 million. District heating is also eligible for subsidies from schemes supporting the construction of, or conversion to, coal-fired boilers. The programmes have been extended for 5 years, DM 1.2 billion being available for grants in this period. It is estimated that this subsidy should provide some DM 5 billion of investment.[21]

The introduction of another energy-carrying infrastructure naturally leads to the idea that areas should be reserved for different carriers according to their suitability. In the case of district heating this is especially promising if the infrastructure can be fed by heat from a power station or industrial site. This idea places severe stress on the organizational, political and legal capacity to adapt. The difficulties are best revealed by an example taken from the city of Frankfurt.[22]

The town of Frankfurt lies at the intersection of the zones of interest of three utilities; RWE, Preussenelektra and Oberhessische Versorgungs AG (OVAG). The demarcation lines between the territories of these companies go through the city; that means that none of them can deliver electricity or offer to deliver electricity outside its zone without written permission from the supplier to the zone on which it encroaches. The actual supply to Frankfurt is provided by three distributor/producers who buy from four utilities; each has a defined territory within Frankfurt. One of the distributors is the Stadtwerke Frankfurt which supplies its load in part from its own power stations and in part through contracts with Preussenelektra. The Stadtwerke has three combined heat and power sites in various parts of the city with a combined output of 340 MW (electricity) and 730 MW (heat); they burn, respectively, coal; fuel oil and refuse; gas. The three district heating areas are not interconnected; they are separated by gas areas. Gas is distributed by two different local utilities within well-defined domains; there are also direct sales by Ruhrgas to the Hoechst chemical works.

An attempt by the town council to bring the energy distribution within Frankfurt and surrounding towns into a single organization foundered on the inviolable demarcation zones of the great utilities. The existing district heating connections represent about 5 per cent of the heat load. Expansion of the connected heat load by the Stadtwerke is prevented by competition from the gas utilities and from the other electricity distributors. There are no legal instruments available for compelling or even inducing consumers to connect. The conflict of interest between the various utilities is particularly poignant as they are mostly owned by public authorities.

These examples give some idea of the organizational difficulties: the vertical diversity which separates the generation of electricity from its distribution is a positive factor in support of district heating, but the horizontal diversity which introduces particular conflicts of interests without means of arbitration is a negative factor.

Among supporters of the idea of regional energy planning there are mixed feelings about how to proceed. Political interests, typically within the SPD, argue for compulsion, not on consumers to be connected but on utilities to offer district heating where it is economic; the rationale is that in many towns there is no local power station any longer and it is not possible for the municipality to supply heat. By this means they estimate 25 per cent, even 40 per cent, of the heat load could be connected by 1995. There is also support for the idea that municipalities should grant wayleaves for district heating, as for electricity and gas. This is not supported by the Federal Government.

The local gas distributors, by and large, claim to be in sympathy with the idea; they also stand to gain. They support a discrete approach. Where gas and district heating are in the hands of a single supplier they imply there is a slow, disguised tendency to optimization anyway. Where the distribution networks are in different hands they rely on intelligent competition, voluntary agreement and political pressure without legislation.

West German cartel laws do not permit the various utilities to come to formal market sharing arrangements; they do permit them to *inform* each other of their future plans in order to avoid double investment. In some places, it is alleged, the electricity supply industry actually promotes district heating as their best chance of competing with gas. The difficulties are not exclusively organizational; money is a problem. The small utilities, though profitable, rarely have access to the kind of finance necessary for a district heating scheme. The great utilities have the money but no interest. The whole problem of how to organize the regional supply concept is presently the subject of study by working parties of the Federal and State Governments with the trade associations of the interested industries.

It is interesting to compare the variable capacity of West German towns to adapt to this idea. Some have managed well, Mannheim has district heating in the centre with an installed electrical generating capacity of 1,000 MW and gas in the suburbs, most have taken the easier option of buying and distributing gas. Much depends on the local institutional structure.

RATIONAL USE OF ENERGY

The rational use of energy received relatively little attention in the energy policy of the Federal Government until the second revision of the programme in 1977.[23] The Government's view was that ensuring economic use of energy was the responsibility of industry and the consumer; this attitude was severely criticized by the IEA in its review of the Energy Policies and Programmes of Member States. The discrepancy between government support of nuclear power through research centres and demonstration plant and the absence of support for conservation attracted unfavourable comment internally. In the second version of its energy policy the Government proposed a joint programme of subsidies with the State Governments. The programme made available DM 4.35 billion over 5 years for the subsidy by 25 per cent of the cost of investment in specified measures to conserve energy in the space heating of buildings.

The public image projected by the Ministry is still that price and the free market are the best means of achieving proper use of energy. Despite this, since 1975 the Government has taken seventy-nine separate administrative actions designed to reduce energy use. These actions include promulgation of standards for insulation in new buildings and in building undergoing extension or reconstruction; set standards of design for new central heating systems and the requirement that existing central heating systems be brought up to a specified performance. The Government has also succeeded in obtaining voluntary agreements with the manufacturers of domestic appliances and automobiles that they will improve the energy performance of their products. The manufacturers of gas and electric appliances have agreed to try to reduce specific consumption by 20 per cent by 1985. The West German automobile industry promised in 1979 to reduce specific consumption in 1985 by 12 per cent; so rapid was its progress that it came back in 1981 with a more ambitious target of 15 per cent. It goes without saying that these 'voluntary agreements' are negotiated by Government under the implied threat of legislation should a satisfactory agreement fail to materialize.

The Ministry is sceptical of the value of the DM 4.35 billion programme. Throughout West Germany it has become known as the 'window programme', because the principal detectable effect has been a rash of beautiful windows paid for, in part, by the programme because the windows are double glazed. The subsidies of DM 4.35 billion are estimated to have induced investment of DM 17–20 billion but it is extremely difficult to find anyone who confesses to believing that technically the results justify the expenditure. The State Governments, being starved for cash and moved but little by strategic arguments, were especially reluctant to continue. They wish that the programme did not exist; it takes time and people; it costs them money to implement for which they are not recompensed. The States tended to react to having the programme foisted on them by making the energy conservation loans conditional on other matters; in Wiesbaden, for example, in order to get the money, landlords were obliged to agree to let some apartments to handicapped people.

Against almost everyone's better judgement the subsidies will be continued when the present arrangements expire. The explanation for this contradiction is that the Federal Government recognizes that popular collaboration on the siting of nuclear plant will be more readily forthcoming if there is evidence of real and sustained support for energy conservation. Details of the continuation have yet to be worked out with the States; the Government has set aside DM 150 billion per year in subsidies; it expects an equal support will be given by tax allowances.[24] The emphasis of the programme will shift away from insulation: specifically it is aimed at connections made within the house to district heating schemes, at heat pumps and heat recovery.

Regardless of the effectiveness or otherwise of government intervention there has been a marked adjustment by the West German economy to higher energy prices, even though West Germany has always been, in terms of specific energy consumption, one of the most efficient industrialized nations in the world. From 1973 to 1980 the consumption of energy grew only by 3 per cent, while the Gross National Product increased by 17.5 per cent. Oil has been substituted in large quantities; from 1973 to 1981 the consumption of oil products in West Germany fell by 23 per cent.

The figures are impressive, but perhaps more impressive is the sense that energy policy is just one part of a permanent process of adjustment which industrialized countries must make to changed circumstances. The Third Revision of the Energy Programme makes a lot of the idea of 'adjustment as a permanent duty'.[25] This realistic perception is shared at all levels of society and by all actors, which gives it a tremendous strength. The trade unions recognize the inevitability of change and act to gain the best deal in that context rather than to resist absolutely. Individuals buy goods on the basis of their energy efficiency. Consumers react with extraordinary speed; to take a trivial example, almost every truck and caravan in West Germany is fitted with a deflector to reduce drag; they are almost unknown in the United Kingdom. Energy consumption is a major selling point not only for cars, but for other appliances such as televisions. Manufacturers appreciate that it is in their own interests to anticipate consumer wishes. It is beyond the scope of this study to enquire why German society is like this, but in any comparison with other European countries it is important to recognize that it is so.

RENEWABLES

To say that support for renewable energy in West Germany is lukewarm would be something of an exaggeration. Indeed an official in the Ministry of Research and Technology gave it as part of his purpose 'to avoid that the potential of the techniques is overestimated'.

There is little support for occasional projects, but the Ministry is well aware of the difficulties of promoting innovation in this area. It is sufficient to demonstrate a nuclear reactor line; it then either goes to market or not. But with solar heating housing, almost every project in different depending on the building, the occupants and the location.

The Government believes that the responsibility for the development of renewable energy systems can be borne by entrepreneurs and will be if they are indeed viable. There is nothing in West Germany comparable to the vast R & D programme in Sweden initiated by the Government for the purpose of preparing the transition to a non-nuclear energy economy.

Most government-financed work on renewables is undertaken with the intention of identifying technologies which can be sold abroad by West German firms, but even here there is nothing to match the scale of the French solar programme, inspired by the same aim. Federal spending in 1980 came to only DM 128 million.

Installation of a solar collector is eligible for a grant under the DM 4.35 billion scheme. The opportunity has been taken up to some extent; in Baden-Württemberg, for instance, there are somewhat more than a thousand units of this type. But as sceptics point out, this effort would have to be increased one thousand fold even to save 1 per cent of the fuel oil consumed in Baden-Württemberg.[26]

NUCLEAR

The main aspects of the present state of nuclear affairs in West Germany are best divided into three parts; the licensing procedure, the nuclear opposition, future prospects.

The Licensing Procedure

The licensing procedure in West Germany appears rather complex; in fact it is much worse than it looks; the following account is greatly simplified.[27] The basic legal framework is defined by the Atomic Energy Act (*Atomgesetz*) of December 1959.[28] The Law is implemented by the States, subject to Federal supervision of both the lawfulness and suitability of implementation. The original intention was to combine the advantages of a decentralized system of implementation, sensitive to local conditions, with the central power of the Federal Government, which would verify that the Law was enforced uniformly. The *Atomgesetz* was principally drafted with the aim of protecting people from the dangers of ionizing radiation; it requires that the scientific and technological status of a proposed development be shown to be the most up-to-date available before a licence be granted. Only the Atomic Energy Law and some associated decrees are legally binding; the technical standards elaborated by the various technical Commissions for reactor safety and engineering have no legal status; they are subject to legal control by the courts who may examine and evaluate them as to whether they are correct and appropriate. The notion that scientific standards should be subject to legal scrutiny gives to the courts great scope for discretion. It can also produce anomalies:[29]

It is incomprehensible for critical citizens that one administrative court, where only lawyers and no engineers are present, demands, for example, burst protection within the framework of the necessary precautionary measures in accordance with the latest technology, and, that only a few weeks later, another court does not consider this burst protection necessary for another similar nuclear plant.

The applicant for a licence is not usually in position to provide all the detailed technical information on the plant at the moment when he applies; a licence is therefore often split into partial licences, starting with a site licence for civil works and ending with a licence to operate the plant. Each succeeding licence application will require more detail than the application for the preceding licence. Often the issue of a licence will be made conditional on design changes or retro-fitting to bring work completed under an earlier licence up to the level considered to be the new state-of-the-art.

Under West German law any citizen has the right to intervene in the courts and object to the issuing of a licence if he believes that his personal rights or interests are affected. This right was incorporated in the Basic Law, or Constitution, after the Second World War and was intended to protect the citizen against the power of the State. Construction work on a site may be authorized while the objection is heard. But a decision by the court may take several years and the utilities therefore run the risk that the work carried out in this period will not be accepted by the courts and will have to be modified.[30] The citizen's right to intervene is not confined to nuclear plant. Indeed the most celebrated case was the application by STEAG to build a large coal-fired plant at Bergkamen; the group opposing the construction agreed to drop its opposition when the company offered it DM 1.5 million. In another instance a 700 MW coal-fired power station to be built at Vœrde in the Ruhr was halted by an action brought by one man.

It is this combination of the citizen's right to intervene and the discretionary power of the courts over technical judgements which is at the heart of the problem over licences. There are however three other points which do not help. They are: the diversity of institutions participating in the licensing process, the natural lack of good sites in West Germany, and the conceptual link which has been created between licences for new power plant and an acceptable means of waste disposal. The points will be discussed in the reverse order.

The link between reprocessing and new licences for power plant came about, as has been described earlier, as part of an effort to concentrate the minds of the utilities on the back end of the fuel cycle. It is now deeply regretted in Government, but there is no going back. It makes the acquisition of a licence for final disposal of waste crucial to the expansion of nuclear power in West Germany. The urgent need for this licence brings the Federal Government into direct conflict with the States, because it is the Federal Government which is responsible for final disposal. The Federal Government does not have the land to do this on its own account; it needs a licence from *one* State to provide a final repository for *all* States. The change of heart by the State Government of Lower Saxony over the site at Gorleben was not legally sound; the State agreed that the project was safe but felt it politically difficult to give a licence to become the 'Federal dustbin'. The Federal Government could have intervened, on the grounds that the State Government only had the power to check if the project was safe and if so it was obliged to give a licence. Politically this would have been unacceptable. The Federal Government has since tried to bribe Lower Saxony with compensating developments, light industry and a university, but to no avail.

The second exacerbating factor is the paucity of technically ideal sites. West Germany has a high population density and lacks good cooling. She does not have the extensive shoreline of France, the UK, Italy or Sweden on which to seek remote sites with good supplies of cooling water. The big rivers have been the carriers of industrialization and the population of West Germany is concentrated along their banks. The utilities would favour riverside locations in the vicinity of the great load centres in the cities, but the conflicts with popular sensitivities are here at their most acute.

The third exacerbating factor is the great number of institutions participating in the decision-making process. The States implement the Federal law under the supervision of the Federal Government. The State licencing authority makes intensive use of independent experts to give opinions and carry out tests; they rely in particular on the TÜV (Technischer Überwachungsverein). These are associations under private law which have for the past century supervised the technical safety of equipment requiring licences; each State has its own TÜV. There are many other advisory bodies. The decisions of the experts have no legal standing; they are re-evaluated by the licensing authorities. The Federal Ministry of the Interior monitors the proceedings and duplicates the technical investigations within its own expert committees. The Federal and State Ministries are subject to the Ministerial and parliamentary control of their respective Assemblies. The whole process is subject to the control of the courts. From this simplified sketch two facts are clear; the process is likely to be slow, and it could give eccentric results if the duties of the participants are not all clearly defined or if there is deliberate political infighting. Both conditions obtain.

The Federal Government is attempting to reform the licensing procedures. Several measures are contemplated. Two are of some interest: the idea of anticipating site planning and the 'convoy system'. Neither involves any legislative change. The idea of the anticipatory site planning is that State authorities in collaboration with the utilities should make a preliminary selection of possible power station sites well before they are likely to be required and that the needs for power production be incorporated into state development plans. The convoy system is an extension of the earlier RWE plan for standardized construction of LWRs. A reference plant design would be checked out in detail by one licensing authority and then subsequent plants would not be subject to the same scrutiny. The non-nuclear aspects of licensing could legitimately differ from State to State. The nuclear and non-nuclear aspects of the licensing procedure would therefore have to be clearly separated. The Federal Government is trying to persuade the States to co-operate, but is finding it difficult. The States are reluctant to give up any part of their autonomy. The chances of their allowing so highly charged a political issue as this to escape their scrutiny are slim. The State Governments have significant interests vested in the present process which they are unlikely to sacrifice to energy policy. The most likely outcome is that they will agree in principle to the idea of the convoy without, in practice, surrendering any of their authority.

The convoy system has now been put underway. In March 1982 the Ministry of the Interior in Bonn gave safety and technical approval to three 1,300 MW PWRs; Biblis C in Hesse (RWE); Lingen in Lower Saxony (VEW) and Isar II in Bavaria (Bayernwerke). The utilities must now seek licences from State Governments.

These reforms of the licensing procedure are bureaucratic matters which the public does not care about and which are unlikely to have much result. The only significant change could come from a revision of the *Atomgesetz,* but the Federal Government is extremely reluctant to go down that path because it would open up the whole question of nuclear energy to political and popular debate and scrutiny, with the most unpredictable consequences. It is a nettle that was conspicuously not grasped in the third version of the Energy Programme in December 1981.[31]

Nuclear Opposition

Opposition to nuclear power sprang apparently from out of the blue in 1975 when the regional authorities approved the construction of a 1,300 MW PWR at Whyl, on the Rhine, north-east of Freiburg in the State of Baden-Württemberg. Fierce local opposition culminated in large demonstrations, occupation of the site and violent police repression. In 1977 a Freiburg administrative court upheld the objections of the protest groups and ordered the inclusion in the design of a second concrete containment vessel. The question was then shelved by both sides and it was only in 1982 that the decision was reversed by the higher administrative court of the State. Objectors now intend to appeal to a Federal Court.

Somewhat similar, spontaneous opposition, occupation and violence occurred shortly afterwards at Brokdorf in the North. Three Mile Island did not help; it sparked off many anti-nuclear protests including a demonstration by 100,000 people in the autumn of 1980 on the lawns of the University of Bonn. These events all received wide attention from the media; the anti-nuclear movement quickly reached a high plateau and has stayed there ever since. No nuclear power plant has come into operation in Germany since 1978. The phenomenon is not confined to nuclear construction, although it is here that most people's feelings run highest. Airports, motorways and other public works have all been blocked. At one time the volume of investment affected by legal proceedings instituted by citizens' action groups was estimated at DM 25 billion.[32] This outburst of opposition in the mid-1970s was part of an important change in West German political life, the origins of which can be detected some years before they began to have this particular influence on nuclear construction.

West Germany enjoyed a student movement in the late 1960s and extra-parliamentary opposition much like that of other European countries. But the movement developed in its own way, rapidly stimulating lobbies of older, middle-class citizens, the *Burgerinitiativen*. These citizens' lobbies were a significant change. German social politics had been characterized from at least the nineteenth century by authoritarian relationships; they made a transition after the War into a political culture with marked material values—most succinctly expressed by Chancellor Adenauer's *Magenpolitik*. The enormous growth of wealth, the tremendous expansion of the middle class, were bound to destabilize conventional political alignments and this adjustment seems to have been precipitated by the student movements.

It is well-established that membership of citizens' lobbies tends to be middle class; civil servants, teachers, white-collar employees, professional people and students predominate.[33] These are all groups who cannot easily identify with the conventional polarization of politics along the axis of capital and labour. The citizens' lobbies are, at least in part, an attempt by this excluded, disfranchised group to create a class consciousness for themselves by action in a novel political dimension.

The lobbies operate mainly at local and regional levels and in so doing they contrast with organized capital and Government which increasingly has shifted to centralized decision-making at a national level. The members of lobbies are often educated and politically informed; they seek a new mode of participation in decision-making which does not simply involve giving loyalty and a free hand to party leaders. They also tend to reject the bureaucratic means by which political parties come to formulate policy and the process of compromise which it entails. The compound objectives to acting at local level, against materialist priorities, with uncompromised motives, in a political dimension not polarized by capital and labour, all find near perfect expression in opposition to nuclear power.

The citizens' lobbies are especially effective where there are strong local traditions and a high proportion of professional classes. Lobbies with an environmental bias will also attract local farmers. Freiburg is a good example: it has wealthy wine growers, strong traditions and a university. There is also a close link between resistance to the building of nuclear power stations and the consequent threat of extensive industrialization. At Whyl the nuclear issue focused resistance towards the State intention to create an industrial area there. Brokdorf became a symbol of the industrialization of the lower river Elbe. In contrast, the proposal by BASF to build their own nuclear heat and power station in the middle of a chemical complex at Ludwigshafen met with no resistance; the idea died subsequently on economic grounds. The militant opposition to nuclear development fights general industrialization but it can create more emotion about nuclear issues.

In their struggle against nuclear power plants the opposition has three main weapons: the ambiguities of the licensing system, the media, and the political tensions of a Federal State. The first of these has been dealt with already. The media is a crucial actor; it conveys information and opinions, sensitises marginal participants and creates awareness of opposition. It is not definitely and comprehensively anti-nuclear in outlook, but the unease which individually minded people feel about organized business and the State has a stronghold among those who work in the media. The coherence of industry and utilities in the electricity sector is strong; a collusion with public authorities is always suspected and the media naturally sympathize with attempts to reveal or fight those combinations.

The citizens' lobbies are skilful at exploiting rivalry and tensions between public authorities controlled by different political parties and in undermining the political confidence of parties in control of marginal constituencies. The governing majorities in many of the Federal States are slim. The citizens' lobbies put up their own 'Green Lists' of candidates and even if it is unlikely that they themselves will cross the 5 per cent barrier required for parliamentary representation they can cut away the margins of other parties. The FDP is especially vulnerable because its essentially liberal constituency is easily seduced and because its votes often fall between 5 per cent and 10 per cent of a poll. The effects of the citizens' lobbies on policy can be substantial; in recent local elections at Gorleben 18 per cent of votes went to various protest groups and the SDP vote dropped from 60 to 52 per cent.

At the conventional political level there is probably more support for nuclear power than at any time since the mid-1970s. The CDU have always been pro-nuclear; the party receives strong support from business and industry and in some CDU-controlled States in the Catholic South it is a regional issue; they lack coal and see no way of assuring themselves of a reasonable degree of autonomy in power supplies without nuclear energy. The FDP, liberal with a touch of nationalism, came round to a qualified agreement after a delicate debate within the party. The SPD has always, especially in opposition, expressed the clearest doubts. Its electoral strongholds are in the North, where coal not only provides an alternative but competes for Southern markets directly or as exports of electricity. Within the trade union movement there was some division between coal-mining unions and pro-nuclear manufacturing unions. That incipient conflict was defused by the agreement in 1977 between the coal producers and the electricity utilities to burn on average 33 million tonnes of hard coal equivalents of coal in their power stations up to 1977, but the general mood of the party remained cautious, with the leaders more sympathetic than the militant members. Even among unions with members from the nuclear industry there were different currents and some division between older people with memories of Weimar, Fascism and deprivation and younger people without that perspective. A union rally in Dortmund in 1977 one month before the SPD party conference in Hamburg brought the question to the forefront of party politics. The eventual party conference fudged the issue, declaring that the nuclear option should be kept open and yet that the future option to abandon it should not be closed. But the unions were more aware of the problem and set up technical committees to assess the potential of conservation, indigenous supply, renewables and the residual demands that must be made on nuclear. At the Berlin conference the party clarified its position: existing nuclear power stations should continue to operate, because the consequences for closing them down could be too great; stations in construction should be completed, but only put into operation when a satisfactory means of waste management was assured or when there existed sufficient intermediate storage capacity to cope with the discharge of irradiated fuel; new stations should only be licensed when a satisfactory means of waste management was assured. The links between waste management and licences was later confirmed by Government. This 'yes, but' verdict of the SPD congress is not as insignificant as it appears; it does mean that for the first time there is agreement among all parties; negotiation with State Governments is now not so grossly tainted by party politics.

The debate within the SPD was carried into the Bundestag. Following the Second Revision of the Energy Programme, the Bundestag set up an Enquiry Commission to investigate the determinants of future nuclear energy policy. The result of intensely conflicting views was a series of compromises within compromises between the antis and pros. The first compromise was to agree that there were two phases of nuclear philosophy: Nuclear I, where the technology was employed as a limited contribution to base load electricity generation, and Nuclear II, which involved closing the fuel cycle, reprocessing, fast reactors and a major resort to nuclear power. The antis forced the statement that one could not know yet whether massive recourse to nuclear power would be necessary until the potential of great efforts in energy conservation and other fuels had been properly explored. The pros were happy to agree to that providing that power stations could still be built and operated. A second Enquiry Commission has begun and will continue the analysis; in particular it will report on whether Kalkar should be completed and operated. It is preparing the decision as to whether or not to join

Nuclear II, but one can be sure that the final outcome of that debate is a long way off.

A discussion of nuclear opposition is not complete without further mention of the part taken by the West German association of trade unions, the Deutscher Gewerkschaftsbund (DGB). The unions have a tradition of recruiting able people to assist with their participation in industrial management and of training their own members for the same purpose; it is natural that they seek to influence government policies and the association has a large bureaucracy for this purpose. The unions informed much of the debate within the SDP and the Enquiry Commission; the compromise reached there reflects the compromise within the DGB.

There is also considerable concern in trade unions about the safety of workers in nuclear plant. There are indeed hard decisions to be taken in determining a balance between the safety of the workers and that of the public at large. If there is a fire within the reactor then the normal practice is to shut off the ventilation to protect the environment; this action could endanger workers. Similarly if there is a rapid increase in temperature, pressure and radioactivity then the containment is designed to lock automatically; the workers may then be trapped. The unions do not discuss these issues publicly, because they do not want to come into coalition with anti-nuclear forces. There is little sense of the anti-nuclear *résistance* which one finds in the CFDT in France.

Future Prospects

The First Revision of the energy programme published in 1974, just after the Yom Kippur War, envisaged the installation of 45–50,000 MW of nuclear capacity by 1985, with nuclear energy contributing 45 per cent of its electricity generation and 15 per cent of primary energy consumption. The Second Revision, in late 1977, envisaged 30,000 MW by 1985. It is now clear that these estimates were unrealistic; no more than 18,000 MW can be available by 1985. The status of nuclear plant, existing, in construction and planned is resumed in Table 5.7.

Advocates of nuclear power sense a new mood; they detect a fear in the population that the economic position of the Federal Republic is declining and that this will ease the resort to nuclear power. Local opposition will continue to challenge through the

TABLE 5.7

Nuclear power stations in Germany

Station	Type	Power Output (MW)	Year of Commissioning
Operating			
Kahl	BWR	60	1960
Karlsruhe	PHWR	55	1965
Jülich	HTGR	50	1966
Obrigheim	PWR	330	1968
Karlsruhe	FBR	20	1971
Würgassen	BWR	670	1971
Stade	PWR	660	1972
Biblis A	PWR	1200	1974
Neckar 1	PWR	855	1976
Biblis B	PWR	1300	1976
Brunsbüttel	BWR	805	1976
Isar	BWR	905	1977
Unterweser	PWR	1300	1978
Phillipsburg 1	BWR	900	1979
Grafenrheinfeld	PWR	1300	1981
In Construction			
Grohnde	PWR	1360	1984
Gundremmingen B	BWR	1310	1984
Gundremmingen C	BWR	1310	1984
Phillipsburg 2	PWR	1350	1984
Krummel	BWR	1310	1984
Vertrop	HTGR	305	1984
Mülheim-Kärlich	PWR	1310	1985
Brokdorf	PWR	1360	1986
Kalkar	LMFBR	330	1986
Whyl	PWR	1360	1988
Neckar 2	PWR	1310	1989
Biblis C	PWR	1310	1990
Hamm	PWR	1300	1991
Planned			
Neupotz A/B	PWR	2×1300	
Vahnum A/B	LWR	2×1300	

courts, but the utilities are beginning to get the hang of that and can contain the consequences. Revisions to the licensing procedure will be of modest assistance. The bulls would predict that four to six new reactors (4–8 GW(e)) would be licensed over the next 5 years. Most utility executives are more cautious, four to six more units over 10 years would, they believe, be a good result and two to three the more likely. The link between licences and reprocessing will not go away.

An unpredictable element is the peace movement. Those who see favourable omens everywhere think that the discussion of nuclear weapons within the peace movement will clarify in the minds of people the distinction between nuclear weapons and commercial nuclear power, with the result that they will more easily accept the latter. It is difficult to tell; there are at the moment contingent links; both appeal to the same emotions and are mutually reinforcing. The spectre of a dangerous nuke is in both cases a powerful image; members of the 'green' movement supported the peace demonstration in Bonn in Autumn 1981. But there is as yet no sign of any coherent anti-nuclear philosophy which demonstrates more than circumstantial connections between the two. The way that relationship evolves will probably determine the development of commercial nuclear power in West Germany in the short run.

COAL

The coal-mining areas are SPD strongholds. The party has given considerable support to the industry, partly by subsidies, partly by pressure on utilities to use more coal and partly by financing research, development and demonstration of new processes which promise to make accessible future markets.

Subsidies

There are a variety of subsidies for domestic coal. The State will contribute to the extra capital costs of building a coal-fired plant compared to a cheaper option (normally oil) or of converting an existing plant to oil. Subsidies are also paid to the utilities for burning coal; these are calculated as a proportion of the extra cost incurred by the utilities in burning domestic coal rather than imported oil or coal. The question naturally arises as to who pays. At one time the subsidies were paid out of general taxation, but some years ago the procedure was changed and the money was raised instead through a charge on electricity tariffs. The utilities argued that it was not correct to disguise this government inspired distortion of free market costs within their tariffs; consequently the increment to pay the surplus costs is entered separately on the bill to the consumer. The extra amounts to between 4–5 per cent on average; it is known as the *Kohlepfennig*. The revenues are paid into a special fund from which the subsidies are then financed. The revenues for 1980 were DM 1,827 million; more than half was paid out as compensation for the additional costs of burning domestic coal rather than imports. Compensation was still paid on the comparison with oil, because the grants related in part to past years; some 15 per cent of the revenues were required to finance capital grants. The Government estimates that some DM 2 billion will be required over the next 4 years for capital grants alone. The framework for paying subsidies to equalize fuel costs has recently changed as a consequence of the new coal burning agreement. The way in which coal producers and utilities arranged the legal framework of these agreements has been described. Here we describe their contents.

The first agreement was signed in 1977, for the period of 10 years between 1978 and 1987; it provided that the utilities would take yearly, on average, 33 million tonnes of domestic hard coal. Consumption in 1980 was 33.4 million tonnes. In January 1981 the agreement was extended until the end of 1995 and the quantities were revised to: 40 million tonnes in 1985; 45 million tonnes in 1990; 47.5 million tonnes in 1995.

The prices at which the coal is exchanged are fixed at a suitable level by the Minister for Industry. The extra cost to the utilities of burning the coal are calculated as follows. For about 11 million tonnes the industry is compensated for the extent to which the price of domestic coal exceeds imported coal. For 22 million tonnes it is compensated on the same principle, but with respect to oil, unless coal/oil price relativities change drastically this subsidy is unlikely to be paid. The coal over and above the run of those quotas is not compensated.

The utilities were much against the contract, they signed under Government threats of legislation in the absence of voluntary agreement. They did obtain a valuable concession: to burn imported coal. Up to 1987 they are permitted to burn imported coal, provided the volumes are no more than half of the volumes of domestic coal burnt; after 1988 the permitted proportion is one to one. About 10 million tonnes of foreign coal was shipped into West Germany in 1980; estimates of consumption by the end of the century are sensitive to what happens with nuclear power, but some forecasts go up to 40 or 50 million tonnes. Some of the West German coal companies, including Saarbergwerke and Ruhrkohle are buying into production abroad, mainly in the US and Australia.

Coal Conversion

Coal was converted to light liquid fuels by the chemists of IG Farben in the early 1920s and the processes employed in three large plants in the Ruhr before and during the Second World War. These plants were then converted to oil refining, and commercial interest in the technology died. The first significant sign of renewed interest outside research laboratories came with the publication of an Energy Technology Programme by the State Government of North Rhine Westphalia in 1974; a State which has a large vested interest in the future of West German coal. In the same year the Federal Minister for Research and Technology released a programme for non-nuclear research, *Rahmenprogramm Energieforschung* (which in 1976 was combined with the nuclear programme in an overall energy R & D policy). Between them these two government initiatives have put DM 1 billion into research on coal conversion technology. Several pilot plants are running or in construction; eight are designed to gasify coal and two are designed for liquefaction employing a modified IG Farben process.

As part of a response to the oil price crisis caused by the Iranian revolution, the Government gave its support to coal conversion and invited industry to submit projects. Fourteen projects were submitted costing DM 13 billion. On cooler reflection the Government came to the view that large-scale liquefaction and gasification of West German coal is unlikely to be economic in the foreseeable future. The only real rationale for development was in order to master the technology for export. There is a distinct embarrassment in the Ministry at having built up expectations of the technology and therefore of the coal industry, which they themselves no longer share. To salve, or compound, its embarrassment the Ministry has made available in its budget for 1982–85, DM 1 billion for gasification and DM 950 million for liquefaction.

The fourteen gasification projects sit on the Minister's desk, waiting for a decision. (Three projects are likely to be funded; the front runners are Shell, Klockner and a Ruhrkohle/Ruhrchemie combine).

There are a few bright spots; RWE is going ahead with its

project to gasify lignite. This is a commercial venture; it is intended to supply synthesis gas for chemical feedstock. The project has two advantages; lignite is cheap, and it has a high content of oxygen. The first is illusory from the perspective of a welfare economist, although it explains RWE's interest; the second is real. There is already uneconomic generation of power from hard coal and economic generation from lignite. Which coal to transfer at the margin from power generation to gasification should depend on the appropriateness of each as a feedstock; costs of acquisition are strictly irrelevant.

There is also recognition that processing of foreign coal will be commercially viable before processing of domestic coal. This is of interest to West German constructors and manufacturers, because they could contract to build process plant in Australia, South Africa or the USSR. It has the classical economic advantage of minimizing transport costs and the modern political advantage of exporting pollution costs. Interesting, but distinctly *sub rosa* at the moment, is the idea of gasifying Soviet coal using West German technology and transporting the product back by pipeline. Discussions on the prospects have been held at Ministerial level, but it is not something which the West German Government has included in its Third Revision of the Energy programme.

In a paradoxical way, the brightest, or at least the most expensive, star in the firmament of coal gasification is the High Temperature Nuclear Reactor (HTR). The first HTR came on stream in West Germany in 1968, before the first PWR; it has an inherent safety potential that is of dubious practical value and it generates power at twice the cost of an LWR. A prototype with a capacity of 300 MW is now under construction and should be commissioned in 1985. The future of this reactor has been in doubt for some years; it is kept alive because of political pressure. The concept is promoted by the government research establishment at Jülich, but more importantly it is paid in part by the Ruhr-containing State of North Rhine Westphalia. The HTR is being presented as the means towards a bright future for German coal; the argument is predicated on the fact that the reactor can provide heat at a temperature which is suitable for gasifying coal. There are problems. Only 20 per cent of the heat input to coal gasification is needed at high temperaturers; 80 per cent is required as low pressure steam. The 20 per cent can be provided from the combustion of char from the process and the 80 per cent of steam is more cheaply available from an LWR. If the process were economic, the materials to provide the coupling between the two processes would still not exist. The idea of using the HTR as a means of gasifying coal is accepted on all sides as a fantasy, but no one likes to say so, as it might persuade some of the mining unions to become anti-nuclear and disturb the delicate balance of nuclear opinion. The HTR is being used as a means of pressuring, on balance, union support for nuclear power.

OIL

There is not much to write about the operation of a free market; this is one of the market's great unsung advantages. There are perhaps two points of principal interest, which relate respectively to the structure of the market and the consequences for government intelligence of not having a direct or indirect State presence in the international oil industry.

West Germany is the largest oil consumer in Western Europe; it burnt 129 million tonnes in 1980, representing 48 per cent of its total primary energy. Much of this was imported as product. 94.7 million tonnes of imported crude oil was run through West German refineries in 1980, along with 4.5 million tonnes of domestic oil. Total primary refining capacity stood at 154 millon tonnes, giving a load factor of some 64 per cent.[34]

The various refiners on the West German market comprise three groups:[35]

1. The great international companies which have been represented for many years; they own some 52 per cent of refinery capacity.
2. West German refiners: VEBA, Wintershall, Union Rheinische Braunkohlen Kraftstoff and Saarbergwerke, with 27 per cent.
3. The international newcomers, many of whom entered the West German market in the 1960s on the back of the switch to North African imports; the group includes European firms (AGIP, Elf, Fina, Total) and American (Texaco, Chevron, Conoco and Marathon).

The petrol and automotive diesel products of VEBA, Mobil and

Wintershall are marketed through a joint, (VEBA controlled), company, ARAL. ARAL is the market leader for these fuels with some 25 per cent of sales.

One of the main features of the West German market is its high dependence on imported products, which is a direct consequence of its open, free market structure. In 1980 imports of products were about 40 million tonnes, almost one third of total consumption. These imports are concentrated by region and product. Regionally they predominate at the coastal ports and along the Rhine; a product pipeline links centres of consumption along the Rhine and Main rivers. By type, the imports are predominantly gas oil; they are imported partly by the refiners, but also by independent traders. These independents have about 15 per cent of the market; they have built up a central buying company to obtain better terms for purchases. At the moment they buy spot and have contracts for products with Belgian and Russian refiners. They may in the future attempt to make crude contracts with producers and contract refining capacity.

The high proportion of imported products is closely connected with the free market. There are always imbalances in supply and demand contracts within the industry and these find expression in spot market sales of products. Most European markets are constrained in some way that damps their response to any change; the West German market being unconstrained is therefore a point in the system where the process of equalization through product sales takes place. On the other side of the coin, the free market gives scope for entrepreneurs to make a living from the inevitable structural imperfections of the oil industry, whatever they may be at any time.

As a result of open access, the absence of price control and the high volume of imported products, the West German market experiences larger price swings than most.[36] Broadly speaking West German prices are lower in periods of surplus, e.g. preceding the Iranian revolution, and higher in periods of shortage, e.g. 6 months later.

It has been claimed by other European Governments that this rapid response of West German prices has deleterious effects for other oil importing countries because it drives up spot market product prices, which in turn puts pressure on spot crude and crude contracts. The system adapts less rapidly on the way down because OPEC attempt to protect their own prices on the downswing. On this view this process of 'ratcheting' is exacerbated by the free West German market.

This argument has not shaken West German confidence in the workings of its system which is claimed to have kept West Germany supplied throughout successive crises. Other countries with controlled markets have also been supplied throughout these crises and one wonders whether commitment to a free market is what really lies behind the policy. An alternative consistent with other sectors of energy policy would be a series of agreements between Government and industry based on voluntary collaboration. These agreements work in other sectors in West Germany because industry is able to organize itself, in continuity with its long history of cartellization. The difficulty with the oil industry is that control of the quasi-cartellized industrial half of the negotiating forum would lie outside West Germany in the hands of the international oil industry. In those circumstances a free market has considerable operational attractions.

The fact that the principal interests of the West German Government in oil policy are to stabilize international markets in times of crisis and to speed up and increase their access to information about the oil industry does not conflict with this thesis. The Federal Government has persuaded the companies to part with statistical information on their operations on a voluntary basis. This move derived from the intense criticism which the Government suffered in 1974 when prices rocketed. The public was easily persuaded that the companies were 'price gouging' and the Government had no means of denying or confirming this accusation with the data available to them. The Federal Government's domestic interest in price transparency has since been translated to higher spheres. It is a principal objective of Germany within the European Community (EC) and the International Energy Agency (IEA). The other international priority has been to try to persuade the member states within the EC and IEA to make careful preparations for crisis management; for example to use compulsory stocks in a systematic way when there is market tension. Both priorities, information and crisis management, could be seen as an attempt to carry to an international level the kind of

organized relationship between Government and industry practised domestically in other sectors of West German energy supply,
but which is not suitable in the oil sector.

PRICING

A principal, perhaps the principal, means by which Government
effects policy is through control of prices. Price control is part of
real policy which may not be consistent and indeed may be in
flagrant conflict with *paper* policy. (The contradiction between the
Italian Government's nuclear expectations and its vicious control
of ENEL's electricity prices is a case in point.)

It is recognized in West Germany that electricity and gas
distribution companies are local monopolies and that the prices at
which they offer their services must be monitored and controlled
by the State. In practice, gas is considered to be in competition
with oil products and there is little legislative action. The fact that
distribution companies are generally owned by local councils is
supposed to guarantee that their monopoly position will not be
abused—why anyone should believe that is difficult to understand.
Tariffs have to be published, so companies getting out of line are
detectable. As already noted, the industry is reasonably
homogeneous depending on much the same marginal source of
supply and without much scope for collusion among suppliers.

More attention in practice is paid to electricity prices. Tariffs for
domestic consumers are published. The Cartel Office studies these
tariffs, but it has powers only to decide whether there has been an
abuse of the market; it compares similar situations to see if there is
evidence of discrimination, it does not compare prices in specific
areas with the corresponding costs of production. Generally the
Office is not thought to be particularly effective in this function.

The States also monitor prices. Their procedure is quite
different. The utilities have to prove that costs justify an increase.
In the past this was a formality; control now is still far from
oppressive but is somewhat more demanding than it was. The
regime varies from State to State. North Rhine Westphalia is
considered to be one of the tougher States; it demands from the
four large utilities operating within its borders detailed accounts of
the costs of their operations. The picture is different for the next
level of enterprises who do not produce much of the electricity

which they supply, e.g. a town like Wuppertal in North Rhine Westphalia has a single power plant of its own and buys in most of its supply; the utility would not be obliged to give very detailed costs breakdowns because most of the relevant information would have been collected from the big four. The general trend at this level is to permit price increases proportional to those of the large producers.

In truth the procedure is largely an administrative check on efficiency; to be anything more would require a depth and breadth of technical expertise which the States do not possess. It is politically desirable for the States to appear to be getting tougher on prices, but the general feeling, inside and out of utilities, is that for the time being and for the foreseeable future the utilities will get their way. In this context the deciding factor is that the public authorities are the shareholders and their revenues are an important contribution to their budgets.

ENERGY POLICY AND FOREIGN POLICY

Chancellor Helmut Schmidt is reported once to have observed, 'For some years now our economic policy has simultaneously been our foreign policy.' The implication of the assertion is that the exercise of economic advantage is a necessary, and possibly a sufficient, means for the procurement of as much as practical of the gross international product and for the stabilization of international and domestic economic activity. Exploration of this idea is far beyond the scope of this study, but there are aspects of West German energy policy which are important, yet which are easily passed over if not viewed in this light.

The most striking example is provided by the economic relationship of West Germany to Middle East oil producers. While France and the UK have tried to exploit traditionally political links with the Arab world in pursuance of economic advantage, the West German Government has, with occasional moments of weakness, allowed its economic advantages to replace political manœuvring. A consequence of the successive large increases in oil prices has been the accumulation by OPEC of exceedingly large surplus revenues which they have directed into industrialization of their economies. This process requires the purchase of capital goods and equipment and the elaboration of infrastructures of all types. A vast market sprung up over night with few pre-existing economic ties. The ability of West Germany to deliver high quality goods on time, to a price, inevitably attracted to her a proportion of these new orders quite in excess of the enforced contribution by West Germany to the producer surpluses. In 1972, West Germany ran a trade deficit with the OPEC producers of DM 2 billion; in 1974 the deficit rose steeply to DM 11 billion. But by 1975, while the majority of industrialized countries were still running heavy deficits, West Germany had brought hers down to only DM 300 million.

It is probably better understood in West Germany than elsewhere that economic and industrial advantages like efficiency and the capacity to adjust are directly relevant to proper management of the 'energy crisis'. West Germany is sometimes said to be complacent about oil and the complacency is attributed to her belief in her ability to buy her way out of trouble. Perhaps a more accurate description of the same general idea would be that West Germany understands that energy is too important a matter to be left to energy policy. It is not a matter of substituting new political relationships for ancient concessions in oil rich states and of substituting new energy forms for oil; it is also a question of adjusting industrial behaviour to a quite different distribution of economic power.

The USSR gas contract is another matter wherein the West German appreciation of the issues involved incorporates belief in the stabilizing influence of economic liaisons. Much as the official organs deny the charge, there can be little doubt that a reliance on the USSR for 30 per cent of gas supplies is dependence. Dependence like everything else operates at the margin and 30 per cent is a large margin. A principal sanction which the industrialized world has on Soviet behaviour is economic reprisal. If the USSR can respond to economic sanctions with suspension of gas supplies then it has an immediate and effective retaliation on the economic level.[37] There are technical arrangements for mitigating the effects of such an action, but West German confidence in the soundness of the deal is based for the most part on the considerable economic incentives to supply gas regularly. The contract requires the USSR to pay for the pipeline up to the border of Czechoslovakia and West Germany. The cost is likely to be DM 20 billion or more, financed by West German banks. The

USSR, according to West German financial experts, requires a steady income of foreign exchange and cannot afford interruptions in supply. One does not have to find this argument convincing to see in it the same basic ideas that, in the long run, sound economics makes sound foreign politics because in an economic bargain both sides benefit and are loath to jeopardize their gains.

WHO MAKES ENERGY POLICY?

The civil servants in the Ministries of the Federal Government are inclined to deny disarmingly that energy policy has anything to do with them; it is formed by the free market, they say; the Energy Programme is not really a programme, it is more of a 'looking back and pointing out how we will go on'.

It is certainly true that the West German Energy Programme, published in 1973 and revised in 1974, 1977 and 1981, has a peculiar stamp to it. The Third Revision contains hardly any numbers, in striking contrast to the energy section of the Eighth French Plan. There is instead emphasis on the need to adjust and on the implications of that need for individual citizens, local authorities, industry, commerce and State Governments. Superficially the most striking absence is of any government forecast. Instead, research institutions are commissioned to prepare forecasts; these institutions are subsidized by the Federal and State Governments, but they are independent. The Ministry claims to have little or no influence over the content of the institutions' report. 'We often do not believe the forecasts, but we have no real competence; we cannot say that our studies say otherwise.' In fact there is evidence that the Ministry is not as passive a participant as it sometimes claims, but whether that matters much is open to question because, in the words of one civil servant, 'We never change our policies on the outcome of the Institutes' work.' There is a great deal to be said for this approach. The notion that policy making somehow consists of endless Tables of numbers of doubtful accuracy and meaning relating to the far-distant future is one of the minor lunacies of the second half of the twentieth century; no amount of evidence about the appalling track record of this practice seems to weaken its appeal. The Federal Government has found a means of incorporating the obligatory Tables in its work without having to take any responsibility for them. This is eminently sensible, especially as the Government is of the view that it lacks the means of control of the economy to bring about any predetermined end.

To accept that the Government's control of policy is limited is one thing, but to swallow the reiterated assertion that policy is the product of a free market is quite another. One can distinguish at least five ways in which Government intervenes: by subsidies, by price control, by administrative action, by voluntary agreements, and by changes to the institutional structure.

The subsidies are massive: central and local government support to the coal industry in 1980 was DM 6.3 billion (DM 6.9 billion in 1979). This sum does not include the compensation paid to electricity utilities for burning extra coal or the subsidies to coal-burning plant (DM 1.8 billion in 1980). From 1978 to 1982 DM 4.35 billion were made available in grants to conservation; over the same period grants of DM 730 million were made available for district heating. DEMINEX received DM 1400 million up to 1982 in subsidies to encourage prospection for oil. Nuclear developments have been aided by state finance of research laboratories and by contracts for demonstration plant. The Federal Government support for the fast reactor has been crucial; it is paying 62 per cent of the cost of the prototype at Kalkar, i.e. a contribution in excess of DM 3 billion.

Price control of the services of utilities is not severe, but this is an act of policy as much as rigid control would be. Electricity is distributed through local monopolies; there is no free market at the consumers' end. How much profit to leave to the utilities, and consequently what financial capacity to permit them, is a political decision.

The Federal Government took seventy-nine separate administrative actions between 1975 and 1980 aimed at obliging efficient use of energy; it may also introduce legislation to permit local authorities powers to implement the regional planning concept. At the same time it has made a continuous administrative effort to untangle the licensing procedure for nuclear plant.

The 'voluntary agreements' between the Federal Government and industrial groups are perhaps the most typical modifications brought to the workings of the free market. They are always made under the threat of alternative compulsion through legislation. Sometimes industry is acquiescent, as with the agreements to improve the efficiencies of motor cars and domestic appliances; at other times it is less compliant, e.g. the agreements between utilities and mines on coal burning. Voluntary agreement is a possibility for implementing the regional planning concept. These voluntary agreements are powerful weapons; they depend on the ability of industry to organize itself, in their organizational demands they are reminiscent of the Cartels and the Coal Syndicate.

The Federal Government has intervened decisively in the institutional structure. The reconstruction of the coal industry in 1968 required Federal and State guarantees for the industry's debts. The Government determined the design of the national oil company; it twice overruled the Cartel Office to obtain the end it desired.

How then can the notion that policy is a matter of market forces be so prevalent in West Germany? It is in the interest of most of the actors involved in policy making to go along with the disingenuous thesis of free market forces. 'Free forces' implies things impersonal, aspects of nature; if they are the spring of policy then all the participants are but acting out their predestined parts and count for nothing in any value judgement that is implicit in the outcome. This is part of the answer, but it is not complete. There exists also a recognition that the free market is an economic instrument among others, which has its place in the proper context. High energy prices induce consumers to adapt their behaviour and they give to the producers the financial capacity to adjust their assets and sources of supply. West German energy policy is driven therefore by market forces operating within a framework determined to a substantial degree by government decision. But in that respect it is like energy policy everywhere; it is scarcely a characteristic of West Germany.

The attempt to understand the importance attributed to market forces in West German energy policy leads then to two propositions, one cynical, one banal. There is a third possibility. The success of the West German economy since the War has its roots in a consensus among the owners of the means of production, not only capital but also labour. Government has tended to let this consensus have its head and step in with peripheral adjustments—*flankierende Massnahmen.*[38] In that sense policy is in large part left to forces outside Government—whether it is accurate to call them market forces is another question.

So which are the actors within the consensus who determine the direction of policy? Where does the initiative lie? There are the obvious choices, the great industrial corporations: RWE, Ruhrgas, KWU. For those who do not like the obvious there are the banks.

Since the beginning of the twentieth century the big commercial banks have been closely involved in the decisions of German industry and they came to be seen as the 'grand strategists' of the economy. The prevalence of this view owes much to Shonfield's analysis:[39]

The banks have always seen it as their business to take an overall view of the long term trend in any industry in which they are concerned and then to press the individual firms to conform to certain broad lines of development. They saw themselves as essentially the grand strategists of the nation's industry.

A moment's thought reveals this to be an essentially plausible proposition. Business men, by and large, reckon they are cleverer than other business men; they always accept restrictions of cartels with some reluctance and are easily tempted to undermine the common good if they detect individual opportunities. Banks in contrast know that one business man is much like the next and perceive a clear need to restrain behaviour. The participation of the banks in the elaboration of the pre-war cartels is undeniable; they took an active part in the electrification of Germany. They still have directors on the Boards of the classic Ruhr concerns and they are especially thick on the ground in the nuclear industry. At one stage the commercial banks had their representatives in one in three of the seats on the Supervisory Boards of the biggest companies in Germany, apart from those confined by law to representatives of the workers. Banks are still the main source of finance for companies in the FRG; the stock market is relatively weak and only the biggest companies have access to share capital. No doubt the banks continue to exercise a substantial degree of control over general business policy. Whether they are still the 'grand strategists' is less sure. Many large energy projects are financed by loans and the banks take a creative role; the negotiations with the USSR on the natural gas pipeline to Russia made considerable demands on the financial institutions.

The preoccupation of the bankers, however, is whether they will get their money back. They study the energy economy and make their decisions on whether a project is sound, but they no longer have the means of directing large sectors as a whole. The old system of a house bank, whereby a firm had an exclusive financial relationship with a single bank, made for collaborative assessments of policy. Firms now go where they can get the best terms and the opportunities for sustained influence by particular banks on sectorial policy is far less than in the past. Even the market share of the big West German commercial banks dwindled; they have only 10 per cent of banking business today.

This brings us back to the obvious, to the great firms as the initiators of policy. The list begins with RWE. If one discounts VEBA, whose size is inflated by other activities, then RWE is the largest energy company in West Germany. It straddles the private and public sectors and penetrates at all levels into the administration, the States, the municipalities, the Federal Government. It has a wide range of affiliation with other electricity supplies; few electricity companies are not related to RWE in some way. It has close links with the coal-mines and the mine-mouth power stations of VEW and STEAG. It is the dominating participant in the nuclear fuel cycle and the only one to be represented at every stage; it is the natural co-ordinator of that exceedingly complex set of industrial processes and the only participant whose own requirements can be determinant on the structure. It has money from its considerable rents from lignite and nuclear; its prices are controlled by its shareholders; technically and economically it has many chances to confirm and extend its dominance in sales and in control of upstream facilities. Moreover, and perhaps most importantly, it has the vision. It has provided leading figures influential in policy making; particularly celebrated is Professor Heinrich Mandel, a major promoter of nuclear energy over two decades and eloquent proponent of the PWR and FBR at critical stages. Its links outside of electricity supply give it the incentive to conceive of a broad policy; in its long-term strategy of replacing lignite in power generation by nuclear and gasifying lignite it has aims for the future which come nearer to a complete energy policy than do those of any other participant. In keeping with its 'extra-commercial' vision, the company has a large public relations activity, is fairly highly bureaucratized and engages heavily in planning and research. It displays consummate skill in playing off many interests.

It is not possible for the Federal Government to make policy in the electrical or nuclear sectors without the consent of RWE. If the Government needs to get something moving it turns to RWE in the expectation that if RWE does it the others will follow; for example the Ministry of Research and Technology turned first to RWE to pick up the future costs of Kalkar.

That negotiation of the coal agreement was possible at all is probably due to the dominant position of RWE within the utility structure. Certainly it was RWE's consent that was crucial. Given that progress with nuclear power is at best highly uncertain, it was clear to RWE that it would have to resort to a higher coal burn. The agreement with the mines reduced by subsidies the perceived costs of that low risk strategy.

The real effect of a free market is that the economic actors are left to their own initiatives and can back their own judgement. RWE has given several decisive twists to the choice of technology and the use of energy sources; the company strongly supported nuclear energy when it was economically doubtful in the 1960s and forced through the choice of light water technology instead of West German or European plant. It has led, world-wide, the search for economies of scale; the high 1300 MW plant at Biblis was planned well ahead of similar plant elsewhere. It has given the necessary encouragement to the Federal authorities in the fast reactor programme and baled it out when the costs got too high. It has taken the lead in coal gasification with its own commercial project independent of government subsidy.

RWE does not exist in solitary splendour; Rurhgas determines where supplies of gas are bought, is the main influence on how the various available supplies are incorporated into an optimal system, and is generally the guardian of the security and integrity of the national gas system.

These dominant enterprises lack the elitist or welfare perspective of nationalized industries in other European centres; they optimize their activities in their own interest, no one else's. The absence of statutory limitations on activity gives RWE especially an opportunity to penetrate and colonize adjacent, strategic areas. In its position in the nuclear fuel cycle RWE comes closer than any utility throughout the world in absorbing completely all the vital nuclear functions. It has no direct presence in reactor manufacture and construction, but it would be easier for RWE to find another supplier than for KWU to do without RWE, so the balance of power is not in any doubt. Anyway, the supply of the reactor is not so crucial a task; the oil industry flourished without making boilers or burners.

RWE may not suffer *étatist* or welfare constraints, but then it does not enjoy *étatist* advantages. It cannot rely, as can EDF, on decisive support from the State in critical matters; EDF has no problem with sites and licences. The results from this reliance on commercial agents to solve problems whose full range and scope is only perceptible on an international plane have been imperfect; impressive in potential, disappointing in actuality. The Government has shown no signs as yet of seeking to reinforce its entrepreneurial vigour with state authority. It is on the future nature of this delicate relationship that West German energy policy will depend.

REFERENCES

1. The early and absorbing history of the Ruhr Syndicate is documented *inter alia* by: F. Walker, *Monopolistic Combinations in the German Coal Industry*, Macmillan, New York, 1904; A. H. Stockder, *Regulating an Industry*, Columbia University Press, New York, 1932; G. Gebhardt, *Ruhrbergbau*, Verlag Gluckauf, Essen, 1957.
2. P. Wiel, *Wirtschaftsgeschichte des Ruhrbegietes*, Siedlungsverband Ruhr-kohlenbezirk, Essen, 1970.
3. Gesetz Zur Förderung der Energiewirtschaft, 13 December 1935.
4. *Gegenwärtige Struktur und künftige Entwicklung der öffentlichen Elektrizitäts-wirtschaft in der Bundesrepublik Deutschland*, Energiewirtschaftliches Institut an der Universität Köln, Duncker und Humblot, Berlin, 1963.
5. P. Wiel, op. cit.
6. F. Tuppeck, 'Ferngastransport in der Bundesrepublik – heute und morgen', *Erdöl und Kohle*, March 1967.
7. G. Gebhardt, op. cit.
8. O. Petzina, *Autarkiepolitik im dritten Reich*, Deutsche Verlags-Anstalt, Stuttgart, 1968.
9. W. Karslen, 'Ausblick auf die Mineralölversorgungslage der Bundesrepublik und angrenzender europäischer Länder', *Erdöl und Kohle*, May 1952.
10. P. H. Frankel, *Mattei and Power Politics*, Faber and Faber, London, 1966.
11. H-W. Schiffer, 'Die Entwicklung der Mineralölwirtschaft in der Bundesrepublik Deutschland im Jahre 1980', *Zeitschrift für die Mineralölwirtschaft*, March 1981.
12. L. E. Grayson, *National Oil Companies*, John Wiley and Sons, 1981.
13. Ibid.
14. W-J. Schmidt-Kuster, 'Das Entsorgungskonzept in der Bundesrepublik Deutschland', *Jahrestagung Kerntechnik 1980*, Deutsches Atomforum, March 1980.
15. O. Keck, 'The West German fast breeder programme', *Energy Policy*, December 1980.

16. P. Wiel, op. cit.
17. A. Wimmelmann, 'Die Steinkohle in der Wirtschaft der Bundesrepublik', *Jahrbuch des deutschen Bergbaus*, 1955.
18. Gesetz zur Förderung der Energiewirtschaft, op. cit.
19. *Die öffentliche Elektrizitätsversorgung im Bundesgebiet, 1979*, VDEW, Frankfurt, 1980.
20. Ibid. See also P. Weil, op. cit., for details of area of Territory.
21. *Dritte Fortschreibung des Energieprogramms*, Bundesministerium für Wirtschaft, November 1981.
22. This example is based upon an unpublished paper: K. Eigenwillig, 'Energieversorgung in Frankfurt, Zwischenbericht', Frankfurt, 1981.
23. *Zweite Fortschreibung des Energieprogramms*, Bundesministerinn für Wirtschaft, December 1977.
24. Ibid.
25. Ibid.
26. *Zur friedlichen Nützung der Kernenergie*, Bundesministerium für Forschung und Technologie, Bonn, 1977.
27. Ibid.
28. Gesetz über die friedliche Verwendung der Kernenergie und den Schutz gegen ihre Gefahren, Bonn, December 1959.
29. J. Bugl, 'Towards a better Licensing procedure', *Nuclear Engineering International*, December 1978.
30. U. Daunert, 'Understanding the structure of the nuclear industry', *Nuclear Engineering International*, May 1981.
31. *Dritte Fortschreibung des Energieprogramms*, op. cit.
32. W. Rudloff, 'The impact of the opposition to nuclear power development', *Nuclear Engineering International*, December 1978.
33. J. A. Helm, 'Citizen Lobbies in West Germany' in P. H. Merkel (ed.), *Western Political Party Systems, Trends and Perspectives*, The Free Press, New York, 1980.
34. W. Karslen, op. cit.
35. H.-W. Schiffer, 'Internationaler Vergleich on Mineralölmarktstrukturen und Politiken', *Zeitschrift für Energiewirtschaft*, January 1981.
36. H.-W. Schiffer, 'Preissysteme und Preisentwicklung für Mineralölprodukte im EG-Vergleich', *Zeitschrift für die Mineralölwirtschaft*, October 1980.
37. H. Maull, 'Erdgas und wirtschaftliche Sicherheit, Zukunftsprobleme für die Bundesrepublik und den Westen, *Deutsche Gesellschaft für auswärtige Politik, Arbeitspapiere zu Internationale Politik*, No. 17, Bonn, July 1981.
38. H. Maull, 'Time Wasted, the Politics of the European Energy Transition' in G. T. Goodman, L. A. Kristoferson and J. M. Hollander (eds.), *The European Transition from Oil*, Academic Press, London 1981.
39. A. Shonfield, *Modern Capitalism, Oxford University Press, London, 1965*.

6

THE INFLUENCE OF INSTITUTIONAL STRUCTURES
ON ENERGY POLICY

INTRODUCTION

The purpose of this chapter is to examine the influences on the choice among energy policy options which arise from the allocation of responsibilities and powers to existing institutions. It is not easy to prove influence. The controlled experiments necessary for scientific study cannot be done. But different European countries have different forms of organization; their different responses when faced with similar technical predicaments comprise a basis for elucidating the complicated relationships between organization and technical choice. The evidence is anecdotal and circumstantial, but by the nature of the problem nothing better can be expected.

The institutions which control the supply and use of energy have a variety of corporate objectives; their operations are subject to a varying extent to the sanction of the market and the law. Public and private companies will plan in part according to objectives set by regulation of statute or formulated internally to anticipate the expectations of shareholders. But there is more than this to the motivation of companies; it is well-known that organizations develop a concern for their own security, future well-being, and growth which is almost organic.

When strictly economic incentive for change is strong enough, institutional influence is of peripheral effect. This was probably the case in energy transitions from animal power to wood, wood to coal and coal to oil; simple technical developments released vast resources at low cost and change was irresistible. The present transition is distinguished by its reluctance; a reluctance which arises because the transition is not pulled by overwhelming economic benefits but is driven by fear of the future. Of the several alternatives to oil none is an outstandingly attractive proposition; there is no obvious choice, In these circumstances the marginal influences arising from the constraints of the institutional structure can be important and the 'organic' objectives underlying the behaviour of institutions can be crucial. The objectives which supplement obligations to statute and shareholder include those:

1. To extend control over markets for products.
2. To extend control over the means of production, especially over the supply of vital raw materials and technology which is either useful or threatening.
3. To extend control over finance.

Much of the dynamic of energy policy in Western Europe is explicable in these terms; the origins of many initiatives, much institutional opposition and conflict stem from these aims. Executives in the business react as if it were quite improper to impute such objectives to their enterprise, but at the same time they are the most astute observers of them at work in their competitors.

Naturally, companies will try to manipulate the process by which society makes choices about the future in a manner which furthers these objectives. To do this they must influence the resolution of the principal contradictions of energy policy in their own favour. These contradictions are:

1. Between cost and security (a high-low risk axis).
2. Between the specific political demands of particular technology and the general political expectations of modern democracies (often a central-local axis).
3. Between the need for long-term planning and the alleged tendency of governments to attend to the urgent rather than the critical (a short/long-term timescale).

The commercial institutions involved in energy supply will attempt to influence the resolution of these contradictions in ways which help them attain their corporate objectives, explicit and implicit. Generally they will seek to formulate and present their aims as economic arguments. Consequently they are most successful when decision-making is restricted to participants who broadly accept the values and criteria of economic analysis; they are least successful, and most uneasy, when matters are exposed to political judgement. The rapid expansion of energy supplies since the War was possible because the particular form of that expansion was not generally seen to raise political questions. Sporadic, temporary difficulties caused concern to a few but generally the combination of ignorance and weakness in producer countries and complacency among consumers was sufficient to leave the technocrats a free hand. Now that energy choices are overtly political, the existing structures cannot cope in the same way.

THE INSTITUTIONAL STRUCTURE OF EUROPEAN ENERGY SUPPLY

The institutional structure of energy supply is a compromise between preferences specified by the technology and the general political traditions and priorities of a country.

Consequently, the structures achieved vary from country to country. One of the most interesting aspects of European energy supply is this diversity of organizational forms. Because national idiosyncrasies in structure can be consistently associated with different emphases in national policies, this diversity is a valuable source of evidence for the relationships which we seek to establish. The operational functions of the energy system are exploration, production, procurement, conversion, distribution and use; the main institutional relationships between these functions are as follows:

1. There is often pronounced vertical integration of the operational functions for the three principal energy vectors; i.e. electricity, gas, and oil. The oil companies are the classic integrated industries controlling the chain from exploration to the petrol pump. Some gas and electricity utilities are strongly integrated, GDF and EDF perhaps are the obvious examples. The structure is rarely as complete as with the oil industry. EDF has no direct participation in the nuclear fuel cycle. Although not generally perceived as such, in some ways the most 'complete' electricity utility is RWE because it has direct and generally controlling interests in exploration for, and processing and reprocessing of, nuclear fuel. At the distributional end, of course, RWE is relatively weak. The relationship between different parts of utilities is different again in Scandinavia. In Denmark the upstream functions are nominally owned by the downstream companies and there is correspondingly a different perspective of the balance between supply and distribution. The Swedish utility structure offers yet another resolution of interests through a rather

tense balance between the State Power Board and other producers and distributors.

These integrated chains have developed to facilitate the flow of energy among themselves and it is natural that they should view their relationship with the user of energy at the downstream boundary as an exercise in marketing. Aggressive marketing ensures that the sophisticated and well-adapted organism for energy supply can be used to ·full capacity and can anticipate growth in the future. EDF is a good example of an energy chain furthering its development by subtle institutional relationships at the downstream boundary; it has created many associates with private French capital with the aim of influencing consumers or of promoting new uses for electricity. When, as is often the case in West Germany, the producer of electricity sells on to a relatively unsophisticated distributor then the opportunities for aggressive marketing of innovative appliances are more difficult to take up.

Associated with the tendency to visualize the industries as devices for channelling ever more energy into the economy is the search for lower costs of generation through economies of scale in conversion and procurement. This choice of priorities can conflict with other possible ways of adapting; it may, for example, mean foregoing specific benefits that could come from integrated physical planning of energy supply to suit local circumstances.

2. The perceived energy sources of the future—coal and nuclear—are not vertically integrated in any comparable fashion; they are the functions at the upstream end of the supply chains. The existing energy chains naturally try to capture or control these sources and incorporate them into their own structure. The petroleum industry seeks to gasify or liquefy coal. The industry seeks to gasify coal, possibly in conjunction with nuclear power. The electricity supply industry tries to penetrate as far as possible into the nuclear industry; RWE's presence has been noted; EDF once tried to take over the Westinghouse stake in Framatome in competition with the CEA; the dispute was arbitrated by the Ministry of Industry in favour of the CEA, but the attempt was significant.

The few institutions involved at this boundary can easily organize negotiations; their motives and expectations can be mutually assessed and there is a reasonable prospect of co-ordinated research, development, demonstration and commercial planning to facilitate innovation within the existing supply structure. Conflicts obviously exist; sometimes they stem from ill-defined boundaries between functions, e.g. the almost ubiquitous struggle between utilities, atomic agencies and reactor constructors, for the architect-engineering of plant and the competition between coal-mining companies, oil companies and utilities for the procurement of coal imports. Sometimes conflicts stem from competition for sources, e.g. for coal to SNG, oil, or electricity. Given strong central government, conflicts can be efficiently and clearly arbitrated at low cost.

3. The supply of electricity and gas tends by nature to be monopolistic. State control by regulation or ownership is recognized as inevitable. The particular form of control chosen can be an important determinant of behaviour. One can distinguish between centralized forms of control, generally with an active welfare ethic and localized forms wherein the emphasis would lie in avoiding exploitation of monopoly positions. France and Italy are examples of the first case; regulation of the industry is based in national ownership of the means of production. The welfare ethic implies that geographically different costs of production should not be revealed in prices, although this principle has cracked under the stresses of the nuclear programme. The system of control in West Germany is quite different. The principal idea is to avoid abuses; if a utility can attract consumers by genuinely lower costs, that is permitted.

Where economic control proceeds through central state ownership of the means of production there tends to coexist the idea that expansion of the means of production can legitimately be eased by coercive legislation. The only countries, in this study, wherein there exists a national right to impose sites on communities are Italy and France. In Italy the legislation has never been used; in France it has never been questioned. In Sweden, Denmark and West Germany there is no such overriding state prerogative. In these three countries there is, by contrast, a municipal presence in distribution. It is interesting that there tends also to be greater tolerance of the idea that legislation can be employed to help physical planning and more efficient use.

4. Where the vertical integration of energy vectors is pronounced there tend to be few horizontal links, i.e. between gas, hot water

and electricity. In these cases the marketing and distribution of energy is governed by the principle of competition, however distorted the application may be in practice. There is little co-ordinated planning and little willingness to accept that there are benefits from co-ordinated planning.

In those countries or parts of countries where the vertical integration is not predominant there are often institutional links between the energy vectors and generally a local authority involvement. Consequently the organization of co-ordinated activities is easier and institutionally more attractive.

5.   In contrast to the efficient institutional interface of the chains with production, the interface with use is weak and clumsy. There is little organization for the systematic collection, analysis and dissemination of experience of energy use; there is no systematic apparatus for co-ordinating the application of finance and diverse technical expertise; there are few organizational economies of replication because different people are involved each time; management and design overheads as a proportion of project cost tend to be high because projects are small and replication is limited; energy is generally a low priority of the user and there is no efficient professional lobby for efficient use. The implementation of energy conservation policies is consequently difficult. The topic is discussed in detail later.

MECHANISMS

Institutions intervene in decision-making by influencing the flow and interpretation of information. Intervening between competing technical conceptions and an economic recommendation are assumptions among others about:

> Technical performance
> Expected costs
> Prices (especially in state monopolies)
> Investment criteria
> Permissible financial norms
> Expectations of future needs
> Expectations of risk
> The legitimacy of coercion

The optimistic assessment of cost and technical performance is an antique and ubiquitous feature of human activity; it is no stranger to the proponents of nuclear or of renewable energy; it causes a distortion only when one organization by virtue of its status is able to press its optimism unfairly by its control of information, by its preferential access to government or by its ability to direct surplus management talent to the preparation of a sound brief. As an economist in EDF remarked to me, 'We are not a state within a state; our dossiers are just much better prepared than others'.

Relative price levels will influence innovation. The prospects for district heating, for example, are sensitive to the relative price of gas; the prospects for cogeneration can be influenced by electricity pricing. Because of the monopoly structure of utilities, and/or their close regulation by government, prices do not usually reflect long-run marginal costs at all accurately; prices are determined by political compromise, hallowed by tradition. For example, the arrangement whereby most domestic electricity in Italy is sold below cost is untouchable because it has been sanctioned by a political compromise with the unions which see it as a partial compensation to the poor for tax avoidance by the rich.

At the time of writing, electricity prices in France are some 20–30 per cent below the marginal cost of supply. To put them up to marginal cost would depress demand; the low prices are causing havoc with the utilities' financial structure, but the logic of the nuclear policy would be threatened if the electricity could not be sold. At least the French, by virtue of their planned steady expansion, do know what their marginal costs are. In many countries it is not so clear what type of plant will be built, when, and at what cost. In these conditions the idea of marginal cost pricing has little meaning. Prices are consequently the result of political and administrative bargaining, strongly influenced by the allocation of responsibilities to actors and their priorities. In particular, the way the process works is dependent on the nature of state control, in the way which has already been discussed.

Another important distortion of the process of economic appraisal is caused by the use of different investment criteria in the public and private sector. A discount rate between 5–10 per cent is usual for public enterprise whereas 15–25 per cent or more is common in private enterprise. These different requirements may be justified when the public and private sectors are investing to quite different ends (e.g. in motorways rather than manufacturing plant) when many of the criteria are subjective anyway, but when the capital ends up in different parts of a specialized system of energy supply and use the result must be a misallocation of resources towards the state controlled supply side.

The extent of public or private ownership also influences access to finance, conditions of finance, constraints on financial ratios and eventually the legitimacy of economic protection. State enterprises often have access to government finance at favourable terms; if they seek external finance then government guarantees have a similar value. The permitted limits of borrowing are suspended for state enterprise; the debt/equity ratio of EDF would be unthinkable in a private utility. It is arguable that profitable development of nuclear power is only possible on a large scale and that the financial consequences can only be tolerated by a state enterprise.

Investment decisions are susceptible to assumptions about future needs. The assumptions of any interested institution will be a compromise between its hopes and expectations. The extent of the compromise will depend in part on the extent to which the institution will be responsible for sorting out the problems which arise and its expectations of political support in that process. Nuclear Energy Agencies are remote from the responsibilities of implementation and there is almost no restriction to their flights of fancy. Utilities have to handle the problems and are therefore more cautious; they will be encouraged to plan for and forecast high future needs for their product if they expect to benefit from government support in overcoming political, financial and commercial difficulties as they arise. The relationship between atomic agency and utility and the extent and nature of government involvement is therefore important in the assessment of the risk of a programme and therefore on the specification of future needs.

The absence or unfamiliarity of an institutional structure will also influence the perception by policy makers of the risk involved in an option. The civil service will on the whole have greater confidence in their ability to assess the outcome of initiatives from existing institutions with proven performance (not necessarily good performance) than those which originate from untried and/or badly organized sources; it will prefer options which involve negotiations with a few parties whose motives they comprehend, so that they can clearly anticipate and monitor the consequences of policy. They will tend to avoid projects involving many parties with diverse, ill-comprehended motives because the negotiating costs are high, monitoring is difficult and assessment uncertain. Money put into nuclear energy will eventually emerge as a power station, albeit 5 years late, twice the cost and half the capacity; there is in all countries great doubt whether the money which has been put by government into implementing conservation has achieved anything at all. In the former case the civil service has some one to blame whereas in the latter it does not.

Another extremely important factor in economic appraisal, which is seldom recognized, is the perception of the legitimacy of coercion. The state which imposes sites for nuclear reactors and transmission pylons but which hesitates to put any restriction on automobiles, 'an untouchable social conquest', is introducing significant constraints into the economic process. Whether the possible restrictions on civil liberties which might arise from the use of plutonium are of more significance than freedom of choice of fuel for space heating is a judgement conditioned as much as anything else by political tradition. This perception of the legitimacy of coercion is an important economic distortion arising out of fundamental political prejudices.

IMPLICATIONS FOR TECHNICAL CHOICE

Energy policy can be defined either in terms of a series of specific technical choices or by the resolution of apparent contradictions. It is easiest to begin with a discussion of particular technical choices before proceeding to esoteric generalizations.

Acceptance of Nuclear Power

One of the more unexpected things about nuclear power is the surprise felt, especially among scientists, in discovering that scientists do not necessarily agree. Whatever the matter in question, it is possible to find scientists and technologists from industry and government and its research establishments to argue one side and others from universities and a variety of peripheral institutions to argue the reverse. How, goes a frequent line of rhetoric, can the common man feel anything but unease when even the experts fight among themselves? How can the political process cope when called upon to arbitrate technical matters of great complexity?

Implicit in these questions is the idea that the unresolved technical matters are the cause and the political conflicts the effect. A little thought suggests that this can hardly be the case. No doubt there are within the domain of nuclear technology matters of genuine controversy. But they are for the most part so obscure that few can contribute usefully to their elucidation; it is scarcely conceivable to imagine political conflict springing naturally from such rarefied matters. Rather, the process is reversed. Technical matters are entrained into social and political currents whose form and direction have been determined over much longer time scales than any technical controversy could expect to last. Technical developments are interpreted in the context of the history of European ideas; it is not so much that nuclear power offers especially intractable political problems, it is simply a perfect symbol for wider social and political conflicts. Accordingly the myths (or perceptions) are created which are the real material of the political process and on the basis of which political choices will inevitably and necessarily be made.

The first era of mystification belonged without challenge to the men of action. Nuclear energy would unite Europe. Jean Monnet wrote: 'The United States of Europe, means: a federal power linked to the peace exploitation of Atomic Energy'. (Jean Monnet, *Les Echos*, special end of year edition, Paris, 1955.) In debates in the French National Assembly it was alleged that nuclear energy would restore to France her position among the great powers. The US-inspired Geneva Conference on the Peaceful Uses of Atomic Energy presented the technology as a symbol of the munificence of the US and the material benefits that her friends could expect. For smaller countries like Denmark and Sweden, nuclear research programmes symbolized a presence in the world of modern technology and industry. To West Germany, command of nuclear energy represented the crossing of the technology gap that had appeared between her and the Allied Powers. These interpretations were hardly challenged at the time and many countries were able to institute nuclear programmes. In some cases, especially Sweden, the programmes were substantial. There was, of course, internal strife. Everywhere, utilities, manufacturers, and government research agencies came into conflict over reactor choice and competed for borderline functions, notably that of architect-engineering. In rare cases scientists made public criticism; this happened mainly in North America. Professor Alfven in Sweden is perhaps the best known European exception. But the opponents were a restrained group; the Bulletin of Atomic Scientist was their medium; it dealt with technical matters according to technical criteria.

The counter-myths to those of the men of action appeared in volume in the early 1970s when specialists began to produce political interpretations of nuclear power for the consumption of members of the intellectual groups to which they belonged. These commentaries were accepted by every good conservative/liberal/ socialist/radical/civil libertarian/trotskyist/environmentalist . . . It was on the basis of these interpretations that the popular political process of mass movements, demonstrations and votes would function. The technocrat might find this deplorable, as indeed it is. But people are always more attached to ideas than to facts; in no society where popular opinion holds sway will political life be governed by facts. The facts must first be digested and absorbed into complex structures of ideas of far wider intellectual dominion; ideas which have been adopted on the basis of analyses and prejudices stretching beyond the consideration of detailed technical controversy.

So how does nuclear energy appear in the light of the principal European ideas? The interpretations of the more modern movements—nationalism and various proletarian-based ideologies—are broadly favourable, but have little else in common. Nationalist sentiments find comfort in a sense of power and independence. The influence of nationalism is manifest throughout nuclear policies. In France, the nuclear industry has been, since its inception, a symbol of French nationalism and this has had an influence on its form and content. The *filière française* survived the onslaught of EDF longer than it might otherwise have done because of the nationalist sentiments of the Gaullists, especially those of their leader. Having taken the plunge and accepted the manufacture of American technology under licence, the French establishment has never failed to emphasize the progress being made in the françisation of the PWR design. The enormous effort being put into the fast reactor programme, by governments of left and right, without obvious commercial benefit, has only been possible because the aspirations and strengths of nationalism provide a means and a motive.

The effective control which can be exercised by a nation over the chain of processes which releases energy from uranium is also important in the nationalist perspective. Nuclear power appears in French energy balances as an indigenous source, even though France is largely dependent on imports of uranium. This mild deception is necessary if the correct impression is to be conveyed.

Consummate practitioners of nationalism as they may be, the French are not alone. In the other European countries, nuclear energy policy has responded in different ways to the need for national identity. The costs of this identification have been large; almost every European nation has laboriously, independently and expensively learnt to build American reactors and set up manufacturing plant for the process. Without exception this plant is under-utilized; it will probably remain so for the foreseeable future.

Nuclear energy is a little ambiguous in terms of the political philosophies arising from, or on behalf of, the proletariat. Common to most interpretations is the sense of nuclear technology as a liberating influence, alleviating the labour of man, creating wealth and a better society. Luddite notions that the technology destroys jobs have been raised from time to time but have never gathered significant support. The main ambiguities arise from the high degree of centralization which the technology is perceived to engender, the reliance on tight organization and strict management. The restriction of decision-making to a few members of an occult capitalist club symbolizes effectively the pernicious potential of nuclear technology to shift the control of events further from the proletariat. One way out of the dilemma is not hard to find; it depends on who controls the means of production. The Communist view is quite straightforward. Nuclear power controlled by the State is acceptable; controlled by capital it is unacceptable. Socialists and Social Democrats tend to more complex presentations of the same sentiment. The French Socialists in opposition, when they were *de facto* men of reflection, opposed the French programme; when they became men of action and took charge their enthusiasm waxed phenomenally. Social Democrat movements in West Germany and Scandinavia have had more difficulty in reconciling the contradictory qualities. In Sweden in particular the Social Democrat leaders have leant with the wind depending on whether the unions, as representative of the proletariat, or liberal minded bourgeois fellow travellers, have had the upper hand in the party.

Still influential on European ideas are the progeny of the eighteenth century—liberalism and radicalism. Liberal conceptions of the rights of man, submerged in the nineteenth century, have resurfaced and are now widely recognized, if not acquired. Liberals in seeking to defend them have become among the most subtly reactionary of forces. With its roots in the eighteenth century, liberalism has always been closer to the land than to the factory and has never had much interest in, or sympathy with, the working class. In France in 1848 the liberals fought against the proletariat; in Sweden the liberals have tended to espouse rural rights, the Social Democrats those of town and industry. The pattern is European. It comes as no surprise that liberal currents of thought tend to see nuclear power specifically as a threat to rural privileges and generally as a symbol of the corruption of noble and tranquil values by indiscriminate industrialization.

The essence of radicalism is to oppose. It is from twentieth century derivatives that some of the most virulent opposition to nuclear energy has sprung. In the 1960s, direct political action through demonstrations, blockades and occupations was unusual; in the 1970s and 1980s, this is commonplace. Opinion polls reveal that quite large proportions (30 per cent or more) of the populations of European countries would be willing to participate in such forms of expression. This high tolerance of activism coincides with the disenchantment of the young with conventional politics. This has been a slow and continuous process; one event where it was very clearly seen was the 'betrayal' in France in May 1968 of the 'revolution' by the Communists. Many young radicals abandoned the conventional left-right polarization of politics and invented new areas such as 'steel' versus 'green'. The phrase 'widows of Mao' was used in France to describe those who continued to espouse conventional radical positions.

The existence of this heterogeneous environmental constituency is recognized by conventional political parties; but generally they have been unable to adjust. Their capacity to represent the constituency is imperfect because the issues cut across conventional lines of political thought. Occasionally adherence to environmental causes is sufficient to overcome the natural barriers with devastating consequences. The Centre party of farmers in Sweden picked up tremendous support from far beyond its natural boundaries as a result of its anti-nuclear campaign.

In West Germany there has been a different effect—the 'greening of parties'—as the SDP and FDP have tried to capture environmental support. It has especially affected the FDP, which is peculiarly vulnerable under the West German voting system.

The 'greening of parties' is noticeable in countries such as Sweden and Denmark where parliament is still significant. In countries such as France and the United Kingdom where parliament has little influence the phenomenon is less marked. French parties do compete for the environmental vote at election time, but purely as a temporary, opportunist measure; they are not affected by it thereafter. In Italy, where the political bureaucracies are important, the local environmental issues are effectively transmitted into decision-making but without appreciable adjustment of party political philosophies.

The theme of this book is that the individual character of European countries has a substantial influence on energy policy. Although there is a common European phenomenon called anti-nuclear opposition, its values are particular to each country and must be seen in large part as an expression of traditional political dialogue. In France the anti-nuclear movement is a manifestation of both the traditional anarchist fringe and the traditional resistance to the highly centralized structure of French institutions. Most participants are young and radical. Some particular developments may be opposed by older, staider people who are specifically affected. Even then they will often invoke the vision of nuclear power as the ultimate symbol of centralization.

The character of anti-nuclear opposition in West Germany is quite different. Here the movement has been shaped by the general resurgence of a participatory political culture that had almost disappeared. In the 1950s and 1960s West Germany dutifully enjoyed high voting rates but little participatory politics. This artificial situation could not last, the resurgence caught up with environmental themes, which lend themselves in many ways to participatory and direct modes of action.

In Italy the situation is different again. In this heterogeneous country over which central political power has waned, nuclear energy is seen as a symbol of the imposition of power by the State. Each region wants the benefits but rejects the means.

The Swedish and Scandinavian movements are (generally) conservative and have a traditional environmental character accompanied by the shadow of country-town conflicts. In these wealthy countries a large enough proportion of the population enjoys the positional advantages of quiet countryside and bright trout streams to make the protection of liberal values a popular cause.

What is it about nuclear power that can create these strange alliances between radicals, anarchists, churchmen, bourgeois groups, regionalists, conservatives? The answer is simple. It is a perfect symbol. The essence of a good symbol is that it means all things to all men. The best way of rallying disparate groups is to give them an evocative ambiguous symbol into which they can read their own aims and expectations. Nuclear energy means oppression to the anarchist, centralization to the regionalist, capitalist exploitation to the proletariat, industrialization to the liberal, a means of class consciousness to the bourgeois, and so on. If this thesis is correct, that it is not the substance of nuclear energy which people oppose, but something else with which they associate it, then the corollary is that the future of nuclear power development depends not on how successfully technical issues can be solved but on whether acceptable political compromises can be struck. Whether compromise is possible, and on what terms, is implicit in the political character of each country. If it were simply a technical matter one could expect in the long-run a convergence of policies on the rational technical optimum. But as the outcome depends on political cultures, and these are diverse, further divergence among European policies is inevitable.

Implementation of Conservation Policies

Energy conservation is really a process of adjustment to changed and changing circumstances. Although much talked about, there is still little understanding of the factors which govern and inhibit this process. Some anecdotes about the difficulties of improving the energy efficiency of industrial structures may help.

A piece of chemical process plant burns natural gas and rejects hot air at 450°C. It is possible to capture and recycle this heat on the same plant by retro-fitting a heat exchanger. Calculation shows that if gas prices were set equal to long-run marginal costs of new supplies then the budgetary price of the heat exchanger could be paid back in 6 months. In fact the firm pays one-third this price for gas under a contract signed several years earlier. Moreover, the overheads on such a small project are high. The costs of ducting, moving pumps, making drawings, fitting equipment tend to be proportionally large for small projects. In this case the effect is to bring the total cost of the fully equipped project to about four times the cost of the heat exchanger. The combined effect of these factors is to bring the payback period up to 6 years, at which point the firm loses interest. The first two morals of this story are that prices often do not reflect future costs and that the overheads on small, complicated adjustment of existing plant are high and simple assessments of the potential for conservation can be misleading. The story does not stop here. In the view of the firm it is also too costly to respecify the next plant, at that moment on the drawing-board. It is thought, however, that the plant after next might have some heat exchange. The third moral is that energy conservation has a long lead time just like supply options.

In a second anecdote, a manager could choose between buying a new machine tool or insulating his factory roof; both investments give about the same return. No reasonable man would not choose to buy the new tool which would keep the organization abreast of new technical development. The moral is that there are intangible benefits associated with investment in new productive capacity which are not to be found in simple cost cutting investments. This is probably why many firms look for higher (and often apparently absurd) rates of return on investment in energy conservation than they expect from new productive capacity. This is a crude way of dealing with real but intangible factors.

In a third case an engineer attempts to persuade his management to choose an efficient industrial refrigeration system, the extra capital cost of which would give a high economic return. A cheaper and less efficient scheme is chosen because the management believe in the capital increment of the efficient scheme but not in the future savings. Energy wastage in this case arises from an organizational deficiency.

In a similar story a profit centre receives capital sanction from its main board for the price of a plant including a heat exchanger. It later discovers it can not build the plant to cost. Rather than go

again through the process of approval the local site managers
decide to take off the heat exchanger, which is not necessary for
the functioning of the plant. Again the cost of precise communica-
tion prevents efficient adjustment.

There are still other obstacles to the efficient use of energy. Use
of energy is characterized by fragmentation. Fragmentation of
demand, fragmentation of supply,fragmentation of responsibility.
Energy use is spread over the entire economy and is finally applied
at many small points in engines, motors, lights, boilers, furnaces
etc. The supply of goods and services promoting efficient use is
also fragmented. It includes manufacturers of insulation, instru-
mentation, controls, heating and lighting appliances, boilers; it
includes consultants of many different specialities. Lastly, responsibility within government is fragmented. Local and central
government share responsibilities in proportions which differ
considerably in different countries. Generally the responsibilities
of government will be further split between departments, typically
departments of housing, industry, transport, education, health etc.

The result is that although it is relatively easy to dream up a list
of desirable actions which would make for a more efficient
economy, it is much more difficult to think of policy actions which
will encourage this adjustment and which can themselves be
implemented by government and its agents. No European country
has yet succeeded in implementing energy conservation policies.
This is often not recognized. Governments prefer to suggest that
they have been successful and there is much obfuscation such as,
'we are using 10 per cent less energy in 1980 compared to 1973
even though economic growth has increased by 5 per cent'. Such
figures are misleading. There has been in recent decades in most
European countries a tendency for the amount of energy used per
unit of economic output to decrease steadily with time. In other
words there is, in this sense, a historic trend to greater efficiency.
Because economies grew, especially in the 1960s, faster than the
decline in specific energy consumption the effect was that total
energy demand increased, although less fast than economic
output. The main change since the early 1970s has been the slow
economic growth. Economies are now growing less slowly than
specific energy consumption declines and the result is a drop in
total energy consumption. It is not correct to point to this as
evidence of an adjustment out of line with historic trends. There is

little evidence from an examination of the specific energy con-
sumptions of most European contries to suggest any marked
improvement in efficiency out of keeping with historic
trends.

The gloomy evidence of econometrics is supported by anecdotal
experience of the implementation of conservation policies. The
Agence pour les économies d'énergie made money available for
industrial projects designed to promote efficiency, but quickly
found that it could not properly monitor and assess the projects
with the necessary accuracy and that those it did study were not
encouraging. The scheme was later abandoned. Large programmes of subsidies in Sweden and West Germany though popular
and politically convenient are not generally thought by those
responsible for their assessment to have been cost-effective. One
must distinguish between the cost-effectiveness of specific conservation measures and the cost-effectiveness of a programme
designed to encourage such measures.

The basic difficulty is that central government cannot exercise
sufficient technical expertise to implement policies directly. It
must rely on others. The best equipped agents are the utilities;
they have well-trained personnel, knowledgeable in the subject
and widely dispersed. In the United States some utilities have
found it so difficult to build new generating plant that they have
promoted conservation programmes with vigour. But in normal
times the large utilities are not enthusiastic about conservation;
they see it as being in clear conflict with the sale of energy.
Utilities with close connections to municipalities may see the
problem differently.

In Scandinavia where the municipalities have a traditional
involvement in energy supply, governments have tried to use the
municipalities to implement conservation policies. Superficially,
this seems a good opportunity, but it is not easy to find evidence as
to whether the attempt is really successful. Certainly the existence
of such means for implementing policies encourages people to try.
The Scandinavian countries do have large government expendi-
tures for this purpose and have large expectations of conservation
in their policies. It is a plausible assertion that countries with a
decentralized utility structure and the means and experience of
implementing policies through municipalities have more chance of
mobilizing information, money and technology to improve the

energy efficiency of the built environment. Whether the assertion is more than plausible is too early to judge.

Physical Planning of Energy Supply

The ideas of cogeneration and district heating which have been practised to varying extents in different European countries have recently developed into a broader concept known as heat planning or regional energy planning. The concept essentially incorporates energy supply infrastructures into the physical planning of the built environment. It replaces the spur of competition between energy vectors by co-ordinated planning as the mechanism for achieving efficiency. The process is perhaps most fully formed in Denmark, where the intention to incorporate relatively costly discoveries of natural gas into Danish energy supply obliged constraints on competition with other fuels. The concept is also favoured in Sweden, West Germany and in some Italian cities.

Physical planning of energy and cogeneration are both, in slightly different ways, threats to the vertically integrated energy supply chains. Cogeneration introduces a new energy vector—hot water—in direct competition with established vectors. Much of the European gas industry sees its long-term future in the gasification of coal and is therefore uneasy about technology which converts coal to thermal comfort via hot water. Local energy planning makes demands for co-ordination of physical planning and energy supply which the existing institutional structures in the different countries are differently equipped to meet. Countries with pronounced vertical integration of utilities are less able to adjust to the idea than are those where the utilities have a local perspective. Planning replaces competition as the means of social interaction of the utilities and, like any other organism, the institutional structure of energy supply resists change and the unknown.

There is a wide variation internationally in the extent to which district heating and cogeneration are practised. The origins of this variation are worth detailing because they offer the clearest case of a marked influence on technical choice by institutional structure. Denmark has the highest proportion of district heated homes in Europe. As has been described, this characteristic is a result of the long tradition of local and co-operative initiative and the formative influence which it had on the structure of the electricity utilities.

The municipalities have, by and large, been able to force cogeneration onto the utilities. When it was thought desirable to introduce natural gas into Denmark, it was decided at an early stage that the industry should not be vertically integrated, but that distribution should be the responsibility of local companies, preferably with local authority involvement. In natural co-existence with this structure was the incorporation of energy supply into a form of physical planning, whereby areas were divided into zones within which the various forms of heat supply would be encouraged or restricted. This concept of the balance of competition and planning arises out of the structure and traditions of the industry.

France, as we have had occasion before to remark, has highly centralized energy and political structures. But there is one revealing gap. The law of nationalization left certain cities with the authority to distribute and sell electricity. It was intended eventually to devolve the responsibility for distribution throughout France to these *régies*. In the event this never happened and the *régies* are seen by EDF as anachronistic. However one of these rare creatures was at Metz where, since nationalization, the municipality has put into effect a highly successful district heating scheme, with cogeneration of electricity. The two other towns in France which have shown interest in cogeneration (Grenoble and Strasbourg) also possess municipally controlled *régies*. These islands in the centralized sea of EDF are perhaps the most striking evidence one could find of the way technical choice is affected by the character of institutions.

Much the same is true of Italy, which has a somewhat similar structure. The interest in cogeneration and district heating which exists in Northern Italy (Brescia, Milan etc.) is confined to those cities which still possess municipal distribution agencies.

Sweden is an intermediate case, where a long conflict between municipalities and the State Power Board forced a draw whereby the municipalities built cogeneration plant, but the Power Board restricted its operation.

West Germany has the most heterogeneous system. The detailed example given earlier of Frankfurt shows how involved the commercial relationships can be among various suppliers to one town. The basic argument is, however, clear there also. Given an interest in energy supply, and the opportunity to pursue it, the physical planning of energy supply is greatest where the municipality has a strong involvement in the distribution function.

The evidence of these comparisons, which by its nature can only be circumstantial, suggests that the institutional characteristics which are receptive to heat planning are that there be no monopoly in gas or electricity distribution and that the municipality be involved in energy distribution.

Energy Research and Development

Research is an activity which helps determine the productive instruments among which future energy choices can be made. There are two principal ways in which the countries studied here differ in their R & D policy. The obvious difference is in content. More interesting perhaps is the difference to be seen in the conception of the role of the State. One can distinguish three quite clearly different conceptions. There is the French concept, in which the State and its agencies have an important responsibility for research and are proprietary over the results; the West German concept in which responsibility for research and development lies with commercial actors and they naturally have the rights to the results; and the Swedish concept in which the State assumes a part of the financial burden but the results belong as far as practical to the community. In the first model the State is the agent of change, defining the paths to be followed and the applications to be made; in the second the State minimizes its responsibility in all respects; in the third case the State assumes responsibility for inducing change, defines the broad directions of work but leaves the specific choice of project to others and attempts to ensure that the new information is available to others to apply. Responsibility for implementing results belongs to commercial actors.

These three models do not exactly match reality, of course. The Federal German Government has financed energy research, notably in nuclear power, but always apologetically, and frequently for opportunist, political purposes, e.g. the high temperature reactor. In France, equally, private actors do their own research and the State has financed demonstration projects from which the results have been disseminated. Detail should not however detract from the validity of the generalization about the attitudes of the three States to their responsibilites for research and their rights to the results.

IMPLICATIONS FOR ENERGY POLICY

A second way of perceiving energy policy is not as a series of technical choices but as a procedure for resolving contradictions. Earlier some contradictions were identified as lying along a central-local axis, a cost-security axis and a long/short-term time dimension.

Central–Local

It is not my intention to define these terms closely. The advantages of definition are clear enough, but the disadvantage is that too precise a terminology will detract from the elusive, but real, general conflict of interests between groups which are in some sense central and others which are local or peripheral. A centralized institution in one context or country may be a local or regional institution in different circumstances or in a different place. But, broadly, there is a boundary separating coalitions of interests that are national in scope and interests that are local or personal.

There are several ways of using the idea of a centre and a periphery as a basis for analysing energy policies. In one sense the whole conception of what constitutes policy depends upon the emphasis given to centralized and diffuse decision-making. One can recognize as opposite ends of a spectrum the 'prescriptive' idea of policy practised in France and the 'diagnostic' idea practised in West Germany. This is revealed in the contrast between the energy sections of the Eighth French Plan and the Third Revision of the West German Energy Programme. The Eighth Plan is a remarkable piece of work detailing the future by volume, by price, by internal rate of return on investment. The future is pinned down numerically in voluminous appendices. The implication is that the State will try to ensure through its agencies that the optimal response to future conditions be achieved. There are limits of course to the ability of the State to do this, and after the change of administration the specific objectives of the Eighth Plan no longer have political support. But the idea of a comprehensive, prescriptive role for the State in policy making is enshrined in the Plan and in the process of making it.

The West German Third Revision, by contrast, contains few numbers and the State itself is careful to avoid making quantitative forecasts. The emphasis is on diagnosis of stresses and allocation of responsibility for adjustment to individuals, companies, local and central government.

In West Germany, as in France, there are substantial discrepancies between practice and the idea. The Federal Government has acquired certain specific tasks which are technically difficult to attribute to others (e.g. final disposal of waste, monitoring of abuse of monopolistic positions); others have been thrust upon it by the process of political compromise (e.g, subsidies for energy conservation, support for the high temperature reactor). The Federal Government also exercises surreptitious pressure to obtain the action it wants from companies and State Governments. But despite these important qualifications the essential principle is, in fact, that responsibility for adjustment lies with the economy at large and not with the State.

Between the extremes of this spectrum lies Sweden where the State prescribes the outcome, but leaves it to others to implement the actions which will achieve the ends. To the extent that there is a link between formulation and implementation of policy it lies in the central funding of appropriate research and development and the 'bribing' of actors (especially municipalities) by subsidies. Italy is situated close to France along this spectrum, which measures only intentions, not the capacity to implement them.

The capacity to implement policies appears to depend on the technological and political demands of an option being consistent with the distribution of technical competence and political power. France offers, as ever, the clearest case. The energy institutions are characterized by a pronounced vertical integration and large monopolies. The electro-nuclear sector is dominated by EDF and the CEA with its subsidiary COGEMA. For coal there are various monopolies attributed to CDF. Natural gas and electricity transmission is monopolized by the state utilities. Even the supply of oil is seen as a state monopoly, albeit delegated to the competent companies.It is accepted that the State has the right to exercise a tight control on the activities of the nationalized companies. The formulation and implementation of supply-side policies comes naturally to such a structure. Among democratic countries France is uniquely capable of planning and imposing a vast nuclear programme. The attempt has also been made to use central institutions to implement demand-side policies. A central

agency for energy conservation has been created; the substitution
for oil in state housing has been undertaken by the state
organization responsible for the construction of the housing, a
similar attempt to substitute coal for oil in industry has been made
by the Association Technique de l'Importation (ATIC). It is no
secret that the effects of French conservation policy have not
equalled the original expectations. This arises from the absence of
a widely distributed local technical competence for energy use
which is actually able and willing to make the necessary physical
adjustments. Such a competence exists of course in the utilities;
EDF has made considerable efforts to influence the behaviour of
consumers but its emphasis lies on projects which increase sales of
electricity or cause favourable change to the load profiles. The
coherence of central decision-making and centralized technical
competence and the absence of local influence on policy or local
technical competence is perhaps the reason why supply-side
policies in France (especially the nuclear programme) have been
successfully implemented and performance on the demand-side
has been less satisfactory.

Denmark, in contrast, has a decentralized electricity supply
structure with a sense of ownership flowing from the bottom to the
top. The distributed technical competence for energy supply fits in
well with energy options that require local, specific, effort. Energy
conservation and energy planning fit well in this structure. On the
other hand, it is difficult for central government to sustain
unpopular policies. Although the municipalities can be reasonably
well disciplined by the central government, the informal groupings
of local and peripheral interests cannot be excluded from
decision-making and have a considerable influence. Important
decisions pass inevitably through the Assembly; coalitions between political parties are made and unmade, changing nature and
direction according to the mood of the people. A rather
communicative Prime Minister has announced on separate occa-
sions that 'Denmark is ungovernable' and that 'there is little
likelihood of a nuclear site being agreed before the year 2000'.
Peripheral influences on policy are profound, but they tend to be
direct rather than exercised through the municipalities.

Sweden is full of apparent contradictions. She has one of the
biggest nuclear programmes in the world (per capita) and yet a
popular referendum has decided that nuclear energy should be

excluded completely from future policy. The declared aims of present policy are to progress towards a system based on durable sources of energy, preferably renewable and with minimal environmental impact. The apparent contradiction originates in the institutional structure which is such as to generate substantial local and central competences for energy supply and almost a conflict between them. The technical balance is matched by a political balance between central and municipal government. The dramatic shift in Swedish energy policy has been possible because the institutional structure permits the formulation and implementation of both centralized and decentralized policies. A passive acceptance of centralized policies in the 1960s has been replaced by an active prosecution of decentralized policies. The central government has shown itself capable of adjusting to this preference and contributing to it through research and development and state subsidies.

The West German experience has some similarities to that of Sweden, similarities that one might not *a priori* expect. The main parallel is the large nuclear programme arrested in full swing. There is also the propensity of local actors to take responsibility for adjusting their behaviour. There is some similarity in the structure of the utilities in that central and locally based participants coexist. The probability of a complete transition to a Swedish style policy is low, given the improbability of concession from the great utilities (RWE, Ruhrgas) and the far less favourable natural resources of West Germany. Essentially, the periphery in West Germany has shown itself strong enough to block the centre without being able to impose alternative policies. The impasse shows no real sign of ending.

In Italy technical competence is located mostly in the bureaucracies of the parastatal organizations, especially ENI and ENEL. Technically the means exist to formulate and implement supply-side policies. ENI has been successful with natural gas projects in Algeria and the USSR; there are signs that some of the many conflicts within nuclear policy are, albeit slowly, in the process of resolution; the importation of coal is beginning to appear as a serious possibility. The parastatal agencies operate in an unfavourable political environment; they are perpetual victims of political patronage and often constrained to bear the costs of adjustment of the national economy to world events. Policies have been blocked by the difficulties of sustained political action within a decision-making system notorious for its intrigue and *ad hoc* solutions. For example, although the National Assembly has given its approval in principle to legislation which attributed to the central government the power to impose nuclear sites on local communities, it has always avoided exercising this authority in specific cases. The party bureaucracies are effective transmitters of local opposition to national politicians. Although this mechanism permits local interests to influence decision-making the quality of opposition is parochial; there is no evidence of an alternative movement with national organization and coherent ideology. The Italian Government appears to be using the regions as a means of dealing with the local communes. It is difficult for national government or the parastatal to deal directly with local communes; the developments which might sweeten nuclear sites are not in their gift. Bartering can proceed indirectly with a regional go-between.

In this way it is probable that supply-side policies in Italy will slowly, and painfully, be implemented. It is much less likely that demand-side policies can be implemented. There is little competence in local institutions for energy supply: attempts to regulate energy consumption, ferocious in aspect, have met with mistrust, not to say incomprehension. A nation which does not pay its taxes is unlikely to be much alarmed by legislation affecting the temperature of its rooms.

If one accepts the thesis that there is a wide variation in the demonstrated ability of different countries to implement different types of energy policy and that this variation is correlated with the institutional structure, then one is led to the conclusion that divergence in energy policies will increase. Institutional structures are good survivors. In France there is continuity back through de Gaulle, to Napoleon and Colbert, if not to Charlemagne. In Sweden the continuity is even more marked. Even in West Germany, with a chequered political history, the ideas governing the interaction of technical and political institutions have survived, almost unscathed, through traumatic events. If these structures are determinants of technical choice then these choices will continue to reflect the disparity of the structures rather than the homogeneity of the technical predicament.

Cost–Security

The need to balance the cost of energy supplies against their security has been paid lip-service since Suez by most European Governments. But almost nothing has been done about it. The principle of security has been used from time to time to defend decisions which Government have felt to be weak or unpopular. The large subsidies paid to local coal industries in France and West Germany are cases where Governments have partially rationalized protection on the grounds of security of supply. There can be no doubt that the real reasons for these decisions have been opportunist; the importance of the Ruhr to the German SPD, the avoidance of high localized unemployment and the accompanying social strife. Having decided for reasons of political opportunism, and local and regional policy, to protect uncompetitive industries it is just as well to inject a positive note by justifying the decision on the grounds of its contribution to the security of energy supply.

The French nuclear programme has somewhat the same quality. It is almost certainly true that the long-term promise of energy supplies secure from easy disruption has been a real influence on French decisions. But it is also true that this consideration was not as prominent as it has been in public presentation of the programme. The reason why one can level this allegation with some confidence is that there has never been any coherent examination of the costs associated with energy shortages, of the probable frequency and duration of such shortfalls, and therefore of the extra benefits to be attributed to secure or domestic sources of energy. In the absence of any such policy, the occasional claim for particular technologies that they are to be preferred because they are secure is injurious. One might modify Dr Johnson: 'Security of supply is the last resort of the scoundrel.'

One action which has undoubtedly been undertaken exclusively to minimize the costs of disruption is the holding of compulsory stocks of oil above the levels required for smooth commercial operation. Schemes have been agreed in the International Energy Agency and the European Community. They are different in the obligations they impose, but for many countries the result is that they must hold extra stocks equivalent to 40 or 50 days consumption of oil. The interest on the oil held and the costs of equipment to hold it amount to some $8 per barrel; for a country consuming 100 million tonnes of oil annually the annual cost of stocks is therefore a little under $1 billion. This is a considerable sum. If this cost is indeed justified by the contribution the stocks make to managing an oil crisis then one wonders whether there are not other means of achieving similar ends which should also be given preference in the form of financial subsidies. Nuclear energy, coal conversion, renewable energies, conservation, all deserve to be developed beyond the point indicated by market forces. Storage facilities for natural gas and robust interconnection of national gas transmission systems permit further additions to security. Countries in a position to offer support to others more exposed to interruption are not encouraged to do so because the consumer of the support is rarely willing to pay for it.

There is no systematic attempt to incorporate security into energy planning. It is necessary to develop a consistent theory in order to allocate resources to the various means of providing security properly and to establish reasonable levels of recompense for countries who undertake specific projects which contribute to the security of others. The interconnection of UK gas transmission to continental systems as a means of helping to stabilize the supplies from the USSR and Algeria is a case in point.

Long–term/Short-term

The most common paradox of planning is that long-term plans are both essential and impossible. They are essential because most modern energy projects take many years to be completed and require heavy capital commitments. In order that these projects are well-adapted to the circumstances of the time in which they are commissioned, the characteristics of that period have to be known. Moreover, in many cases and especially with nuclear energy, the success of a programme depends on many separate projects and the intentions of many participants. In this case, either the participants must share a common vision of the way the future will evolve or they must co-ordinate their activities to mould the future to the form they think desirable. Long-term plans are in this sense essential.

Yet the most casual examination of past efforts to plan energy policy or forecast future developments will reveal how discouraging is past experience. A rash of studies in the late 1950s, inspired by concern over dwindling availability of European coal, can be seen in retrospect as nothing more than attempts by interested parties to force certain choices by sketching a future, implicitly the only acceptable future, and demonstrating that the achievement of that future would depend on immediate commitment to the preferred choices.[1] There were at that time two principal camps, the nuclear camp and that of domestic coal. In fact, of course, neither could sustain their views in practice. Long-term plans to protect domestic coal industries against imports of oil were scarcely worth the paper they were written on; the French Plans of the 1960s are the best documented, but by no means the only, example.

More recently, in the late 1960s, forecasts have been dramatically wrong and misleading for different reasons. They have indicated rapidly rising consumption of energy, especially oil, which, prolonged until the end of the millenium, would exhaust reserves of hydrocarbons. Though indicating a genuine predicament, the forecasts were of little help in detecting what would be the actual outcome. One recalls that Cassandra could foretell the future only because no one would believe her. In fact there is an inevitable process of adjustment, which though it may not be the best process, will certainly have the effect of ensuring that the future is different from any extrapolation of trends.

One way of dealing with the evidence from past attempts to plan or forecast is to refuse it. One can then continue to put faith in the analogous efforts being made today. To take this way is to accept the overriding need for coherent sustained planning and to give less importance to the second half of the paradox. Another way is to accept rather more the impossibility of detailing the future and to give less importance to the first half of the paradox, the need for long-term planning. This way could be consistent with the diagnostic style of policy whereby the principal uncertainties and tensions of the future are made known to all and a range of participants are encouraged to take their own decisions on the basis of this diagnosis.

It is evident that these two ways of resolving the paradox tend to distinguish energy policies into classes with much the same membership as the central-local axis. The reasons are not hard to find; where decision-making is concentrated centrally it is both difficult to accept the idea of fallibility and difficult to delegate decision-making. Where central control is weak there is less point in fabricating detailed prescriptions for the future because the means of implementation do not exist. If local competence is high (which is not a necessary consequence of weak central control) then the opportunity exists of delegating responsibility for long-term adjustment.

What constitutes local in this context can be curious. It may just mean institutions outside the state, as with the utilities in West Germany. It may mean genuinely local institutions like municipalities or even local lobbies and pressure groups. The most important perception which this analysis permits is that responsibility for long-term adjustment need not be the exclusive preserve of the State or corporate enterprise but can be effectively dispersed. The situation in the 1950s and 1960s whereby citizens permitted a large degree of discretion to central decision-makers has come to be interpreted as signifying that only central decision–making is effective in dealing with matters like energy, global in scope and long-term in implications. French indicative planning is the model to which this train of thought leads. Although the French formulated the process most explicitly, the general tendency to accept technocratic planning was evident throughout Europe; Sweden had at the time the largest per capita nuclear programme. Resentment at the process has recently grown rapidly, stimulated undoubtedly by the special characteristics of nuclear energy, but, once established, spreading to effect all large developments. The extent to which this resentment has been able to prevent the implementation of centrally formulated decisions and the extent to which opposition has been able to formulate alternatives, vary considerably from country to country. The most interesting case is Sweden because the alternative process is best established there. Not only has the referendum prevented construction of nuclear plant, but popular resentment has been able to support positive alternatives. It is apparently accepted that the decision to reject nuclear energy imposes the responsibility to find other means of adjusting and to sustain that effort over a long period. It is early to judge, but the expected slow reversal of nuclear opposition has not materialized; marginal developments such as uranium mining and heat-only reactors have been resisted; alternatives such as peat and wood have been actively promoted by local lobbies. If it does turn out that the Swedes can sustain in individuals and local institutions a sense of the long-term need to change then it will establish and prove a process quite different from the models generally thought possible. It is an important experiment.

REFERENCES

1. N.J.D. Lucas. Energy and the European Communities. Europa Publications Ltd. London, 1977.

INDEX